Out of the Desert

Out of the Desert

*My Journey from Nomadic Bedouin to the
Heart of Global Oil*

ALI AL-NAIMI

PORTFOLIO
PENGUIN

PORTFOLIO PENGUIN

UK | USA | Canada | Ireland | Australia
India | New Zealand | South Africa

Portfolio Penguin is part of the Penguin Random House group of companies
whose addresses can be found at global.penguinrandomhouse.com.

First published 2016

003

Copyright © Ali Al-Naimi, 2016

The moral right of the author has been asserted

Picture Credits: 1, 9, 20, 25: Saudi Aramco; 2: Saudi Aramco/Fahmi Baswari;
3: Saudi Aramco/Thomas F. Walters; 4: Saudi Aramco/V. K. Antony; 5: Saudi Aramco/
A. A. Mentakh; 6: Saudi Aramco/Shaikh M. Amin; 7, 8: Saudi Aramco/Abdullah Y. Al-Dobais;
10: Saudi Aramco/F. Al-Dossary; 11: BILAL QABALAN/AFP/Getty Images;
12: King Abdullah University of Science and Technology; 13–16, 23, 26: Courtesy of
Ali Al-Naimi; 17: © OPEC 2009; 18: David Bohrer/The White House; 19: © OPEC 2005;
21: UN Photo/Eskinder Debebe; 22: Theo Anderson; 24: Saudi Aramco/Hadi Al Yami

Set in 13.5/16 pt Garamond MT Std
Typeset by Jouve (UK), Milton Keynes
Printed in Great Britain by Clays Ltd, St Ives plc

A CIP catalogue record for this book is available from the British Library

ISBN: 978–0–241–27925–0

www.greenpenguin.co.uk

This book is dedicated to my wife, Dhabyah.
Without her love and support,
none of this would have been possible.

Also, to my wonderful children,
Reem, Rami, Nada and Mohammed,
and to their children, who give me faith in the future.

Contents

Contents

CONTENTS

Quotes about Ali Al-Naimi

James C. Oberwetter (US ambassador to Saudi Arabia, 2003–2007): 'You hear about people who walk with kings and who walk with the common man. That's a perfect description of Minister Al-Naimi.'

Daniel Yergin (Pulitzer Prize-winning author): 'He's a wise man. And there are not a whole lot of wise men about.'

Sherard Cowper-Coles (British ambassador to Saudi Arabia, 2003–2006): 'He is highly intelligent, disciplined, and ruthless when it came to defending his country's national interest. In terms of comparisons to British energy ministers, he was a giant among pigmies.'

James R. Schlesinger (US energy secretary, 1977–1979): 'He is a very affable man. He is attuned to what I'd call the American spirit. I hope that doesn't get him into trouble.'

Alan Greenspan (US Federal Reserve chairman, 1987–2006): 'He's the most important man you've never heard of.'

John Watson (CEO, Chevron): 'When I first met him, he was already a legend. But he was very personable and made me feel comfortable. He has Americans pretty well figured out.'

Ernesto Martens (Mexican energy minister, 2000–2003): 'He should be recognized worldwide for his work on making sure that the world didn't suffer for lack of oil.'

Sam Bodman (US energy secretary, 2005–2009): 'When I think of Ali Al-Naimi I think knowledge. Knowledge of the industry, knowledge of the political scene, understanding the way the world economic markets work.'

Dick Cheney (US vice-president, 2001–2009): 'He's been a very confident and professional individual to represent the Kingdom on issues of great importance to the United States. He was always a man of his word. And he's a good shot.'

Khalid Al-Falih (CEO, Saudi Aramco, 2009–2015): 'People look in the rear-view mirror and say: "Yes, it can be done. Of course, you can come from office boy to a CEO, it's easy to do. It's easy to build a mineral industry. It's easy to build a university." But at the time, it was impossible. For anybody else, it would have been impossible.'

Abdallah Jum'ah (CEO, Saudi Aramco, 1995–2009): 'He has this great humility. And humility is a strength.'

Ali Baluchi (Saudi Aramco, 1949–1990): 'Ali has an elephant's memory.'

Sa'ad Al-Shaifan (senior vice-president, Saudi Aramco, 1997–2003): 'He is never afraid to try something. He would take chances and that takes courage.'

Abdalla el-Badri (OPEC secretary general): 'If you want to improve yourself you have to work hard, you have to start from scratch, nobody will help you. No father, no mother, no uncle, nobody, you are alone. You have to make it yourself. When you realize this, it's really a good lesson to everybody.'

Harry Alter (former government representative, Saudi Aramco): 'He saw through the transition of Aramco from a foreign concessionaire to its recognized place as a Saudi industrial giant. That alone would serve as a legacy for anyone.'

Stan McGinley (former legal counsel, Saudi Aramco): 'He was instrumental in the evolution of the relationship between the US shareholders and the government. That was a critical thing.'

Bill Richardson (US energy secretary, 1998–2001): 'Al-Naimi is the most influential energy official in the world. He is one of the most honest, circumspect, elegant individuals, who put his country first but was very mindful of the American/Saudi relationship.'

James B. Smith (US ambassador to Saudi Arabia, 2009–2013): 'People who are critical of him would say he's "my way or the highway". But he has laser focus on issues.'

Abdullah Al-Attiya (Qatari oil minister, 1999–2011): 'He can kill people with silence.'

Robert Jordan (US ambassador to Saudi Arabia, 2001–2003): 'He is unsurpassed in the world in terms of his level of expertise and authority and responsibility.'

Stephen Gallogly (former US State Department official): 'Naimi is unflappable. He helped build an image of Saudi Arabia that people can count on it. If you're in the business of selling oil, you don't want people to worry about it. You want them to take it for granted.'

Bill Ramsay (former US energy official): 'He would often be swamped with reporters but never took the bait. Every now and then he'd poke his thumb at the US, but we probably needed to hear it. When he had something to say, he'd say it. At OPEC meetings, he's a little island of tranquillity.'

Maria van der Hoeven (head of the International Energy Agency, 2011–2015): 'He's very proud of his country and his background. He cares about energy poverty. He has personal experience of it.'

Charles Hendry (British ambassador to Saudi Arabia, 2010–2012): 'He oozed authority and expertise, which could be quite intimidating as a transient UK politician.'

Nasser Al-Mahasher (CEO, S-Oil Corp.): 'Minister Al-Naimi is a national hero. He's dedicated his life to the growth of Saudi Arabia.'

Rex Tillerson (CEO, ExxonMobil): 'I spend all of my time thinking about what it is going to be like in ten or fifteen years, because I have to start working today. I think Ali Al-Naimi is very much of the same mind.'

Luis Téllez (Mexican energy minister, 1997–2000): 'I don't think people realize how important he has been for the world, bringing stability to global energy markets. He understands both sides of the equation.'

Adrian Lajous (CEO, Pemex, 1994–1999): 'Many ministers are frivolous. Not Mr Al-Naimi. He was serious. Predictable. Cautious. You knew where you stood with the guy. There are people who understand but cannot perform. He performed.'

Luis Giusti (CEO, Petróleos de Venezuela, S.A., 1994–1999): 'We had confrontations, for sure. But they only made me respect him more. He's a brilliant guy.'

Fatih Birol (head of the International Energy Agency, 2015–): 'To use a football analogy, he can read the game.'

Mahdi Al-Adel (engineering specialist, Saudi Aramco): 'He stands as a beacon of hope for young Saudis. His story would make a great film.'

Christophe de Margerie (CEO, Total, 2010–2014): 'He has something few people have: a vision. Even if it's wrong!'

Introduction

I was born in 1935, in the eastern deserts of modern-day Saudi Arabia. My mother was a Bedouin and, for the first eight years of my life, we travelled the region with our extended family seeking water and a place to graze our live-stock. My first job, aged four, was tending baby lambs.

The image seems romantic, but it wasn't. It was a precarious existence. We had little water, food was scarce and there were no modern sources of power. You can't flick a switch in the desert. The weather and conditions were harsh – blisteringly hot in the summers and freezing at night in winter. I didn't own a pair of shoes until I was nine years old. But then you didn't need shoes in the desert. This life made you tough. We were survivors.

Then, in 1938, American prospectors struck oil. Life in Saudi Arabia would never be the same again. Through luck, and some ill-fortune that befell my close family, at twelve years old I began working as an office boy at this strange US oil company, then simply called Aramco. Almost seventy years later I'm still here.

All of us Bedouin kids were quick learners and hard workers. We had to be. My enthusiasm was appreciated and I was lucky to be encouraged into education, first in Saudi Arabia, then in Lebanon. I then studied geology at Lehigh University in Pennsylvania, and followed this with a masters at Stanford University in California.

All this set me up for a life in the oil business. I returned to the Kingdom in November 1963 and started to apply my knowledge in a bewildering range of jobs. I must have done something right, because I was soon getting regular promotions.

People ask me the secret of my success and I tell them: hard work, luck and making my bosses look good. The idea is simple. If your boss looks good, he might get promoted – and you can take his job. It certainly worked for me.

In 1984 I became the first Saudi president of Aramco. In 1988, the year the company was renamed Saudi Aramco, I was installed as the first Saudi CEO. It was, by any measure, quite an achievement for a Bedouin kid.

But I didn't have time to celebrate. In 1990, the first Gulf War kicked off, directly threatening Saudi Arabia and its huge oil reserves. Thanks to the courage of Saudi citizens and leaders, and with vital support from our allies, the battle was won. And thanks to the hard work of Saudi Aramco employees, the oil kept flowing.

Meanwhile, I began to look east. China was on the rise and Saudi Aramco sensed a growing opportunity for future growth across Asia. It was a fascinating time for me, exploring new cultures, meeting new people and grappling with negotiations that took me well outside my comfort zone.

Then, in 1995, aged sixty and looking forward to retirement, a call came from the king asking me to become Saudi Arabia's oil minister. That's not an offer you turn down.

So began a new odyssey lasting more than twenty years, meeting world leaders, grappling with oil politics and overcoming various international and domestic challenges. In 1997/8, oil prices collapsed to under $10 a barrel, leading to a hectic round of global diplomacy. By 2008, prices spiked at a staggering $147. Cue more negotiations and tough decisions.

It's been a rollercoaster. I've never looked back. And I'd do it all again.

As for my motivation for writing my autobiography, let me be clear: I didn't do it because of my ego, I didn't do it for the glory and I certainly didn't do it for the money.

For many years people asked me to tell my life story but I didn't have either the time or the inclination. To be honest, I'm still not sure it's a good idea, but I understand that I've had an interesting life and career, and I appreciate that other people are interested in it.

The reasoning behind this book is simple: if one young person who reads it is inspired by my career, then I've done a good job. Saudi youth, male and female, and in fact all Arab youth, could use more positive role models. There are many already, but I hope I can be added to the list. If I, a poverty-stricken Bedouin kid born in a desert, can make it, anyone can.

More broadly, the Arab world is often misunderstood. It receives a lot of media attention, but much of it is negative because of the seemingly endless squabbling and fighting throughout the region. But that's not what we're really about. The Arab people are like all people. We are concerned about our families, our kids, our health and their education. The Arab people are fun loving, good natured and tremendously loyal.

I hope this book can, in some small way, make that better understood.

1. Start of a Journey – 1935

I can still clearly see our family's black tents huddled together on the sand. As a young boy, I never let them out of my sight. Those tents and the large connected families they sheltered were the centre of my universe. Beginning when I was four, my stepbrother Mohammed and I were sent out each day to tend to the family's lambs. We kept the flock of as many as 150 close to our desert camp. Even so, we often came home with one or two fewer than we had started out with at daybreak.

After a few days of this my uncle on my mother's side took charge. 'Ali, I think there's a wolf that's eating your lambs.' I thought he might be right, not that I could count, or read or write. We set out to kill the wolf, tracking him to a cave in a cliff out in the desert.

My uncle gathered a bunch of bushes from the surrounding desert and told us to stack them in the cave entrance after he went in with his old-fashioned rifle to kill the wolf. He told us that if we heard a gunshot and the bushes didn't move, then he would have killed the wolf. If we heard the rifle and the bushes moved, then we would know that he had missed and the wolf, now frightened and angry, would be after us. We tied up our thobes, or ankle-length robes, and were ready to sprint for our tents. We were too young to realize that the wolf would have no more trouble running us down than he had catching the lambs.

The gun went off. After a moment of dread out came our

uncle pulling the dead wolf, fattened from feasting on our lambs. It was later skinned and pieces were given to us boys to taste. The meat was very salty as I remember, but we were told that if we ate a piece of the meat, we would become courageous and heroic. So, of course, we did. And to protect us from evil spirits, what we called jinns, our uncle gave us each a wolf's tooth tied to a string to wear around our necks. Mine remained there for years.

The world I was born into in 1935 had remained all but unchanged for hundreds of years. The family's efforts provided enough to eat, but little more. The rhythms of seasonal migration were set by nature, by the endless search for water and grass for our camels, sheep and goats. It was a way of life largely untouched by the modern world. To say we didn't understand modern finance and technology would be an understatement; most of those in this tribal culture had no knowledge that such things existed at all. I could just as easily have been born in the 1830s, the 1730s, or possibly even the 1630s and had a very similar bare-footed boyhood to the one I experienced in the Saudi Arabia of my youth.

The harsh desert sun, the night-time moon and stars and family gatherings around a communal fire were our schoolrooms; the gossip shared in coastal trading towns and date-palm oases our internet. The fact that we were poor and undernourished mattered little since that was all we knew. It was a good life because the family, and the tribe it was part of, was always together.

Our young country was only three years old when I was born. It had been forged by King Abdul Aziz ibn Saud over the previous three decades. With patience and courage – and relying on little more than camel-borne troops brandishing swords and rifles – he assembled a kingdom from a collection of autonomous and semi-autonomous regions spanning the Arabian Peninsula, an area as large as the United States east of the Mississippi. It was the fulfilment of a family destiny centuries in the making.

The Al-Saud, or House of Saud, had been a leader among Arabian tribes jousting for authority across the region since at least 1720. Starting from its base in Al-Diriyah just north of Riyadh, the Al-Saud's influence gradually expanded. During the nineteenth century, challenges increased as the family confronted tribes backed by the Ottoman Empire. At the same time it was wary of aligning itself too closely with the other global power operating in the region, Great Britain.

In a crushing blow, our founding king's father lost the family's capital of Riyadh in 1891 to the rival House of Al-Rashid from north-central Arabia. From the despair of that loss, Abdul Aziz vowed that he would be ultimately victorious. To hone his fighting and survival skills, he lived first with the proud Al-Murrah tribe on the edge of Arabia's Rub' Al-Khali desert.

Beginning in 1896, he and his father became guests of the Sheikh of Kuwait for several years. At that Gulf trading post, our future king continued to prepare himself as a leader, observing at first hand the value of being a keen negotiator with Arab and non-Arab alike. By 1902 he was ready to forge his destiny. Backed by a small band of fighters, the young Saudi led a daring night-time attack to drive the Al-Rashid from Riyadh. By avenging his father's defeat and assuming leadership of the Al-Saud, Abdul Aziz took the first step on a thirty-year march to statehood.

Although my tribe was blissfully unaware, the government in Riyadh was feeling the effects of the Great Depression that was ravaging more developed countries during the 1930s. In its early years, Saudi Arabia relied heavily on the many foreign pilgrims who came annually to the Muslim holy cities of Mecca and Medina. Their number had dwindled from close to 100,000 in the late 1920s to about 20,000 shortly before my birth.

Fewer pilgrims arriving for the hajj meant a reduction in customs duties and levies for King Abdul Aziz, who was the custodian of these holy places. That money was badly needed to build our new nation. Yet the king remained determined to make his new country flourish. Unbeknownst to all but a handful of Saudis close to His Majesty, a search was already under way for a new source of income. The fruits of that search – what would turn out to be the largest known reserves of crude oil in the world – would shortly begin to transform not only Saudi Arabia but also the global economy itself.

Whether I have the wolf's tooth to thank or not, I have been fortunate to witness this incredible transformation first hand and almost from its beginning. My country and I for all practical purposes were joined at birth. After decades rising through the ranks of the oil industry here, I was named the first Saudi CEO of our national oil company, Saudi Aramco. And from 1995 to 2016 I served as the Saudi Minister of Petroleum and Mineral Resources, representing the Kingdom in the Organization of the Petroleum Exporting Countries, or OPEC.

In my role as oil minister I travelled the world, met with some very impressive heads of state and, in consultation with our king, helped shape Saudi Arabia's global oil policy. (Some would say for the better while others would disagree.) Many oil producers blame Saudi Arabia for oil prices plunging 50 per cent in a few months beginning in late 2014. Perhaps instead they should look in the mirror at that fellow who is producing so much oil. Who would have thought critics would long for the days when people blamed Saudi Arabia for *higher* oil prices? But let's not get ahead of ourselves.

With each day my generation of Saudis is passing. Our grandchildren and great-grandchildren, with their smartphones pressed to their noses, have grown up in our kingdom's modern cities. The lives we knew under the sun and stars of the desert sky are nearly as alien to young Saudis as they must seem to anyone raised in the West. Yet that past is worth remembering, and handing down to generations to come. What follows is the story of a Bedouin boy, a commoner from a humble background who came of age as his world was changing, and he changed with it. I, like most of the boys I grew up with, was no stranger to hard work. That part of my character most certainly helped me rise within this new Saudi world. But I was also extremely lucky.

For the first eight years of my life I was a nomad. My family and my clan were Bedouin, or Bedu, derived from the Arabic word for desert dwellers who travelled in family and tribal groups. A number of families would compose a clan. A number of clans coming together would form a tribe. Although the numbers would fluctuate, we moved across the deserts and scrublands of the Arabian Peninsula in groups of fifty to a hundred or so. Tribes have roughly defined areas, called dirahs, reserved by tradition for their livestock. Wells within these areas are for the exclusive use of these tribes. Taking water from another tribe's well, especially during a drought, could be considered an act of war.

We lived in spacious box-shaped tents made of black goat-hair, called bayt al-shar in Arabic, which means 'house of hair'. The tribe followed the seasons and we moved our flocks to find grass and water. The tents were typically open on the downwind side and usually divided by cloth curtains into three sections, one for the men and for entertaining male guests, one for the family and one for cooking. The loosely woven material let the breeze pass through and kept most, but certainly not all, of the sand out. Rugs were our floors.

As we trekked from outpost to outpost along the shores of the Arabian Gulf, we would come into contact with others, mostly Arabs like ourselves. But our lives centred almost exclusively around our families and tribe. Marriage between cousins was commonplace. We ranged consider-able distances, from Kuwait City on the northern border of Saudi Arabia to the sprawling date-palm oasis and ancient town of Hofuf more than 500 kilometres to the south and east. There we would barter our sheep, goats or camels, along with their milk or wool, for grain and other dry goods and staples.

The Bedouin were not well understood, and often feared by outsiders. We were certainly tough. Paul Harrison MD, after visiting the region, wrote the book *Doctor in Arabia*, published in 1940. He quite rightly stated that 'the Bedouin sees the world through eyes that are different from our own'. That's true even today. He went on:

> The Bedouin for the most part lives with his goats. He guides them and protects them from enemies . . . He wanders all day long with them over mountains and *wadis*, and shows them where the best food and water can be found. In return

he lives from their milk and meat and skins and hair. Each lives with the other, and from the other, and for the other, partners in the freest and hungriest life in the world.

I don't remember it being so hungry, but he did make one other astute comment. He said, 'There seems to be no limit at all to their endurance.'

My father, Ibrahim, belonged to the Al-Naimi tribe and my mother, Fatima, to the Ajman, both very prominent tribes in the Arabian Peninsula. They met while my father was working with her brother in the pearl-diving business, and they married quite young, when she was perhaps just fourteen. By custom I took my father's tribal name, but was born into and lived with my mother's tribe because my father divorced her several years later, while she was pregnant with me.

That may sound shocking to those unfamiliar with traditional societies, but to the Bedu, the broader family – parents, grandparents, aunts and uncles – has always been the core of tribal culture. My mother was not ostracized for being divorced; she was simply brought back into her family, as were her children. There, she married my stepfather. My father had other children by other wives, but my half-siblings and I had no contact.

My mother was a kind, stout woman under a metre and a half tall, dressed like most Bedu women in black with simple silver jewellery. She gave birth to me in a small village called Ar-Rakah, which is now part of the sprawling city of Al-Khobar on the Arabian Gulf coast. It was popular with the Bedu tribes for its year-round supply of artesian well water available to all the tribes in the area.

Reflecting both custom and necessity, I was born in the

7

family tent. There were no hospitals in the region, though there were the equivalent of midwives who helped with births. I was the fifth of five children: Yousef, Maryam (the only daughter, who died before I was born), Ali, Abdullah, and me, little Ali. It was not an easy environment in which to raise children. The lack of vitamins in our diets left us susceptible to many diseases, and life expectancy was short. The Bedu were undersized compared to more settled populations in the Middle East, and furthermore, taking after my mother, I was a small boy among a small people.

After I was born we moved to a region north-east of Riyadh called Summan. When the rains come, Summan is a very fertile place with plenty of grass for the livestock. For that reason, we spent the winter and spring there before migrating in search of water, both for us and for our animals. We had plenty of meat and milk, but in those days no vegetables or fruit beyond dates.

Days started with the predawn call to prayer. If we weren't near a mosque, prayer rugs were lined up on the ground facing Mecca. After prayers, the male tribal elder banged together the mortar and pestle used to grind the coffee beans. I remember that sound even today. He was calling us to a simple breakfast of rich-smelling coffee with dates to eat. Camel's milk was reserved for the small children.

With no formal school to attend, we boys found plenty of time to explore the desert. And get into mischief. We would catch small lizards, called damusas, and roast them on sticks. Later I would learn how to make small traps to catch birds and roast them as well. We used to take small sticks and poke them in holes to see if a lizard would come out. Bored, I relieved myself in one of these holes one day and I heard a noise. Suddenly a lizard without any legs shot out. I ran back to our tents screaming that something was behind me. A Bedu hunter named Gannas killed the snake, which turned out to be a very rare and very poisonous desert cobra. Years later I was pleased to hire his very talented sons to work for me at Saudi Aramco.

As children, we did as we were told. Unlike the common practice in other religions, Muslim boys aren't typically circumcised soon after birth but later. I might have been five years old or so when a group of us were stretched out side by side on the floor of one of our family tents. They didn't tell us what was about to happen. My mother said something about looking at the ceiling of the tent and a man, not a religious leader, came along and snipped each one of us with a sharp instrument quickly and cleanly in turn.

Desert life also had its amusing moments. My mother's dowry in marriage to my stepfather was a beautiful white camel. The family built a small platform called a hawdaj that sat on top of the animal like a saddle and carried my mother and me and my brother Mohammed. A camel's broad foot works well in sand, but they can have trouble crossing salt flats, or sabkhas, which are often covered with slick mud. On the way to Hofuf one day our camel hit a slick spot. Its front and back legs both flew out from under her. The frenzy of activity and arm-waving involved in getting us off the camel and the camel back on its feet and us back on the camel would come back to me years later in the midst of pulling an oil company truck out of a hole after it had sunk up to its axles in the mud.

Although physically similar to the rest of the Bedu boys, in our society I was considered different because my father had been in the pearl-diving business and lived in villages along the Arabian Gulf coast. To the Bedu I wasn't Bedu. I was hadhari, which translates as civilized or cultured. Being an outsider was sometimes hard to bear, but it also may have helped mould me into someone capable of seeing opportunities beyond those offered by traditional society.

In that world, being called civilized was not much of a compliment. The proud Bedu considered their nomadic way of life – a life based on elaborate honour codes, oral histories handed down from one generation to the next and feats of bravery – as the essence of what makes an Arab an Arab. They looked down on those who were yoked to their fields or village houses like beasts of burden. The Bedu also had an aversion to anything that involved the sea, including eating fish and shellfish and pearl diving. When I later took up baseball I realized that I started life as a Bedu with two strikes against me.

My outsider status did have a few advantages, however. Even as a child I was always considered a guest. So when a sheep was cooked for guests and served on a bed of rice, tradition held that I be given the head. I would always run with it, but I never got very far. The other boys would catch up with me and try to wrestle the head away. We would fight for who was going to pluck the eyes out and who was going to get the tongue and so forth. What usually happened, unfortunately, was that the head would pop out of my arms and roll in the sand. We would then crack open the skull and share the brains, which were the real delicacy.

One day when I was eight years old my mother told me that I needed to move back with my father and his family, the Al-Naimi. She was divorcing my stepfather, which in Saudi culture is a relatively simple process, and had decided not to stay with the Ajman tribe. Given these circumstances, she must have decided it was time I got to know my father. I had not been sure what to expect. We travelled by camel to my father's home in an area near the coast in Al-Hasa, the site today of the Dhahran airport. I was relieved to see that at that time the Al-Naimi were living in tents similar to the ones I had been living in.

I was curious about what had been my father's business. Pearling, as it was called, had been one of the primary sources of income for the city states and regions lining the Gulf for centuries. Divers traditionally worked in teams during the pearling season, June through September. The best swimmers with the biggest lungs would take baskets and plunge to the bottom from host boats in search of oysters in the shallow coastal waters. The divers wore nose plugs and tied a rope around their waists. Some could stay under water for up to two minutes. They would give a yank on the rope and their partner in the boat would haul them and the basket of oysters on board. Profits were split among the diver, the hauler and the boat captain. Brokers and middlemen would buy and resell the pearls across the region as well as in Europe.

I would soon learn that my father had, in fact, been out of the pearl business for many years. He was, for all practical purposes, unemployed. The growth of the Japanese cultured pearl industry in the early 1930s, coupled with reduced demand as a result of the global depression, bankrupted many such enterprises in the Gulf region.

The collapse of the Gulf pearling industry ended centuries of employment opportunities for coastal people in the area. But eventually it became clear that this dark cloud had a silver lining. Those who laboured in the pearl business had no fear of hard work. As a consequence, many of the tribes whose family names had dominated the pearling boats would soon figure prominently among the early employees of the young Saudi oil industry. Both I and my immediate successor as Saudi Aramco CEO, Abdallah Jum'ah, are sons of pearl divers.

While I was growing up, so was my country. We didn't really appreciate exactly how much, and how fast, things were about to change. My friend Nassir Al-Ajmi, also a Bedouin, and someone who would go on to become an executive vice-president at Saudi Aramco, summed up the outlook of us boys at the time:

> I came from the desert. By the age of seven I knew everything that my father knew. I thought that was it. But then you see all the new equipment and machines. It's not a camel, it's not a donkey, it's not a horse, it's not a sheep and it's not a goat. Then your mind begins to tell you that you don't know everything. You want to know more and that's how it started.

He's right. And once it started, there was no stopping it.

2. The Oil Beneath Our Feet – 1935–1945

Ever since the formation of Saudi Arabia, the king and his advisers had been watching oil industry developments in the region. They paid close attention to nearby Bahrain, whose sheikh was a long-time friend of the king and where oil had been discovered a few years earlier. Geologists advising the king reasoned that oil could very likely be found in our kingdom as well. This was welcome news to a country badly in need of cash to build a nation and serve its people.

In the spring of 1933, even before Saudi Arabia was a year old, our king granted a concession to Standard Oil of California (Socal) to explore for oil across much of the vast Kingdom. To fulfil its mission, the oil company created a subsidiary, California Arabian Standard Oil Co., referred to as Casoc. This was the small seed from which today's mighty Saudi Aramco has grown.

To get the best financial terms for the Kingdom, the king and his advisers cleverly played the American company off against its rival, the British-controlled Iraq Petroleum Company, IPC. The king and many Gulf leaders tended to distrust the British, given their history of imperial designs on the region.

Records from the time show that the British themselves didn't see a lot of potential in Arabia. The British political agent in Kuwait from 1929 to 1936 was Colonel H. R. P. Dickson. In

1931, he wrote a paper, 'The Future of Arabia', in which he described the place as 'little more than a gigantic desert'. While he accurately set out the then perilous financial situation in the Kingdom, he also asserted, 'When Ibn Saud disappears, Arabia will probably dissolve into chaos.'

As for the Americans, who were already supporting the oil industry in Bahrain, they were seen in a different but hardly more positive light. They were opportunists interested solely in the money to be generated from selling oil. That assessment may or may not have been accurate, but another factor weighed in America's favour. As *Collier's* magazine reported the king saying to an American oil industry adviser at the time, 'You are so far away.'

In negotiations for the concessions, two factors were at play. To meet the Kingdom's pressing financial needs, the Saudi negotiators wanted to get as much money up front as possible. But history records that they were also focused on national development. About two-thirds of the way through the thirty-seven articles of the concession agreement, Article 23 represented a key building block in the shaping of Saudi society for decades to come. It stated: 'The enterprise under this contract shall be directed and supervised by Americans who shall employ Saudi nationals as far as practicable, and in so far as the company can find suitable Saudi employees it will not employ other nationals.'

As development accelerated over the years, many of my fellow Saudis and I would push the oil company to live up to this commitment.

The first Saudis hired in significant numbers were little more than day labourers. In late 1934, a few hundred built a pier out into the shallow Gulf at Al-Khobar, near the city of Dammam, so oil company ships could deliver supplies. By

the spring of 1935, the year of my birth, they began constructing the first camp at the base of the nearby jebels (small
hills) forming part of a geological formation known as the
Dammam Dome.

The geologists working for Casoc reckoned that those
hills, which closely resembled the oil-bearing jebels in
Bahrain, were the most promising sites for drilling exploratory wells. Indeed, initial results were promising. Yet that
news brought little comfort to the workers, as conditions
were fairly primitive for everyone involved. Most Saudi
workers, all men, lived away from their families in barastis −
dormitories with roofs made of woven palm fronds. The
king also had a mosque built on site.

The unique − indeed, extraordinary − navigational skills
of several Bedouin tribesmen allowed them to rise above the
status of day labourers. Using landmarks and the sun and
stars to find their way across the desert, they were of enormous assistance to the oil company geologists as they mapped
the region. One guide, Khamis ibn Rimthan, was in such
demand that the king had a family member seek him out in
southern Iraq − where he had fled in the late 1920s when his
tribe was on the losing side of a battle with the future king −
to return and help the geologists. No hard feelings; tribal
alliances often shifted to adjust to changing circumstances.

I've heard acquaintances from the United States refer to
Daniel Boone and Davy Crockett, famous frontiersmen and
iconic Americans. To my generation of Bedouin, Khamis, a
slight, wiry man with skin seasoned by the desert sun, was
the Saudi equivalent of Boone and Crockett rolled into one.
His desert trekking prowess was legendary.

One occasion became a legend in itself. To map out a specific area of desert terrain, American geologists needed to

plot a straight line many kilometres long. The sophisticated optical instruments they normally used required them to fix on a single point in the distance – it could be anything, even a rock or a bush – record that reading, move to that point and repeat the process. But the particular area in which the geologists were working was literally without features: their instruments had nothing to fix on. To their astonishment, Khamis said he could do it, and so set out on his camel, with sceptical geologists following behind. Nearly fifteen kilometres later, their tools would confirm that Khamis had deviated only less than twenty metres from a perfectly straight line. Without using compass or sextant. In other instances, he would regularly pinpoint the location of water wells he hadn't visited in years.

But beyond simply making the exploration process easier, his service taught all involved a greater lesson. Thanks to his skill, intelligence and hard work, Khamis showed that a Saudi could work side by side with the best of the foreign geologists and engineers and win their respect. He was treated as an equal, and thus greatly influenced the culture of the emerging Saudi oil industry.

In the early years, Khamis was often paired with the equally legendary Max Steineke, another inspiration of mine. This gregarious, broad-shouldered American outdoorsman enjoyed nothing more than being out in the desert with fellow geologists and Bedu guides. Town and camp life was not for him. From the American side, he set the standard for what our peoples could accomplish together.

I was trained as a geologist at Lehigh and Stanford Universities, and feel I've developed in the years since then a keen eye for what makes a good oil man. Steineke stood head and shoulders above all others. He had an unparalleled scientific knowledge combined with an intuitive ability to read the rocks and terrain and all but sense where oil was going to be. I can remember as a young geologist in training in Saudi Arabia reading his log books from the 1930s, marvelling how he could get so much right based on so little information. Our best geologists today working with state-of-the-art 3D subsurface imaging could still learn something from Max Steineke.

Assigned by Casoc to Saudi Arabia, Steineke's talents were soon put to the test. Months passed and drilling on the Dammam Dome failed to produce enough oil to support development of the area as a commercial enterprise. Despite geologists' earlier estimates, it turned out that the layer of rock that produced oil in Bahrain only forty kilometres or so away did not contain oil beneath the Dammam Dome. By late 1936 workers on the Dome heard rumours that the Casoc executives back in San Francisco were wondering if they were throwing good money after bad by continuing to drill for oil halfway around the world.

Steineke, who became Casoc's chief geologist in 1936, in the meantime had started what was known as a structured drilling programme that would become a model for global oil exploration for decades to come. He ordered relatively shallow wells drilled across several different regions in the far-flung oil concession. Core samples from these wells were compared to study what likely oil-bearing strata continued from one well to the next. The greater the indication that rock likely to contain oil extended beneath an area, the greater the likelihood of success. In later years many of the wells were turned over to the Bedu as water wells for their flocks.

As the fate of the oil enterprise, and of my country, hung

in the balance, Steineke continued to range across the unforgiving desert. He constantly searched for clues that might provide a hint regarding the location of the vast wealth he seemed certain was trapped beneath the sand and rock.

One of my early predecessors as president and CEO of Saudi Aramco, Fred Davies, recalled being hauled out into the desert one day in 1936 by an excited Steineke. Due to the blowing sand and oppressive heat, Davies could barely see a few hundred metres in any direction. Steineke gestured wildly at jebels that were kilometres away. He insisted that the inclines of the jebel tops indicated the two Americans were standing on top of a dome or uplift created by a vast underground structure capable of trapping oil. Then he pointed to a particular limestone outcropping from the Eocene era at their feet. Such formations typically were buried hundreds of metres below the surface in this region. That it sat on the surface, the layers normally found above it eroded away over the aeons, provided another indication of an uplift. The combination of this evidence, he assured a dazed, sweltering Davies, made that spot the site of 'the next Saudi Arabian oilfield'. Sure enough, drilling later at almost that exact spot would confirm the location of what would be called the Abqaiq field, the second largest oilfield in the country.

After viewing well-known sinkholes outside Riyadh in the spring of 1937, Steineke combined his surface and structured drilling observations to draw some striking, though still tentative, conclusions. These sinkholes exposed sedimentary layers of rock deposited over millions of years. Steineke noted that a layer of relatively impervious anhydrite stone lay atop more porous limestone zones, the type that often contain oil. If that layering held true at some unknown depth beneath the Dammam Dome, then possibly this anhydrite cap was helping to trap oil in the limestone zones.

Steineke's conclusions remained hypothetical, but his combination of wilfulness, enthusiasm and sheer knowledge convinced the company to continue drilling. After a time all Casoc's efforts were focused on a single well, No. 7. It was slow going. Drill bits broke and other equipment failed under the harsh conditions. It wasn't until November 1937 that the drilling produced pieces of anhydrite from a depth of more than 1,200 metres. This stone, if indeed it stretched as a layer for hundreds of kilometres back to Riyadh, could be the cap needed to contain oil beneath the Dammam Dome.

Steineke urged the company to press on, but several more months of relentless effort produced no oil. The situation grew so bleak that in early 1938 Steineke was called back to Standard Oil of California headquarters in San Francisco. Facing the company's senior officials, it would be up to him to argue that yet more time and more money would draw oil from the Arabian desert.

Finally, Steineke's hunch proved right. On 4 March 1938 a telegram reached San Francisco with the news that Well No. 7 – which King Abdullah would later name the Prosperity Well – was producing oil at the rate of more than 1,500 barrels a day at the unprecedented depth of nearly 1,500 metres. The porous limestone containing the oil would later become known as the Arab Zone. Earlier wells on the Dome were deepened and also struck oil. We were in business.

The success of Well No. 7 and the discovery of the Abqaiq field might have been enough for some geologists. Not Steineke and his team. While I was still learning to tend our flocks of sheep, another future Aramco president and

CEO, Thomas Barger, was one of four geologists working under Steineke in early 1940. They had been intrigued by a bend in a dried-up riverbed called Wadi Al-Sahbah, which served as a dividing line between the two areas they were mapping south-east of Riyadh. Waiting for Steineke to join them one afternoon, they compared notes of their recent work.

Geologist Ernie Berg had taken it upon himself to explore the bend in the eastward-trending riverbed, or wadi. He pointed out his measurements tracing the inclines of flat-topped jebels in the area, which suggested that a structural uplift in the region caused the wadi to turn to the right, or south. And where there were structural uplifts, as Steineke had told Davies a few years earlier, an oil reservoir might be trapped beneath. When Steineke joined his young team in the field, he instantly recognized the significance of Berg's measurements. Later calculations by Steineke and Berg confirmed the uplift. Over time the geologists realized that they had discovered the southern reaches of what would turn out to be not just the Kingdom's largest oilfield, but the largest oilfield in the world: the Ghawar field.

In my early years with Aramco, I envied and admired Tom Barger. He had worked directly with two of my inspirations, Khamis ibn Rimthan and Max Steineke. In *Out in the Blue*, a collection of Barger's letters covering his work in Saudi Arabia between 1937 and 1940, he salutes the two and captures what made them so special:

> On the desert, Khamis was never lost. For in addition to his sixth sense, a sort of infallible, built-in compass, he had an extraordinary memory that could recall a bush that he had passed as a young man or the directions to a well that

someone had told him about ten years before. Under the desert, among the strata of rocks and sediment that are the geologist's domain, Max was much the same as Khamis, able to relate an outcropping he might find on the coast to a paragraph in a thick geological report that he had read years earlier. Figuratively as well as literally, they both seemed to know where they were and where they were going next.

What the two couldn't know was that fate would decree their remaining time on this earth to be short. Khamis worked with the oil company in a variety of positions until he died of cancer in 1959 at age fifty. In 1974 a newly discovered Saudi oilfield was named after him, a rare honour indeed.

While still a student I had the honour of spending some time with the revered tracker. We were flying in a small company plane over the northern portion of the Rub' Al-Khali desert known as Neban. Even though Khamis was showing signs of age and illness, his tracker's keen eye was as sharp as ever. As our plane was banking into a shallow turn, he pointed down. 'Ali, you see this dune? Two years ago we camped there.' I looked out the window and saw nothing but a series of smoothly curving dunes. 'Uncle,' I said, using a title of respect younger Bedu employ when addressing their elders, 'how can you tell? I don't see anything.' He simply nodded. 'There are marks if you look closely,' he said.

In 1951 Steineke was given the American petroleum industry's highest honour, the Sidney Powers Gold Medal Memorial Award. At the award ceremony, he was heralded for 'the structural drilling method, which was so widely applied later in Saudi Arabia and has resulted in the discovery of so much oil. The methods he developed in the area probably resulted in the discovery of greater reserves than the work of any other single geologist.'

The following year Steineke, battling a prolonged illness, died at age fifty-four. The main guest lodge still in use at the Saudi Aramco headquarters complex in sight of the jebels on the Dammam Dome is named Steineke Hall in his honour.

Although it was not an official act of the oil company, Khamis ibn Rimthan and his fellow Bedouin trackers bestowed an honour on Steineke that at least equalled the Sidney Powers Award. Barger, in *Out in the Blue*, records that during one of their last exploratory trips together, Khamis told Steineke that a stumpy, steep-sided jebel that the American had learned was called Um Ruqaibah, Mother of the Neck, no longer bore that name. The Bedu now called it Usba Steineke, Finger of Steineke, after one of the geologist's fingers, part of which had been amputated after becoming infected. The great geologist had truly left his mark on the Saudi landscape.

The success of Well No. 7 sparked both an oil boom and the beginning of remarkable social change in Saudi Arabia. As the 1930s ended, the oil company was hiring Saudis by the thousands instead of the hundreds. Bedouin families from across the country converged on the oil camp in search of steady jobs paying three riyals a day – a tidy sum for Bedouin and pearl diver alike. Black tents dotted surrounding hills. Over time, some workers were given training to take on semi-skilled jobs.

On 1 May 1939 King Abdul Aziz personally opened the valve that sent the first shipment of Saudi oil out to a tanker moored in the Gulf at the oil company's Ras Tanura terminal. It was a symbolic gesture, but one of enormous significance:

our underdeveloped kingdom's first commercial connection to the outside world. The course of Saudi Arabian history was forever changed as the dreams of King Abdul Aziz were gradually becoming reality.

The Kingdom was making great strides, but the plight of Saudi workers was not so quickly eased. An intense fire on the Dammam Dome at Well No. 12 on 8 July 1939 reminded everyone involved just how dangerous the oil business could be. The cause of the blaze remains a mystery, but its intensity became embedded in our collective memory: the forty-one-metre-high derrick sitting atop the well melted in about ten minutes.

Initial reports focused on the heroic, ten-day effort to extinguish the blaze. At first the toll in human life was reported as one American and one Saudi. Eventually it was determined that four Saudis perished, but three of the four remain unidentified to this day. If anything positive came from this tragedy, it was that our oil business began practising what all great businesses practise: learning from its mistakes. Poor record-keeping and safety procedures were corrected. The experience also laid the groundwork for the Saudi government's approach to workmen's compensation and other labour issues in the postwar years.

Saudi Arabia's march to join the modern world was not happening in a vacuum. By the summer of 1939 pre-World War II political jousting had already reached its shores. Representatives from Germany and Japan visited the Kingdom in the late 1930s in search of oil concessions as they prepared for war. The king clearly favoured continued close relations with the American oil company, however, and a supplemental concession agreement was signed in July 1939, with much-needed added payments into the Kingdom's coffers reflecting the fact that crude oil production was now under way.

As the war intensified, development of the Saudi oil industry slowed dramatically. Blockades in both the Atlantic and Pacific oceans restricted shipping, and supplies to support the industry were hard to come by. For the same reason, Saudis across the country coped with soaring prices for basic imported foodstuffs, including sugar and rice. By 1942, with America in the war following the Japanese attack on Pearl Harbor, the oil company workforce had been trimmed by half to 1,600 Saudis, eighty-two Americans and eighty-four other foreign employees.

Despite all this, the Saudi oil operation managed some limited development. Three wells were drilled in the newly discovered Abqaiq field by January 1943. Ironically, supplies of petrol were scarce. Casoc, in fact, turned to Khamis ibn Rimthan to organize a camel train to deliver supplies to the remote drill site. But executives were reluctant to commit the company to further large-scale projects. The Germans were advancing across North Africa and many feared they might continue on into Saudi Arabia. As a result, most activity was shut down and facilities closed.

Plans were even made to disable or blow up wells and destroy other equipment and facilities rather than let them fall into German hands. In case the oil men's worst fears were realized, an escape route was plotted through the barren Rub' Al-Khali desert to the British port of Aden at the southern tip of the Arabian Peninsula. Even during the war's darkest days, however, Casoc, with the king's blessing, shipped oil by barge to Bahrain in order to help meet the Royal Navy's needs in the region.

As it became clear that the tide of war had clearly turned

in the Allies' favour, the oil company and the Saudi government began thinking about how to position its oil business for the postwar world. Aiding this effort was the fact that the American government was also beginning to show interest in and support for the nation's well-being. This relationship was echoed in the name of the oil company, which was changed to the Arabian American Oil Company, Aramco for short, in 1944.

Steps were taken to affirm the countries' bilateral bonds. President Franklin D. Roosevelt, though exhausted and in ill health, met secretly with King Abdul Aziz in February 1945 on board a ship in the Suez Canal Zone. Roosevelt was on his way home from the historic Yalta Conference, where he, Winston Churchill and Joseph Stalin had met to determine the outline of postwar Europe. Though Roosevelt would die in a matter of weeks, his gesture of friendship set the tone for relations between the two nations for decades to come.

Saudi Arabia was on the brink of a new economic dawn.

3. Coming of Age – 1945–1953

For me and my generation of Saudis growing up poor in eastern Arabia, the most important event in our lives during the 1940s didn't take place on the battlefields of Europe or the war-torn beaches of the South Pacific. Our vision was more immediate, and by necessity restricted to those things that might promise – or even suggest – a brighter future for ourselves and our country.

My generation's portal to a better life was the front door of a plain house in the coastal town of Al-Khobar. It belonged to oil company employee Hijji bin Jassim. Beginning in May 1940, he rented out a room in the house to the company to serve as its first school for Saudis. Jassim, an interpreter and translator, was also the first instructor.

From the beginning, the development of Aramco was directly tied to the betterment of Saudi Arabia. As such, Jassim's one-room schoolhouse amounted to a modest but significant milestone. Now that oil production was under way, informal on-the-job training was no longer enough. And while four government-run schools were operating in the province at the time, they were 135 kilometres away in Hofuf.

The first company school started with nineteen men and boys who knew at least some English. It quickly grew to fifty. Another school opened in Dhahran, just west of Al-Khobar, in an area called Saudi Camp, where most company employees lived. Soon 165 students were attending classes in that school after working hours. (Although many girls were home-schooled in groups during this period, the first government schools for girls did not open until the early 1960s.)

The school that opened the next chapter in my life, the Jebel School, started in Saudi Camp in 1941. It served mainly those working as houseboys, office assistants or in similar entry-level positions who were too young to attend the other schools that met in the evenings. In the spring of 1944 it was moved along the coast up onto the original oil camp site and located in a former bunk house built from coral-rock cut from the shallow Gulf waters nearby.

The Jebel School was on Main Street in the oil camp, a wide, rutted dirt road lined on either side with dusty trucks, across from the district manager's office and next to the accounting department. This solid building and its location sent a message to us boys: Saudi Arabia was serious about educating its young men. If I was going to be part of this vast transformation taking place before my eyes, then absorbing everything offered in these classrooms was critical.

When I was eight, my mother sent me to live with my father. I quickly became close to my brother Abdullah, who was a student at the Jebel School. Five years older than I, he was tall, thin and very handsome. I became his shadow. After my father, he was the first of many paternal figures in my life. I remember thinking, 'I have lost my stepbrothers but now I have a brother here. He will take care of me.'

I quickly realized that my life was about to change. Abdullah woke me up one morning and said, 'Ali, get up, I want you to come with me.' I told him that I was happy right here. He said, 'Let's go to school.' I asked him what a school was, to which he replied, 'You come with me and you will see young men like yourself.'

Along with many other boys of his age, in addition to his studies at school Abdullah already had a job with Aramco as an office boy. He joined early in the second wave of Saudi hiring that began in 1944, as a building boom got under way at our Ras Tanura refinery on the Gulf, initially to meet demand for oil from the US Navy operating in the Pacific Ocean. In 1945 more than 8,000 Saudis were hired by Aramco – five times the number who had been on the payroll only two years earlier.

After the end of the war, increased global demand for oil further accelerated the growth of the USA's oil industry. By the late 1940s three other American oil companies – Texas, Standard Oil of New Jersey and Socony-Vacuum, the former Standard Oil of New York – had joined Socal as investors in Aramco. They brought much-needed additional capital and expertise to bear on developing Saudi Arabia's national resource.

There was also continuing social change, and ever so gradually I began to sense that I could be part of it. Abdullah and other boys working for Aramco went to the Jebel School for four hours in the morning, starting at 7 a.m., and worked for the company for four hours in the afternoon. Now I was joining their ranks. We walked the fifteen kilometres to school side by side. Even though as a student I now had footwear, all of us Bedu boys carried our leather sandals over our shoulders when we walked in the desert or along roads to keep from wearing them out.

I have a distinct memory of walking into the school in my

thobe and sandals, and feeling like I was the hairiest, dirtiest and poorest boy in the class, even though we were all poor. I was probably also the shortest.

The teacher was a big, thickset Scot, his freckled face all but hidden behind a coarse red beard and moustache. And his booming voice! 'THIS IS A WOLF, THIS IS A FOX, THIS IS A CAT!' He held up pictures as he shouted the animal names in English. Of course I knew a wolf when I saw one. Now I knew what to call it in English!

Most of our time was spent studying English, Arabic and basic arithmetic. The sciences would come later. Our first textbook was British, Ogden's *The Basic Way to English*. We were like sponges, and most of us learned quickly. Since my formal education in English and Arabic began at the same time, to this day I rarely translate between the two languages in my head.

It is hard for me to overstate the impact this simple Jebel School had on me and my country. In educating us boys, Aramco may have been operating out of what I would later learn to call enlightened self-interest, but whatever their motivation, the result was astounding.

The oil company wasn't focusing on my generation by accident. They understood that they were making a long-term investment in both our future and that of the Kingdom. In a 1973 article on the schools that remains unpublished, a veteran company government relations employee, William Mulligan, accurately described what was at stake: 'It hadn't taken the American oil men long to figure out that the complexities of the oil business were only going to be mastered by men with full educations and that the only Saudi Arabs who had a proper chance to obtain full educations were the young ones. From the start, the Jebel School was for boys, not men.'

Boys from the families of diplomats in Riyadh or merchant families in Jeddah over on the Red Sea had always had access to a formal education. Now, suddenly, a broad cross-section of Saudi society, at least among boys, could also see learning as a ready path to success. And we were not all bound for the oil industry, though that was clearly the Kingdom's highest priority. Many of my fellow students later assumed important roles in business and finance, both within the Kingdom and in other Gulf countries. Several of our Saudi teachers, too, advanced into other important jobs.

I confess I had big dreams for such a small boy. Maybe I had something to prove because of my size, but I always wanted to be the one who was working harder and doing better than the other boys. One day one of the teachers was asking each of us what we wanted to be when we grew up. Most of the answers were typical for our age and sex, like fireman, teacher or drilling foreman. I don't remember where I even heard the word, but suddenly I blurted out, 'I want to be president of Aramco!'

It would be a long while yet before that wish came true, but I achieved another of my dreams much sooner, when I was just twelve. In 1947 King Abdul Aziz made an official visit to the area, lasting several days. It was the custom at the time, and still is, for the king to meet local children on such occasions. For whatever reason – perhaps because of my nomadic background – I was among those chosen, and I even recited a poem from memory. I no longer recall the poem, but I do remember the king as being a very imposing and kind man. And I have met every king since.

*

We students, even though we were young, understood how important this opportunity to get an education was for us. There was very little fooling around. In *Saudi Aramco and Its People: A History of Training*, Vince James, an American school principal who moved to the Kingdom in 1946 to take over the Jebel School, recalled, 'We really had no disciplinary problems. The Saudis were there to learn. I would say they were more eager to learn and grasped things as well or better than the average American kid.'

The three years I spent going to school with my brother in the morning and then following him on his rounds as an office boy in the afternoon were among the happiest in my life. I joke that I started my career in the oil business taking papers from one side of a desk to another. When I became president of Aramco, I spent a lot of my time doing the same thing!

I visited my mother in her tent in the desert now and then. I confess to thinking of myself as a pretty sophisticated young man. I could speak English and speak and write Arabic and I was good at arithmetic. Plus I worked for Aramco – even if at the time I received no pay. She was proud of me.

While my skills in language and mathematics began to set me apart from traditional Bedouin culture, my heritage remained valuable nonetheless. Life in the desert teaches many lessons. Resources are scarce and conditions can change dramatically in a very short time. Survival requires preparedness. Although at the time I was far too young to fully imagine what might lay ahead for me, my Bedu background had already taught me the values of preparation and resilience. And now, in addition, I was getting an education.

But nothing could have prepared me for Abdullah's death.

He was only seventeen when he died of pneumonia. With no antibiotics available to us then, he had little chance of survival. I was at his side in the American hospital in Al-Khobar when he died at midnight. We buried him in a matter of hours, as is the custom among our people.

I was about twelve when he died. (I don't know my exact date of birth, which is common among those of my generation born in the desert. In any case the lunar, Hijri calendar we followed did not make it easy to translate dates into the Western, Gregorian version.) Someone from the oil company called me into his office after my brother had been buried. 'Ali, you know this business,' he said. 'We will employ you.' I asked what that meant. He said they were going to pay me for what I had been doing for the past three years with my brother. I agreed, though I almost failed my company physical because I was afraid of the needle they used to give injections. It took my father, an uncle and a third man to hold me still.

I was now officially an Aramco employee, as well as eagerly continuing my studies. And, though still little more than a boy, I was my family's chief breadwinner. My salary was ninety riyals a month, which seemed like a lot of money back then. I took my salary home, to my father, just like all the other boys who worked for Aramco. My father was over sixty by this time and, weakened by decades of hard work, could no longer provide a regular income to support the family. From my earnings, he gave me ten riyals for myself, twenty riyals for my mother and ten riyals for my stepmother. He kept fifty riyals for the family.

My first career at Aramco came to an abrupt halt nine months later, when the Saudi government issued a new set of labour laws. That was a good thing for the Saudi people, but unfortunately it meant that Aramco could not employ boys until they reached eighteen.

So out I went, looking for work to support my family. A cousin was in the contracting business and working on an aircraft hangar at the US military airbase being built near Al-Khobar. (That airbase, greatly expanded over the decades, would play a vital role in the first Gulf War of 1990.) I told him I was eager for work and could do many things. He hired me and sent me up on the roof to check that workers weren't slacking off or sleeping on the job.

I was not as sure-footed as I thought. I had not been there long when I fell from the roof of the hangar. Miraculously, mattresses on the floor cushioned my fall and I was unhurt, but my cousin said he couldn't have looked my father in the face if I had been injured, so I was released from my second job in as many weeks.

Undeterred, I decided to look for employment elsewhere at the American airbase, which seemed a good place to find work as I could speak English. I found an officer and told him I was handy. How about a job? I confess to feeling embarrassed today when I think back and realize that I never knew his name or rank and simply called him 'father'. That's how young I was. Nonetheless, he agreed and I was now on the US government's payroll. I'm not sure how much I was paid since it was in American dollars, which I had never seen before.

In addition to appreciating the work I was doing, the officer seemed to like having me around. He would fly in every week from Rome and bring me a big red Italian apple, which I dutifully took home and shared with the family. It was a novel addition to our diet.

He also taught me to gamble by tossing coins to land

closest to a line. I was pretty good. I took my winnings home to my father. He was horrified. 'Ali, this is gambling, this is forbidden, you shouldn't gamble.' He threw the money away. When I told the officer he said, 'Don't worry. I will show you another game that is not gambling.' He took out a pair of dice. You can imagine my father's reaction when I told him about that!

Unfortunately, my career with the US military was also short lived. One week, the officer was late getting off the plane from Rome. Impatient and excited, and wondering if I was going to get another apple, I darted onto the tarmac to meet him and came dangerously close to the whirling propellers. The other officers said I was going to get myself killed, so my patron had to let me go.

My next career move was to work for another Saudi contractor in the area. He had been hired to paint some huge processing tanks used to stabilize the oil from the Dammam wells by separating the sulphur out of it. He knew my father and agreed to hire me as a clerk. Again, I was asked to spy on the workers painting the tanks and write down who was sleeping on the job. Maybe these contractors thought a small boy like me could move about unnoticed. It took only about two weeks for the workers to figure out what I was doing and beat me black and blue. The contractor went to my father, complimented me on my abilities, but said that I was likely to get killed if I stayed.

If failure had been on the school curriculum, I would have got an A. I lost four jobs in four months. Yet at the same time I had learned a lot about myself. I knew I was quick and adaptable and that the more I stood up for myself, the more people respected me. Size and, I hoped, age weren't everything.

Back I went to Aramco. I told the company official who met with me that I had worked for them for nine months. I stood up as tall as I could and puffed out my chest. 'I am really not twelve or anything like that,' I assured him, deepening my voice. 'I am twenty years old. But I am a Bedouin and a Bedouin is short and little. My father didn't have much hair, so I don't have much hair on my face. And I need a job.'

'Ali, we know you,' he said. 'You are a good boy, but you have to have permission from your government.' I saw an opening. I asked for a letter stating he would hire me if the government would allow it. And so he gave me one.

My luck was starting to change. One of the officials working for the governor of the province was my former government-appointed Arabic teacher Abdullah Al-Malhooq. He would later continue his rise in service to the Kingdom, as ambassador first to the Sudan and then to Greece. I told him what I needed, repeating my claim that it was upsetting for a twenty-year-old to be taken for a boy of twelve. Of course, he knew I wasn't twenty. But he agreed to keep me moving through the system by sending a letter to a Dr Hassan, an eye doctor in Dammam. Abdullah Al-Malhooq said, 'If Dr Hassan says you are seventeen, I will give you a work permit.' 'Seventeen is easy. I'm easily twenty. You will see,' I told him.

Frank Jungers, a former chairman and CEO of Aramco who would do much to advance my career and that of many Saudis in later years, writes about this 'ageing' issue in his memoir:

Saudis who wanted to be hired by Aramco – especially the brightest or those with parents trying to get them a job – would claim that they were eighteen, the minimum hiring age. Most of them would not know what eighteen actually meant in those early days, but they were nonetheless eighteen! When asked their age, they would say: 'Yimkin 18.' (Yimkin means maybe.)

So that's why getting the doctor to say I was seventeen made sense. Seventeen was yimkin eighteen, especially if the job prospect showed promise. In my mind I was at least yimkin eighteen.

Finally, I had my appointment with Dr Hassan. He checked my eyes – trachoma that could lead to blindness was widespread among Saudis and others living along the Gulf at the time – and my teeth. Then he told me to strip down. I protested, knowing what was coming. He said, 'Look, if you want me to age you I have to check you, please.' He checked. He didn't find much. He wrote down twelve years old on the form he was filling out.

I started crying. Tears of deeply felt frustration and anger. But I also saw his sympathetic reaction and argued my case. 'I am really not twelve. I am twenty, but I will settle for eighteen,' I said. He revised twelve and put down sixteen. I said, 'Dr Hassan, look OK not eighteen, I will accept seventeen.' He was wavering. 'Can we agree on that?' We did. I rushed back to the Aramco personnel office with the form saying I was seventeen. And since seventeen for a boy like me could be stretched to yimkin eighteen, I was rehired. My starting date was 6 December 1947.

I was no longer an office boy. Based on my previous experience, and perhaps my display of courage and persistence in job hunting, I was hired as a junior clerk. And I went back to school for four hours a day starting at seven in the morning.

In addition to languages and maths, we also had special classes in shorthand, bookkeeping and typing. I learned I was an excellent typist. I think I was the fastest typist in Saudi Arabia at one time. I used to type on a Remington mechanical typewriter at the rate of 120 words a minute. I was so fast they used me in the oil company steno pool to type letters. My English was OK at the time, but I didn't understand all of the words. I just banged that typewriter as fast as I could. I sat on a pile of dictionaries in order to reach the keys. The Western ladies in the pool cooed over little Ali like a flock of doves. I have to admit I liked the attention.

I continued to work four hours in the afternoon although, probably because the company realized how young I was, I spent two of them playing catch with one of my bosses. I took to American baseball and learned to play shortstop, the position between second and third base. At the time I thought the short in shortstop referred to my height. We had quite a competitive baseball league with Saudi men and boys playing alongside Americans. And we played year round. That cultural seed took root and persisted long after many other traces of American life had vanished from the oil camp. To this day the Little League baseball team from Dhahran is often a contender in the Little League World Series.

One of our English teachers, Fahmi Basrawi, organized the baseball team. We students didn't realize that he had not known anything about either the language or the sport before arriving in the oil camp. His story shows the opportunities open to young Saudi men and boys like us who were willing to take risks.

Basrawi had been a clerk in the Jeddah police department when he answered a vaguely worded newspaper advertisement for an employment opportunity. The recruiter noted that Basrawi could read and write Arabic, and offered him a job on the other side of the country as an English teacher in the Jebel School, for twice what the police department was paying him. When Basrawi said that he couldn't speak, read or write English, the recruiter said don't worry. We will teach you.

Our teacher made the cross-country trip riding on wheat sacks in the back of a truck for nearly two weeks. It wasn't easy back then for trucks to make their way through what is known as the Dhana sands, a stretch of desert between Riyadh and Dhahran where beautiful wing-shaped dunes that move as much as three or four metres a year often closed the roads. Drivers spent almost as much time digging their trucks out of the sand as they did driving on the poorly maintained highways. Once Basrawi arrived, no one was there to teach him English. So he memorized ten or so English words a day from pictures in our textbooks, staying a lesson or two ahead of his students. He ultimately became not only a successful teacher but also a baseball coach loved by all the boys. Basrawi, a handsome man with a close-cropped moustache, would go on to be the star host of a game show on Saudi television.

Years later Basrawi described me to an Aramco interviewer as a 'very serious boy'. He added that I was 'one of the brightest in the class' and that I was very punctual and did my homework without having to be asked. If only he had put that in a report card I could have shown to my father!

We Saudi boys also played soccer, as the Americans called it. Of course, most boys love sports, and I was no exception. What I didn't realize while playing alongside these Americans was how these activities expanded my vision and understanding of people quite different from myself. When I arrived at Lehigh University in Pennsylvania years later, the head of the geology department complimented me on my ability to adjust so quickly to American culture. I told him I had adjusted years earlier while working for Aramco.

The men I played catch with were another set of fathers in my life. One, Keith Cave, used to call me the Mayor of Thuqbah, the small village where we had moved after my brother died. I stayed in touch with him for years after he moved back to America.

Another boss, whom I always called Mr Rafferty, was a kind man who made me his personal project. As I said earlier, many of us Bedu had nagging diseases because of malnutrition and other reasons. I had lesions on my scalp. The treatment among our people at the time was to burn the lesions with a hot iron. I can feel the scar beneath my hair and recall the intense pain of this 'cure'. Rafferty diagnosed the problem as a vitamin deficiency and told me he had just the right medicine. He forced spoonfuls of cod liver oil down my throat, which I can still taste when I think about it. It was terrible, but it worked. After a week, the sores went away and I found new energy.

By 1948 my English was so good that I was selected to be in the first batch of Saudi employees to be sent to Long Island, New York, to teach Arabic to Aramco employees before they came to the Kingdom. My family was very impressed, but also worried about what America was going to be like. My stepmother was determined that I be suitably dressed. So she took me on a dhow, a traditional shallow-bottomed Arab sailboat, to an Indian tailor in Bahrain. He made me two or three white suits like the new Indian Prime Minister Nehru used to wear. I was quite dapper.

Then bad luck again befell me. I ran into Don Richard, the head of the education department. I suppose the person who selected me for the trip had not seen me in the flesh. Richard took one look and said, 'Ali, you are too young to work in the States.' He then drew a line on the wall. 'When you are that tall we will send you,' he said. Even today I would not reach that line. I was disappointed, of course. I have no idea what happened to the suits.

I had a lot of growing up to do over the next few years. One of my most embarrassing memories from this time is about my pride and joy: typing. For some reason I did very poorly on a class typing test in 1951 or so. I don't know why, but I made a lot of mistakes. I threw a temper tantrum and remember telling our instructor, Helen Stanwood, that it was the typewriter's fault. I got so mad I picked up the machine and smashed it on the floor. It disintegrated.

At about the same time, we all took tests to see if we qualified for a government scholarship to a summer course at the American University of Beirut. As I went into the testing room, Miss Stanwood said, 'Ali, I know you are going to do very well but please build no hopes.' I was devastated. To this day I don't know if it was because of my age and size, or my typing temper tantrum, but I was not selected for the scholarship, even though I did extremely well on the test.

This rejection further fuelled my determination to

succeed. But before I could control my destiny, I had to learn to control myself. I made a commitment never to lose my temper again. Since then I don't recall ever again becoming really annoyed – though some overly aggressive journalists covering OPEC meetings might take issue on that point.

4. Stepping Out – 1953–1959

My fortunes turned in 1953 when I was finally selected for the American University of Beirut scholarship, after having been twice rejected earlier. At AUB I received my first exposure to the physical sciences, chemistry, biology and advanced mathematics. Until then, I had no knowledge of algebra or anything like it.

The lush grounds and stately buildings of the AUB campus were a stark contrast to the modest dwellings and dusty offices of the oil camp and nearby towns. And while Beirut is hot during the summer, it is nothing compared to the heat and humidity near the Arabian Gulf. Even though it felt as if we were at a summer resort – indeed, many Arabs during this period vacationed in the hills outside Beirut and in western Syria – we knew we had work to do.

At the end of the course we took a test, and I finished among the ten best. Aramco then sponsored this top ten for another summer course, this time at Aleppo College. Again, we were visiting a beautiful city and campus. Tragically, it has all been destroyed by the Syrian government forces during the recent war. What a waste.

The ten of us returned to the Kingdom in September 1953. At roughly the same moment, Aramco workers in the area of Al-Hasa went on strike. We were not involved directly, but it was a major dispute and almost every family in the region was affected one way or another.

The strike had its roots in nearly a decade of mounting

labour tension between the oil company and its Saudi employees. In July 1945, Saudis walked off the job at the Ras Tanura refinery for several days. Aramco increased wages modestly, particularly for low-level workers, and operations resumed. Just a month later, however, as many as 9,000 workers in Ras Tanura as well as in Dhahran, the heart of our operations at the time, downed tools. Their major complaints involved working conditions, pay, living arrangements and the fact that foreign workers, notably Italians who arrived during the war, were treated better than Saudis.

The government sided with the Saudi workers, which was good news for them but clearly frustrating for Aramco. What's more, the government demanded that the oil company negotiate with representatives of the Saudi workforce, overturning the previous practice of listening to complaints one individual at a time. The government's action put the oil company on notice that, unlike other oil-producing countries in the region, the Kingdom was not going to take a hands-off approach to labour relations. The workers returned to their jobs, and after months of negotiations Aramco agreed to improve working conditions, build permanent bachelor dormitories (replacing many but not all of the tents used by workers) and to construct a hospital in Dhahran.

Another brief strike followed in 1947. Workers and the government continued to complain about the obvious discrimination in the living quarters available to Americans compared to Saudis. The company responded over the next few years with improved conditions in the camps, and the start of a home ownership programme for Saudis so that workers could live with their families.

Many well-meaning Americans had trouble understanding what so many local people were complaining about. Had we not been living in our own goat-hair tents just a few years earlier? Resentment lingered and grew. One of my long-time personal friends and oil company colleagues, Hamad Jurifani, started working at Aramco at the Ras Tanura refinery in 1951. He clearly felt like a second-class citizen:

'They had the community, you know, with the nice houses and so on, on the beach. And they housed the expatriates. The Saudis, they were divided into two levels. Those that are higher grades are put into homes with fans, but no air conditioners. And the rest are put in tents. And, I remember, four people to a tent.'

Adding to the tension between Aramco and the government was the fact that the oil company had closed the Jebel School in 1950. It had been renamed the Arab Preparatory School in 1946 and the Arab Trade Preparatory School in 1947, but everybody still called it the Jebel School. Aramco reasoned that it was time for the government to take over public education.

The government responded, claiming that Aramco had failed to support the Kingdom's effort to meet the needs of the growing population in the oil-producing region of the country. In January 1953 Crown Prince Saud visited the oil company facilities, an assessment of regional education being one of his top priorities. Prince Saud was highly influential, and would become more so when he was named king later that year following the death of his beloved father, King Abdul Aziz. Aramco, which had a special department devoted to relations with the government in Riyadh, was hardly naive. It got the message. Later that month, Aramco agreed to a plan for the oil company to start building schools in the region for as many as 2,400 students.

Saudis embraced this education agreement, but it was

not enough to stop workers from continuing to demand better pay and work conditions. In May 1953 more than 150 Saudi intermediate-skilled workers and others signed a petition addressed to Aramco management, insisting on cost-of-living wage increases and improved living conditions. They also said that not enough Saudis were being promoted to senior positions, and that Saudis were discriminated against in the camps. The company refused to meet with them en masse, but agreed to talks with a smaller group on 30 June. Aramco then rejected their claims.

In early September, the regional government labour office backed the workers' position. It did not call for a strike, of course, but many workers walked off their jobs shortly thereafter. A few weeks later the Saudi National Guard was called in to break the strike. Several workers were imprisoned. It was a harsh lesson for all concerned.

A government panel began an investigation, taking worker testimony in October. By November, the company had agreed to most of the workers' demands, and eventually the conflict resulted in further improvements to Saudi labour laws. Even though my group was already on a fast track for advancement by the company, I don't doubt that the strike helped our cause as well as that of the average worker. It also led to more equal treatment of Saudis in terms of housing and other benefits.

It was nonetheless a slow process. Abdullah Al-Tariki was a rising star in our government's oil ministry throughout the 1950s. Tariki, who received his undergraduate degree from the University of Cairo and a masters degree from the University of Texas, would be one of the first two Saudis appointed to the Aramco board of directors in 1959, and would become the Saudi government's first oil minister when that position was created in 1960. In 1954, while stationed in the Eastern Province, Tariki insisted on living in Aramco's senior staff community in Dhahran. At the time the community consisted almost entirely of American and other Western families. It was a short stay, and there was no doubt among many American oil company officials that Tariki rightly felt discriminated against.

Our scholarship course was cancelled because of the strike. In 1954, the company created the Advanced Clerical School so we and other students could continue our education within the Kingdom. It was not located in the main oil camp but nearby. I was especially eager to study more in the sciences and maths.

At that time, the Aramco personnel department was my sponsor, grooming me to be an employment counsellor. But I didn't think this was the right career choice for me. I met with the head of personnel, Bill Bowman, in late 1953 and told him what I was thinking. He said, 'Ali, we spent money to train you to be a counsellor. You have been given a higher job grade.' I told him I was too young to counsel people. That was probably the first time I used my youth as an argument in my favour! The truth is I simply didn't want to do it.

I told him I wanted to study geology and go into the exploration department. There were lower-level Saudi workers in Exploration at the time, but no one on the senior staff track, and I wanted to be the first. Beyond that distinction, I was well aware that experience in the exploration department had been the route taken by many previous presidents.

Bowman agreed to let me speak to officials in Exploration. My first stop was the office of L. B. Milam Jr, who ran departmental operations. He was a kind man and would later become yet another father figure in my life. Years later he would die in a Texas hospital bed holding my hand. That day, as he gave me advice, I was taking notes. Milam noticed the strange symbols I was transcribing, stopped me and said, 'Ali, aren't you confused? I thought you wrote Arabic from right to left, not left to right.' When I told him I was writing in shorthand we had a good laugh.

The decision to put a Saudi on the department fast track was important enough, I guess, that it had to be taken very high up the ladder, to the general manager who supervised Exploration. Scott Segar was a short, stocky man from Billings, Montana, known for his bluntness. 'Why do you want to be a geologist?' he asked me. 'This is dirty work, you'll be on the rigs all of the time,' he added, not appreciating the fact that I and most of my generation had grown up in the desert.

Suddenly I found myself saying out loud what until that moment I had kept to myself. I felt as if I was back in the Jebel School. 'That's OK,' I said. 'I want to be president of the company.' That caught him by surprise, but only for a moment. 'Son,' he said, 'that is as good a reason as anything I've ever heard. Welcome to Exploration.'

As a test, they dispatched me to the Rub' Al-Khali desert to work with geologists on what is called a stratigraphic test well. This is the kind of well we drill to learn more about the rock strata in the area. It was the first well we drilled in Obailah, and at 5,000 metres deep, using aluminium drill pipe, it was the state of the art at the time. After two weeks in the desert, with its towering rust-coloured sand dunes, I became very sick. Despite being confined to the hospital for a week, they could not discover what was wrong with me. No doubt our people in the old days would have assumed I was being punished by jinns or other evil spirits for some sort of transgression. Maybe simply for tempting fate by venturing into a barren region that was never intended to support much human life. I never did find out my ailment, nor did the experience keep me from trekking across some of the most barren reaches of our country in years to come, but I have been near-sighted ever since.

Once I was out of the hospital, I went back to school instead of returning to the desert. They didn't think I had failed my field test, but nonetheless thought it made more sense for me to continue my formal schooling.

I did fail another field test of sorts, but this time with my family. My cousin Salem, who was about my age of twenty and who lived in a town near Thuqbah, was planning to get married. He offered to lend me a car so I could drive the family to the wedding and the reception afterwards. He asked me if I knew how to drive. 'Of course I know how to drive,' I lied. When he showed up with his car I covered up my ignorance by saying that since we had only old pick-up trucks out in the field he needed to show me how to work the gears and the ignition of his sedan. I could barely see over the steering wheel.

I had watched plenty of Saudis far less educated than I was drive trucks across the desert. How hard could it be? I loaded my father, my uncle and my brothers into the car, filling the front and back seats. We had no seat belts back then, of course, which was a pity. My uncle was suspicious. 'Ali, are you sure you know how to drive?' he asked. I said, 'Of course, don't worry.'

The local roads back then were little more than trails. And like out in the desert they often were filled in with sand. No problem, I thought, I had seen plenty of Aramco truck drivers steer through loose sand by turning the steering wheel sharply in the opposite direction to which they were sliding. So that's what I did when we came around a sharp bend and there was a sand dune blocking our way. The trouble was, I oversteered and we rode up the side of the small dune and the car flipped over with its wheels spinning helplessly in the air.

No one was badly hurt, but they were all angry, especially my uncle. He chased me out across the camel pasture next to the road until he ran out of breath. We all walked the rest of the way to the wedding. Salem greeted us warmly, and then said, 'Where is the car?' I said it was somewhere back in the dunes, letting him think we had simply had a breakdown. Later, a group of us turned the car back over and another relative drove it back to Salem. I would have to wait another five years and travel halfway around the world to get behind the wheel of my next car.

Our work, and much of the region in general, was disrupted in 1956 by the Suez Crisis. In July, the Egyptian Army seized the Suez Canal, setting the stage for an international crisis.

The British, French and Israelis attacked Egypt on 29 October. They were forced to pull out quickly after US President Dwight D. Eisenhower publicly denounced the invasion and threatened to withdraw US financial support. Nonetheless, Saudi Arabia and other oil producers responded by cutting off oil supplies to Britain and France. Because of the clear stance taken by both America and Saudi Arabia, Aramco facilities were spared damage from rioting that occurred in other oil-producing areas where the British had an interest.

When I returned to the exploration department after a

holiday in the mountains outside Beirut, Lynn Milam had a surprise for me. He told me he wanted me to go back to Lebanon. I was one of five students picked to go on a scholarship to the International College at AUB to finish our high-school education and prepare for college. If we succeeded, we would be the first group of Saudi students the oil company sent to college in the States. All expenses paid.

The man who was running the course was named Paul E. Case. He was a big, tall man with glasses and close-cut curly hair, and, once again, very fatherly toward us all. His wife was very gracious as well. They made it their job to teach us about American culture. The Cases would invite us to their house to talk about American customs and habits, down to details including how to behave at the dinner table and hold your knife and fork. For about a week, Mrs Case cooked different meals for us each night. She showed us how to cut our meat with a knife and fork American style, an exotic practice for those like ourselves with little or no exposure to other ways of living.

Paul Case made it clear, however, that there was much more at stake than our table manners. We were guinea pigs, he said. 'If you succeed we will continue this programme. There may be hundreds later, but the programme depends on you.'

Not having benefited from consistent, formal high-school education to this point, we felt the pressure. We were very strong in some subjects and weak in others. Two of our group had to repeat a year to graduate from high school. Despite that setback, they both became successes, one in banking in Syria and the other as a Saudi Arabian businessman.

The three of us who did graduate, myself and Mustaffa

Al-Khan Abuahmad and Abdullah Busbayte, were worried that the course would be halted because of those who did not make the grade. But Case was, in fact, proud of what we had achieved. I modestly think the fact that I ranked as class valedictorian helped in his decision. While we waited to go to America we were actually able to take additional classes at AUB as college freshmen and sophomores. I chose general education courses, including the work of Muslim scholars from the Middle Ages, notably Ibn Rushd (known as Averroes in the West) and Ibn Khaldun, author of the *Muqaddimah*, (*An Introduction to History*). Before we left for America, we were joined by a fourth Saudi student, Hamad Juraifani.

We were now prepared for the next big step in our lives and our development as adults. It was also a milestone for Aramco and the Kingdom. The oil company committed itself to developing qualified Saudis to become fully educated and trained industry professionals. At the same time our country was committing itself to an even faster pace in developing Saudi society and improving the lives of our people.

Life would never be the same again.

5. To America – 1959–1961

I wanted to go home. That's what I told Paul Case when I called him in Dhahran from the Aramco offices in midtown Manhattan. We had been in America for only four days, but I was suffering from acute culture shock. I rode in the elevators in my new suit, a Western style one this time, and said 'Salam alaikum' to everybody and nobody said 'Good morning' in return. New York may be a city of immigrants, but in 1959 nobody looked or sounded like us.

Manhattan was too fast and too confusing, even for a group of college-bound engineers and geologists. On our first ride on the subway from Times Square we ended up somewhere on Long Island and the New York City office manager had to retrieve us in his car and bring us back to Manhattan. 'This is a terrible place,' I thought to myself.

Case told me to be patient. Aramco had been wise to arrange for the four of us to attend a six-week summer orientation course for foreign students planning to attend American universities. We also took a quick trip to Washington DC to see America's capital and learn more about American history. I think I took a picture of every government building and monument. The Washington Monument made us think of the father of our country, King Abdul Aziz.

The orientation course was at Bucknell University in the central Pennsylvania countryside, where we benefited from a much slower pace of life than Manhattan. The course primarily emphasized speaking and reading English. My English was good enough that the people running the course asked me to try to teach it to a doctor and a group of nurses from Brazil, although I probably learned more Portuguese than they learned English.

Just as important to us was the chance to be further exposed to American culture, especially the kind of things young men were interested in. I even learned to dance the jitterbug! Within a few weeks of arriving at Bucknell, I was willing to give America a second chance.

That autumn the four of us went our own ways to attend different universities. I started taking classes at Lehigh University in eastern Pennsylvania. Most of my bosses at Aramco had been from Texas or other states in the south or west, but I owe my choice of university to a man who had grown up in the eastern US, a geologist named Don Donoghue, who had a doctorate in geology. I got to know him one summer working in a shack at the oil camp labelling rock core samples from test wells. It was hot, dusty work, but I learned a lot about the rock strata in different parts of the Kingdom thanks to Dr Donoghue.

He wanted me not only to be educated in the eastern US, but also to attend a smaller school so I wouldn't get lost in the crowd. 'I want you to go to a decent university,' he said. 'Go to Brown or Lehigh. They are good small universities.' I didn't know anything about either, so I asked him how I should go about making a choice. He said, 'Easy, flip a coin. Heads Lehigh, tails Brown.' It came up heads and so I went to Lehigh. If I had known at the time that Lehigh was still an all-boys' school, I might have chosen differently.

When I arrived at Lehigh I moved into Price Hall, at the time a dormitory housing thirty to forty students of various backgrounds and religions in the old part of the campus built on the side of South Mountain. The greystone university buildings were darkened by the soot from the nearby Bethlehem Steel mills that were still in full operation at that time. Worker housing in the town of Bethlehem was built quite close to the school, so Lehigh did not feel quite as isolated as Bucknell.

Back then universities still did a lot of freshman hazing. Ours was pretty mild compared to stories I heard from students attending other colleges, especially those who joined fraternities. We wore on our heads brown beanies called dinks until the annual Rivalry football game in October with nearby Lafayette College. We also had to pretend, at least in my case, to smoke corncob pipes.

We were serious about our studies. Lessons took place six days a week for those of us taking lab classes. Sunday was the only day off. We were very competitive. I was anxious not to let down Aramco or my country, and took a heavy load of science courses. The other boys had to answer to their parents, who were paying for their tuition. Many of them also faced being drafted into the US military if they flunked out. I did well, but it was hard work. The head of the geology department when I arrived, Dr Richard Gault, was a demanding and excellent master. His number two, Dr Donald Ryan, was also a very good teacher.

Despite our competitiveness, we helped each other out. With my combination of shorthand and typing skills I was the best note-taker among my peer group. If someone could not attend one of the classes I also was taking, I would often share my lecture notes after I typed up my shorthand version.

Most of my friends were Americans. There were only

twenty or so foreign undergraduate students at Lehigh during that time and I was the only Saudi on the campus. That said, there was one other Saudi guy, Mahmood Taybah, also sponsored by Aramco, who was married and lived off-campus. We became good friends.

Another sixty to ninety foreign students were in graduate programmes, mostly in engineering. Because I started my education late, I was at least four years older than most of my classmates. A group of us attended football games and wrestling matches together, and went to the movies once a week. Then, as now, for religious reasons no movies are shown in public in my own country. I confess that as boys in Al-Hasa some of us used to sneak into the outdoor movies, mostly westerns that the Americans showed in the oil camp. John Wayne was our hero.

At Lehigh we also went to dances with students from other colleges in the area. I wanted to put my new jitterbugging skills to use. Elvis Presley was the most popular singer in America, but I never liked him. I thought the nickname Elvis the Pelvis fitted him well.

For a time I was president of the international club at Lehigh, and one of my responsibilities was to arrange dances called mixers, where we invited girls from nearby women's colleges to join us. At Lehigh we would dance with partners of the opposite sex, of course, a practice strictly forbidden in Saudi Arabia. For me, dancing with women was fun, but certainly something I didn't expect to continue after college. Besides, I was not interested in a romantic relationship. I always knew I would eventually marry a girl from back home. That was our custom.

American customs were different in more ways than one. When I'd been undergoing orientation at Bucknell

University another Arab student and I had become friendly. We would meet on campus and talk about our homes, cultures and that sort of thing. It is customary for Arab men to hold hands as they stroll along talking in such circumstances. We had done so, and the following weekend it seemed harder than usual to find a girl to dance with me. I asked one of my American friends why. He looked at me and laughed. 'Ali, they think you are gay.' That was my first introduction to the word in this context, and I didn't understand. 'Well, I am gay. I'm happy. Why is that a problem?' I asked. He explained, and then I understood. I was also proud of telling people I was a socialist. This was not long after the McCarthy era, when all things left-wing were considered 'un-American'. Again my friend pulled me aside and checked that he heard me right. 'Yes,' I told him, 'I like to be with people and to talk with people. I'm a socialist.' He corrected me again. 'You mean "sociable". Socialist is something different!'

Americans are often surprised to find out that we Saudis have a sense of humour. Maybe it is the stock media images of Saudis in traditional dress and wearing sunglasses that make us look so serious. But I had already learned from my years at Aramco that Americans and Saudis both like a good joke.

Bethlehem had several events to help foreign students become familiar with the town and area, and local people were equally interested in getting to know something about us. I was invited to a women's group meeting for foreign students shortly after the fall semester started. I wanted to make a good impression. Based on how nervous some of the other foreign students looked, I thought humour would be a good way to break the ice. A lady asked me how I got to America. Did I come on a camel? The other women laughed.

As a matter of fact, the plane we flew from Saudi Arabia to the States was a propeller-driven Douglas DC-4 owned by Aramco and known as the 'Flying Camel'. Back then it took us four days to get to America. So I said to her, 'Yes, I came on a flying camel.' She was amazed. She got the joke after I explained it.

On another occasion I met a man who was a member of the Amish religious community centred near Lancaster, Pennsylvania. They live separate from the rest of society most of the time. He looked me over and said, 'Son, where are you from?' I told him, 'I am from Saudi Arabia.' He thought about that for a minute and asked me, 'Whereabouts in Pennsylvania is that?' So I told him it was near Bethlehem.

That first winter in America was a shock. The Americans in Aramco warned us Saudi students about the cold and snow we would see if we went to college in the northern part of the States. But I still wasn't prepared for the wind whistling around the college buildings at night as I returned to my dormitory after an evening at the library. I had what I thought was a winter coat when I had tried it on back in Dhahran. As it got colder, this coat simply was not thick enough for Pennsylvania, so I went into the town of Bethlehem to buy something warmer. I was sent to the local Army & Navy surplus store, which carried leftover clothing and equipment from World War II. At that time similar stores could be found in almost every American city of any size. I bought a thick wool jacket for what I thought was a good price.

As I strutted into one of our science lab classes, I was quite proud of my new purchase. One of my closest friends and fellow geology major, Peter Van de Kamp, who had grown up not too far away in New Jersey, quizzed me about the coat. When I said what it cost, he told me I had been taken advantage of. I didn't understand, so he took me back to the store the next day and bargained with the salesman for the same coat. He negotiated a sales price that was a fraction of what I paid. I was angry, mostly at myself.

It was a valuable lesson. Just because I wasn't haggling in a souk back home didn't mean that prices in the West or anywhere else weren't negotiable. Decades later when contractors thought oil-rich Saudi Aramco could afford to pay a high price for everything from concrete to precision ball bearings, I always had the same advice for our managers: negotiate, negotiate, negotiate!

I got a first-hand look at American family life thanks to my friend Peter, who invited me to his family's home in New Jersey for the Thanksgiving holiday. To make me feel at home, Peter's mother offered to cook me rice along with the traditional dishes of turkey, stuffing and potatoes. I showed her how we washed it three times at home and then brought it to a boil.

Peter and I helped his father with chores in the yard, including chopping wood. They were a little surprised at how quickly I mastered the axe. I told them I had grown up under the open sky and always enjoyed outdoor work. I felt like one of the Pilgrims at the first Thanksgiving in America.

When spring finally came to America I played baseball and soccer. I surprised my American teachers with my baseball skills, but as a foreign student the Americans expected me to be pretty good at soccer. Fortunately, I was. I had good footwork and passing skills and set up my share of goals.

My most memorable experiences from my education in

America occurred outside the classroom. As geology majors we were expected to take part in field work during the summers. During my first full summer in the States I was assigned to a University of Wyoming project in the Medicine Bow Mountains.

To travel more than halfway across the country from Pennsylvania to Wyoming, I convinced Aramco that I needed to buy a car. They agreed, and allocated enough money for a Volkswagen Beetle. I bought what I thought was a beautiful sky blue Bug, took some driving lessons, since I didn't want to flip another car like I did back home, and was ready to go.

Peter Van de Kamp was going to the same summer project, so he rode along. We were quite a mismatched pair. I was dark-haired and five-three and he was a blond Dutchman almost a foot taller and had to fold himself in half just to squeeze into the car. It was a long trip, since there were very few four-lane interstate highways or turnpikes at that time. We would drive all day and then pull over and roll out our sleeping bags in a nearby cornfield or pasture. The following morning we would buy breakfast in the nearest town and continue on our way. I scheduled a quick visit to Yellowstone and Teton National Parks before we were due to arrive at the project camp in the spectacularly beautiful Rocky Mountains of south-eastern Wyoming. I was amazed to see deer, elk and antelope watching us during our travels that summer.

The University of Wyoming programme is still one of the premier geology field camps in America. It's a formal course in geology but largely held outdoors. Students learned how to examine rocks and how to measure their properties, as well as the essential skill of map-making. We would pace off in a direction and map the terrain using compasses, making notes about the rocks we saw along the way and marking their positions on our maps. We also learned to use aerial photographs and topography.

The first week, we were in the base camp and lived in small cabins. A large building was used as the refectory and for evening lectures. Among the university faculty teaching the course was the famous and highly respected Samuel H. Knight, a professor from the University of Wyoming and an expert on Rocky Mountain geology and dinosaur fossils. Columbia University also had staff participating in the course. The following four weeks we went out to separate areas to do our field work and lived in tents.

Geologists are explorers by nature. That summer, in addition to examining exposed layers of rock from hundreds of millions of years ago, Peter and I decided we wanted to observe the local communities as well. We would drive on weekends to nearby towns. One weekend we decided to drive to Laramie and take part in a three-day celebration called Jubilee Days. The celebrations included a rodeo (my first), lots of carnival attractions and food barbecued over charcoal.

I, of course, wasn't familiar with local customs, and Peter had spent almost his entire life on the eastern seaboard, so he wasn't sure what to expect out in cowboy country either. We did not realize how strange we must have looked to the locals. Even our car was foreign and had out-of-state licence plates. Those facts plus the obvious amount of beer being consumed by the local jocks should have warned us that we were headed for trouble.

We were driving down the highway leaving Laramie and headed back toward Medicine Bow National Forest when we realized that we were being followed by a car full of young men. They were clearly after us and, based on the way their car was swerving, highly inebriated. The little air-cooled engine in the rear of my Bug was no match for the big American V-8 they had under the hood. They were closing in on us.

Suddenly I saw red lights flashing in my rear-view mirror. A large black-and-white police car pulled alongside and an angry officer waved us over to the shoulder of the highway. The car full of young men kept on driving. 'This is it,' I thought. 'The local authorities are in on the plan to chase us down.' Not only was my career with Aramco over. I was worried about getting out of there with my life.

The officers told me to follow them into the next town, Centennial, Wyoming. They told us that we were going to be the guests of Centennial for the night. Our sleeping quarters were the town jail. Only later did it dawn on us that they were locking us up for our own good. They must have seen the car chasing my odd little blue Volkswagen and realized we were in trouble.

I very sheepishly called my course supervisor to tell him what happened. He was so angry that I was going to embarrass Aramco that at first he threatened to call Saudi Arabia and have me thrown off the course. But he calmed down and agreed to keep it our secret, as long as I stayed out of further trouble. I did my best.

Language and cultural issues remained a challenge. Peter and I celebrated our freedom the next morning by going to a local café for breakfast. Almost everyone we saw was as blond as Peter. Their families had all come from Sweden, we learned later. When the waitress came over I looked her straight in the eye and said, 'I would like the antelope.' She looked surprised and said, 'We don't have antelope.' I said, 'Yes you do. It's right here on the menu.' Some restaurants in the Wyoming countryside featuring game did, in fact, have antelope on the menu, but this wasn't one of them. She said, 'Oh, you mean cantaloupe.' I remember Peter looking out the window and smiling. He didn't want to embarrass me further.

Later that summer, before returning to Lehigh, I visited the next group of Saudi students going through the orientation course at Bucknell. In only its second year, the course had expanded to include eleven students sponsored by Aramco, more than double our original group of four. It was an impressive crowd. Included were Nassir Al-Ajmi, my fellow future senior Saudi Aramco executive, and Khalid Ali Al-Turki, who would later leave Aramco and go on to become one of our country's most successful businessmen.

I took pride in the fact that our group of guinea pigs had been considered a success. We opened the door for this group and the thousands of Saudi students, most sponsored by the government, who have followed over the decades. I was grateful that my night spent in Centennial, Wyoming, had not resulted in a black mark on our record of achievement.

As 1960 drew to a close, we Saudi students were not alone in feeling a new sense of opportunity. Across America, change was in the air. It was a new decade and there was to be a new president. Dwight D. Eisenhower had been respected around the world, but was definitely part of the older generation. The candidate prompting the most excitement was the young Democratic senator from the state of Massachusetts, John F. Kennedy.

Kennedy won the presidential election that November and took office in January 1961. He was young and energetic. When you saw him on television or read about him in the newspapers, he made just about anything seem possible. Kennedy helped make the early 1960s in America a time of optimism. The sense of potential he conveyed also brought forth an increasing amount of student activism.

Students across the country protested against racial discrimination in the southern part of the country during this time, and demonstrations against the war in Vietnam would soon follow. We had meetings on campus and there were some student rallies. But in general, my impression was that Lehigh was rather apolitical while I was there. We had very few African-Americans on campus at that time and most students focused on their studies.

I and my fellow Saudis were in America to learn, but we were not immune to the sense of political awakening and activism. A number of us had been exposed to at least some history of Arab nationalism at the American University in Beirut. In my student backpack, I often carried a copy of the Lebanese-Egyptian author George Antonius's *The Arab Awakening*, an influential book on the subject published in the late 1930s. We were proud and loyal Saudi subjects, but at the same time we were proud of Arab accomplishments throughout the Muslim world.

During this time, Crown Prince Faisal, half-brother of King Saud and heir to the crown, was seen in our country as a force for modernization. He was named prime minister in 1958 to help the Kingdom adopt much-needed modern management structures and to control spending. He resigned that position in 1960 in protest at resistance to his efforts, but supporters among the royal family and the ulema, or religious leadership, had him reappointed to that role in 1962. The royal family named Faisal as king in 1964, and Saud stepped down. As a result, the pace of change in the country quickened. Of particular note was the opening of schools for girls.

While I was going to college in America, Aramco was growing rapidly back home. I was in regular contact with fellow Saudis who were working full-time at Aramco. They were advancing ahead of me in job classifications. Some were already ranked as foremen, a position I had been offered at one point if I had chosen not to go into the undergraduate course. As a result, they were making more money than I was. They were also getting married and starting families.

I envied their happiness and prosperity, but I was determined to make the most of my time in America. I was progressing rapidly at Lehigh, taking extra classes, and I had the college credits that I'd brought with me from Beirut. I realized that I could graduate early.

Rather than return home at that point, what I really wanted was to continue my education and get a masters degree while I was in America. I knew that many senior Aramco executives had advanced degrees. That would be an important way for me to get ahead. And as I mentioned earlier, the Saudi model for my generation of ambitious students, our first oil minister, Abdullah Al-Tariki, had attained a masters degree from the University of Texas in the 1950s.

I faced a major hurdle. Aramco started the programme of undergraduate education for Saudis in America with my group. At that time they saw no need to educate us further. They wanted us to come back to the Kingdom and put our new skills immediately to work. The business was expanding rapidly and they were having trouble finding enough skilled candidates to fill important jobs. They wanted a return on their investment.

I eventually convinced Aramco officials that it would be a good thing for me to get a masters as long as I was already in the States as an undergraduate. They insisted on one important condition. They would only give me one year after graduating to get a masters degree. That was a problem: most geology masters courses were two years long.

The geology department at Lehigh agreed that I could use my senior year to finish my undergraduate requirements and at the same time have my work count toward the first year of a masters in geology. They helped me identify several graduate programmes that might work for my situation, including the prestigious geology masters course at Stanford University in California. Like the American students, I took the Graduate Record Examination, the GRE, then left for another summer of work and travel.

That year, 1961, will also stick in my memory because my father, who had long been unwell, died. It hurt me to realize that I would not be able to return in time for the funeral. And even if the funeral had been delayed, I did not have enough money to travel to the Gulf and back. For someone who was raised as a member of a close-knit tribe, that was a sad time. Not all the choices related to improving my life and career were happy ones.

6. Adventure and Education – 1961–1964

In the summer of 1961 I headed off from Lehigh to work for the US Geological Survey. At first we went to Washington DC for two weeks, then were assigned to work in the field. I went to Albuquerque to take part in a programme that was evaluating underground water basins in Arizona and New Mexico. It was work that would be of particular help to me in my career back in Saudi Arabia.

More important for my education was the fact that the programme was run by Professor Stanley Davis, head of Stanford's geology department. A well-known Iraqi professor, Mahdi Hantush, was also part of the programme leadership team. I was not shy about my interest in Stanford. I asked Professor Davis, 'What would it take to get into Stanford?' He said, 'Work with us for two weeks and I will tell you what you need.' I don't think I ever worked harder for two weeks any time in my life than I did that summer.

After that two-week period, I went back and asked if he thought I had a chance of getting into the masters course. He said, 'Yes, very well. All you have to do is write to me. Write to me and I will take care of it.' Due to that chance meeting, and some hard work, I was accepted by Stanford. My good friend Peter was not, even though his grades were better than mine.

When I was in New Mexico that summer I had another incident with restaurant menus. This time I was not mistaking cantaloupe for antelope. I could not read anything on the menu because it was in Spanish. I walked into a Mexican restaurant in Albuquerque and because of the way I look the waitress assumed I was Mexican. That was OK with me, but when I asked for a menu in English she looked at me like I was crazy and walked off. I insisted I couldn't read Spanish but she didn't believe me. I finally pointed at an item on the menu and was served tamales.

While I was eating, an Arab couple walked into the restaurant. The husband was on the faculty at the University of New Mexico nearby. I hurried over to their table and introduced myself. It was good to have someone to speak Arabic with. I asked them in Arabic to please tell the waitress that I was not Mexican and would like a menu in English. They understood and said it had happened to them as well. There were not many Arabs in the south-western US at the time. I finally got my English menu and was able to order the rest of my meal, and enjoyed the company of my fellow Arabic speakers.

I don't remember looking up from my books very often during my final year at Lehigh. I felt the pressure to perform well for my Lehigh professors as well as the Stanford geology department. I was also preparing for the next stage in my personal life.

One exception to my heavy load of science classes was a course on art appreciation that I took to meet my subject distribution requirements for graduation. Our art history professor, Richard Redd, was also a painter. He conveyed a love of art that I still carry with me, although I have no artistic inclinations myself.

For the final test we were to be shown thirty-nine slides of paintings. We had to name the artist, give the date of the painting and describe what it symbolized. The weekend before the test I drove up to New York City and did my homework in a number of museums and galleries. I took pages of notes in a very organized, scientific fashion. I basically memorized all the answers. I am proud to say I ended up getting 100 per cent on that part of the test, which left Professor Redd very confused as to why I didn't continue with art studies.

We were required to pass tests showing we were competent in two languages in addition to our native language in order to graduate from Lehigh. The administration decided that since I was so proficient in English, it was going to be considered my mother tongue. Great, I thought, then my first choice for another language was Arabic. Before the test I brushed up on my Arabic grammar, which can be very tricky.

They brought in an instructor from another university to test me, since Arabic wasn't offered at Lehigh at that time. The first question he asked me was, 'What do you know about Ibn Khaldun?' I was really happy with that question, since I had read his work at the American University of Beirut. I was also a little surprised that the instructor spoke to me in English. 'I guess I am going to speak in English, then,' I said. 'Yes, I don't understand Arabic,' he said. I knew I was going to do well, especially since his second question was about another favourite author, Averroes.

My second foreign language was German, which I studied all three years at Lehigh. I chose it after meeting a few students from Germany who became good friends of mine. A Lehigh faculty member quizzed me, in German, and I passed the test easily.

At graduation that spring I was ranked in the top 25 per cent of my class at Lehigh. The dean, Glenn Christensen, would later note: 'To stand in the top quarter of his class is a solid achievement in any college. To stand in the top quarter of a class so carefully selected as Lehigh's, and while one is also studying in a foreign language, is a highly laudable accomplishment.' My hard work was rewarded. I vowed to myself to work even harder in the future.

After a long, hot graduation ceremony in Grace Hall I met up with Peter Van de Kamp and a few other close friends around the flagpole on campus, a traditional meeting place at Lehigh. We shook hands, hugged and wished each other well. We talked about our summer plans.

Mine would be a bit busier than most. Between graduation from Lehigh and starting my second year of graduate school on the Stanford campus in California, I first spent a month in Copenhagen living with a host family. It was something I had wanted to experience, and I knew it was now or never, because I would then be heading back home to meet my future wife for the first time, get married and return with her to the States. It would be her first trip away from home.

Arranged marriages were common among my generation. For many Saudis they still are. Even though friends back home were already married, I had vowed that I would not join them until I had my degree in hand. Six months before graduation I knew that I basically had the degree. It was time.

I wrote to a distant Al-Naimi cousin in Bahrain who used to teach in one of the company schools near our refinery complex in Ras Tanura. I had known his brother while at the American University in Beirut. I knew they had a sister, and since the brother I had met was quite handsome, I assumed his sister must be beautiful, although I had never seen her picture.

So I wrote to the older brother as the senior member of the family (their father had passed away) and told him I was coming home for two weeks and I wanted to betroth and marry his sister.

I flew home and a few days later went to Bahrain to meet the older cousin. He welcomed me into the family home, and into the family, even though we were already cousins. He said he was aware of my progress as a student and he was impressed. 'May I see my prospective wife?' I asked him. 'Of course,' he said.

In came this dazzling beauty of sixteen or seventeen – like me, she was unsure of her exact age – with dark curly hair. Her name was Dhabyah and she was in her last year of high school. I liked what I saw; she liked what she saw. We were engaged on the spot. A judge was summoned, we signed the deed and legally we were husband and wife. We have been married ever since.

I immediately headed back alone to Saudi Arabia across the shallow strip of the Arabian Sea that separates us from Bahrain. That does not sound romantic, I know, but I had a lot to do. Arranged marriages at first are as much about family as they are about the bride and bridegroom. I had to tell the rest of my family, who had to this point known nothing of my plans.

I called my mother and told her I was married. She asked, 'Who is she?' That meant who was her family. I told my mother who Dhabyah's father was and she said, 'Oh, this is a fine family, I know them.' I repeated that conversation with one of my uncles and several cousins.

On 1 August 1962 I rented a shallow-bottomed dhow and took the whole family from the Kingdom's Eastern Province on the short trip to Bahrain. This was decades before the causeway that now links our two countries was built. The following day we had the wedding at Dhabyah's family's home. It was not very elaborate, just a large party that included my three brothers. Since we were marrying within the family there was not much of a dowry to speak of.

The next two weeks we kept busy. We spent the first week in Bahrain with her family, then we went over to Ras Tanura to stay at my brother's house. The area has a lovely beach even though the housing complexes were developed not too far from Aramco's first refinery.

As strange as it may sound today, that was my wife's first time away from home. She had never even travelled to Saudi Arabia, although you can see it from Bahrain. She spoke English with an Indian accent, having a teacher who, like my first tailor, was part of the large Indian community on the island. She had only the vaguest idea of what it might mean to travel to America, but she was about to find out.

I had one major problem to iron out before we went to America. The extra bursary the oil company had granted me for graduate school did not include any money for a wife. I had not told anyone I planned to get married.

I told my boss, Lynn Milam, that I couldn't leave my new wife at home. For us to have an amicable marriage she needed to come with me and see some of the world. Lynn said, 'Ali, you are like a son to me. I agree with you. My wife and I will throw you a private party to celebrate your wedding. I will invite the vice-president of oil operations. He is the one we need to get to agree.'

So we had the party and everybody was wearing white to stay cool because it was August. White slacks, white shirts, white shoes. That was the Aramco summer dress. We got the idea from the British, who called it their summer kit.

Milam arranged for the VP to be served plenty to drink so he was in a good mood. Then I went and sat with him and made my case for taking my wife with me. He said he would be happy to sign a letter of approval for the director of training the next day. I was there in his office first thing the following morning to pick it up.

The director of training, Bill O'Grady, read the letter and was furious. There was nothing he could do. He had to do what the VP wanted. At the same time, he had a letter of his own that he made me sign as a condition of the company approving this arrangement. I had to agree that Aramco would bear no expenses related to my wife's stay in America beyond her airline ticket. That included health costs or pregnancy. I told them she was healthy and was not going to get pregnant, so why not?

We flew to New York after a few stops in Europe. This was a commercial plane, not Aramco's 'Flying Camel'. The first thing I did was to take Dhabyah to Macy's department store in midtown Manhattan. I bought her some additional Western style clothing so she would feel more comfortable in this new country.

My friend Peter picked us up in my little blue Bug. I had left it with him for safekeeping when I went back to get married. I introduced Peter and a few other lady friends from college to Dhabyah. She turned to me and asked in Arabic, 'Who are these women?' I assured her they were friends of Peter's.

We had about ten days to drive across country to Palo Alto, California, before classes started at Stanford. Our first stop was the Lehigh University campus. Dhabyah was impressed with the university and Price Hall, where I had

72

lived. Our cross-country tour led through the Allegheny Mountains, then across the sprawling fields and prairies of the Midwest. In Ohio one woman at a stand selling apples and cider made a fuss over how beautiful my young wife was, insisting that she looked like Sophia Loren. In fact, it was a good thing we had our marriage licence with us. More than a few motel owners looked very closely at this young man of twenty-six and his very beautiful, very young teen-aged wife.

We stopped to marvel at the Mississippi River. I explained that Egypt had the famous Nile, and this was America's equivalent. On we drove for days, and finally into the Rocky Mountains. I talked about geology as we drove past examples of sedimentary layers of rock that once were flat and now stood on end.

It was a good thing we were both fairly small. The car seemed very full of baggage and things we bought along the way. Finally, we came down out of the mountains, drove across California and arrived at the Stanford campus. We did not know it, but the vast swathe of fruit-tree orchards we drove through on the approach to Palo Alto in 1962 would later be known as Silicon Valley.

My year at Stanford was even busier than my last year at Lehigh. Professor Davis personally welcomed me into the geology department and could not have been more encouraging. The work was demanding and the hours long. I took a weekly course load of thirty-six hours, with six of the hours covered by writing my thesis. The typical load was half that amount.

While I finished my masters, Dhabyah completed her high-school education in Palo Alto. She became friendly with some of the other young women among our neighbours where we lived in rented apartments in nearby Mountain View and Menlo Park. While I was consumed with work most days, we did manage a few trips to some of the spectacular natural beauty the western US has to offer. We drove to the Grand Canyon in Arizona, and with another couple made the relatively short trip to Yosemite National Park in California.

It is an understatement to say that my wife and I were naive about married life. After a month in Stanford she got sick. I took her to the Stanford hospital even though Aramco had insisted the company would not pay for any medical costs. I didn't know what could be wrong. She was so young and beautiful and healthy. After about an hour a doctor came out to see me. 'Congratulations,' he said. 'You're going to be a father!' I was stunned and delighted.

Our daughter Reem was born at the Stanford hospital on 23 July 1963. Naturally, my wife and I were over the moon in love with our first child. In fact, we were lucky in that she was a relatively easy baby. That was a good thing because I was in the middle of writing my masters thesis and our small one-bedroom apartment was beginning to feel a little crowded.

True to my agreement with the company, I was on the hook for the cost of the pregnancy and birth. I remember that the hospital bill for the birth of Reem was $900. I paid it, and I kept all the paperwork. Years later, back in Saudi Arabia, I filed a claim against Mr O'Grady to recover the cost. I won and received close to $4,000, which included interest, from the company.

I received my masters that September. I thanked Professor Davis warmly for giving me the chance to study at Stanford, but I was in such a rush to return to the Kingdom and start working again that I didn't even stay for the graduation ceremony. He later wrote to the company about me, saying, 'He has impressed all of us. He is not only a dedicated student, but also a personable individual.' I was very flattered.

We returned to the East Coast of the US by early November to catch our flight back to Saudi Arabia. I sold my car in California for the same amount it had cost me when I bought it, despite all the miles we had travelled. I was fortunate that the Bug was a very popular model in California in the 1960s.

We carried Reem snuggly wrapped in a bassinet. We said goodbye to Peter and his family in New Jersey and flew back home from Idlewild airport in the New York City borough of Queens. It would be renamed John F. Kennedy airport following the assassination of the president a few weeks after we left the country. It was an act that shocked the world. Looking back, it seemed as if that assassination was a warning that the world was becoming a more dangerous place.

7. Back to Arabia – 1964–1974

Now I had a formal education, it was time to leave the US and get back to Arabia. My wife and daughter moved into the senior camp neighbourhood at Dhahran. In previous years it had been used almost exclusively by American and foreign nationals and their families. I was in exploration and production, E&P, working as a geologist at job grade 11, the lowest level of management. I was in charge of certifying people to drill water wells in the Eastern Province. Our neighbours in our row of small ranch-style homes were all American. We were accepted into the social life of the community without any trouble. Dhabyah became good friends with a number of the other young mothers in the camp.

At twenty-nine years old, more or less, I was the most senior Saudi in E&P in 1964. A few Saudis older than I was were ahead of me in job grade in other departments. Zafer H. Husseini, who had joined the company in 1952, was named a manager in the products distribution department in 1965. He was the first Saudi manager in the entire company. His well-deserved promotion kept the rest of us focused on working even harder to get ahead.

My career briefly took an unexpected twist the following year. In 1965 I contacted an older friend who was the president of King Fahd University, which had recently been created in the Eastern Province to train professional engineers and others in related fields serving the oil and other natural resource industries. He knew that my speciality was

groundwater. He contacted his friend, the Minister of Agriculture, and said if you ever need someone to replace your
Deputy Minister for Water Resources, I have the right man
for you.

The Minister of Agriculture contacted me and after a brief
discussion offered me a government job in Riyadh. It was to
be director general, in line to be the next Deputy Minister
for Water Resources. He offered me 3,000 riyals a month,
nearly double my Aramco salary. At the time, working for
the government in such a position was considered among
the most prestigious jobs a young Saudi man could aspire to
hold. Then, as now, the government was the largest employer
in the Kingdom.

I went to my bosses at Aramco and told them it was too
good an offer to turn down. I told them that I would like to
remain on the Aramco employment roll but have one year
without pay while I tried the government job. If I liked it, I
would resign and stay with the government. They said, 'Fine,
Ali, if that's what you want.' They also agreed to lend me
10,000 riyals so I could rent a house in Riyadh. I told Dhabyah. She said, 'Whatever you think is best for us.' With that
blessing, off I went to Riyadh. She and the baby remained in
our house in Dhahran until I could get settled.

Wanting to demonstrate what a conscientious worker I
was, on my first day I showed up at the ministry at 7 a.m. Not
a soul was to be found, not even the watchman. I called
Aramco's government relations office in Riyadh, which was
run by an American named Harry Alter. He answered his
own phone. When I told him my situation, he said, 'OK, you
don't know the government. Why don't you get in a cab and
come to our office, have coffee with us, and then we'll take
you back?'

At about 11 a.m. I returned to the ministry and met with the director general I was about to replace. He said, 'Welcome to the ministry. Here are the keys to the office. There is a safe that you put the valuables in.' Then he left.

I had imagined myself joining the government to work for our people and help develop our country. I hardly had time to put down my briefcase before I was confronted with what I thought of as my first customers. These were private contractors and land owners who wanted me to give them the approval to drill water wells. Everybody had a piece of paper to be signed, and under the previous occupant of my office they clearly hadn't had much trouble getting approval. What was missing were the engineering and related details of their drilling programmes.

My training at Stanford and at Aramco presented a problem. I told my audience, 'I can't sign these papers. I need to see programmes, the casing programme, the cement programme, how many feet of pipe you are going to run to the well. All of that.' They said, 'No that's not the way we do business.' I said, 'Well, I'm going to do business this way.'

They were frustrated and I was frustrated. After two more days and no sign that I was going to be able to change their business practices, I was finished. I tried to get a seat on Saudia Airlines back to Dhahran, but they were all booked. I ended up hiring a cab for 200 riyals to take me home. Due to the condition of the highway it took most of the day to get there.

My bosses at Aramco were sorry to hear that it hadn't worked out. I paid back my loan, and went to work as a geologist in an area called Jiham, where we were drilling for oil. Two weeks or so later I received a call from Dhahran. The Minister of Agriculture had called, angry that I had abandoned my new position. He was in Jeddah, where the Saudi government meets during the summer, so I was ordered to fly there straight from Jiham.

I met the minister, who like me was from Al-Hasa, in one of the government offices in Jeddah. He said, 'Ali, what happened?' I said, 'Your Excellency, I can't work in your environment.' He said, 'You know I could have you imprisoned for what you have done.' I hadn't really thought my situation through, but I realized that he was right.

Even so, I knew I had done the right thing by refusing to sign whatever form crossed my desk. The right thing for me, and also for the future of our country. I told him, 'Your Excellency, you know me and I know you. We are from the same province. I don't think you chose me to be like the rest of your employees. You wanted me to perform and I can't perform in that environment, OK? So it's up to you. If you want to put me in prison you can, but I don't think it's going to do any good. You won't have what you wanted.' He liked that logic. He said, 'OK, let's shake hands and say goodbye.' I left and went straight back to Jiham and our drilling programme.

My next experience was more light-hearted. I went from being threatened with prison to being accused of being possessed by jinns, the types of evil spirits my wolf's tooth protected me against in my youth. The occasion was also when I learned to shoot a gun.

One of our drivers at the drill site was from the Ajman tribe, the same as my mother's. I called him Uncle Abdullah, since he was a tribal uncle, though not directly related. He asked me one day if I had a rifle. I said I not only didn't have a rifle, I didn't know how to shoot. In his mind I was an insult to the tribe. 'You can't be a part of the Ajman tribe and not have a rifle and shoot,' he said. So the next time they were changing out the drill bit, which took eight to twelve hours back then, we drove to the nearest trading post in Riyadh and bought a lightweight .22-calibre rifle and some bullets for target practice.

We placed several tin cans on rocks and took turns shooting at them. I missed most of the time. Uncle Abdullah was not happy. 'You're a terrible shooter,' he said, shaking his head. Fortunately, we had an American drill foreman whom we all called Red and who liked to shoot, and he took me under his wing. I practised repeatedly but still didn't think I was very good.

One day my uncle was taking me in one of our Aramco pick-up trucks to go hunting. A crow flew by, and I instinctively aimed my gun through the open side window and actually hit the bird in mid-air! Uncle Abdullah hit the brakes. 'Do you think I am stupid? Why did you miss all the cans and now you can shoot the bird out of the sky? You are a sharp-shooter all of this time. Why are you fooling me?' He wouldn't talk to me for three weeks.

We reconciled, and he took me hunting for a large bird called a bustard that used to be found across the desert in our country before it was over-hunted. We saw one in the bushes and Uncle Abdullah directed me to crawl as close as I could get and then shoot the bird. As we got closer the bird, although alive, didn't move. I decided I would get as close as I could. I eventually walked up to the bird and picked it up without firing a shot.

'Now I want nothing to do with you,' my uncle said angrily. I asked why. He said, 'You have jinns in you. You did something to that bird.' I realized later that a snake probably had bitten the bird and it was paralysed. My uncle wasn't interested in my explanation. We never went hunting again.

I confess there were times early in my career when I thought I might have made a mistake not sticking it out with the government. At the time, my generation of Saudis felt that Aramco was not paying enough attention to our progress through the ranks of the company. Instead, we were being transferred from job to job to fill vacancies left by retirements or transfers rather than to give us the training and experience we needed to succeed. Our American bosses did not always understand our desire to prove ourselves.

We seemed to be receiving two different messages. The senior leaders of Aramco, including the geologist Tom Barger, who was appointed CEO in 1961, wanted Saudis to be prepared to advance through the Aramco ranks. One of Barger's rising stars, Frank Jungers, also advocated aggressive training and advancement goals. But too many times that ambition ran into the reality of company bureaucracy and the need to make short-term decisions to get the work done or solve an immediate problem.

The outside world was also influencing the decision makers at Aramco. The creation of the Organization of the Petroleum Exporting Countries, OPEC, in 1960 by Saudi Arabia, Venezuela, Kuwait, Iran and Iraq gave these oil-producing countries a great sense of control over their nations' most valuable natural resource. That created added momentum for Aramco to maintain good relations with the Saudi government and not put its oil concession in jeopardy. And that meant training more Saudis at all levels.

Ahmed Zaki Yamani was a well-regarded thirty-two-year-old Saudi lawyer when in 1962 he was named to succeed

Abdullah Al-Tariki as the Saudi oil minister. Over time he would become a household name around the world as the face of Saudi Arabia's oil industry, and as the most dynamic representative in OPEC. He was known for aggressively advocating for the Kingdom both on the world stage and with the Aramco owners. At the same time, he was a relative moderate regarding the rising interest among oil-producing countries in nationalizing their domestic oil industries. He recognized the value of foreign expertise and capital when it came to getting the most out of our resources.

I first met Minister Yamani and his predecessor Abdullah Al-Tariki at an oil industry conference in Cairo in 1965. At thirty years old I was presenting my first research paper, 'The Groundwater of Northeastern Saudi Arabia', based on my research on groundwater resources in the main oil-producing region in the Kingdom. I was drawing on work performed by earlier oil company geologists, who were the first to study the subject in Saudi Arabia. Since there has been no permanently flowing river on the Arabian Peninsula for more than 5,000 years, knowledge about groundwater takes on paramount importance in the Kingdom.

Both Yamani and Tariki applauded my presentation and congratulated me on my work. They were impressed by my willingness during the question-and-answer period to confront a critic, an older British gentleman. He insisted, erroneously, that seawater encroached on some of the aquifers, or underground water sources, in the region. This had been the prevailing wisdom in the decades before Aramco did its pioneering drilling and research programmes in the area. In the minds of my fellow Saudis I represented the new generation of Saudi technocrats. We were using our education and research skills to debunk the discredited world view that characterized the era when colonial powers held sway in the Middle East.

In 1966, my eldest son Rami was born. I couldn't have been prouder. Like most tribal cultures ours is traditionally patriarchal. The birth of the first son marks the continuity of the male line and is celebrated. Indeed, while my name formally includes bin Ibrahim, son of Ibrahim, intimates and friends would also address me as Abu Rami, father of Rami.

So the family was growing and I was advancing. By 1967, I had advanced four pay grades and was anxiously awaiting my next promotion when global events overtook my career concerns. After months of rising tensions in the Middle East, the Arab–Israeli Six-Day War broke out on 5 June. As news of the conflict swept through the Arab world, Saudi workers at many Aramco facilities walked off the job or didn't show up for work on 7 June. Unlike during the Suez Crisis, the US was seen as taking Israel's side in the Six-Day War and American oil installations in Saudi Arabia and elsewhere in the region were threatened.

Groups of protestors, mainly students from the nearby College of Petroleum and Minerals, marched into the oil camp, which was only lightly guarded at the time. What followed became known as 'Rock Wednesday', when protestors threw rocks at several cars' windows and burned a few others as well. They marched on to the American consulate between the oil compound and Al-Khobar without causing any significant damage to company property or harming anyone.

It might have been a coincidence, but I was asked to move into the public relations department later that year. Because of my knowledge of geology and drilling and production as well as my command of English, I became a public relations escort. I met with international reporters and took them around our facilities and familiarized them with Saudi Arabia.

I got tired of that job after about a year. I was offered the position of PR manager if I stayed, with the promise of eventually becoming vice-president of public relations if I did well. Vice-president was a very senior position, with fewer than a dozen in all of Aramco at the time.

My wife and I were close friends with our neighbours Bob Wilson and his wife. Bob was a brilliant mathematician with a PhD in economics. We would regularly get together for meals and we went camping in the desert areas not far from the oil camp. I asked Bob for advice about my career. He said I should come over for dinner the following night. He promised to bring the organization chart for the company and we would go over it.

We arrived the following evening. The chart was a revelation, with departments branching off from each other like constellations in the night sky. I had never seen it before. Bob drew my attention to one constellation on the chart that was, at that time, clearly a dead end: public relations. That settled *that* career decision.

At Bob's suggestion, I explored switching my Aramco career to the economics department. I had twenty-one credit hours of economics at Lehigh, after all. After a few months I realized that there was no place for me. Besides, that department operated in too rarefied an atmosphere. I needed something more down to earth.

I went back to the exploration and production department in the summer of 1968. Dan Sullivan, a big Irish-American with huge white eyebrows, was waiting for me. Before I could say anything, he laughed and said, 'Ali, you want to go back to work?' I told him I was ready to return to E&P.

He offered me a position in the small community of Abqaiq about sixty-five kilometres outside Dhahran. In the middle of the desert, Abqaiq is something of a pipeline crossroads between some of our largest oilfields. Over the decades we have invested tens of billions of dollars in our processing facilities there. Even today, Abqaiq processes an important percentage of the world's oil.

In the late 1960s, Abqaiq was important but much smaller, offering little in terms of a residential housing compound. The company was in the process of consolidating much of its housing in Dhahran. But that wasn't the worst part. I was a grade 15 geologist, but the company was offering me a grade 9 job as senior supervising operator. Further, I was starting in the middle of August, the hottest and most humid month of the year in the Eastern Province, when the temperature regularly tops 43 °C (110 °F). In 1956 it had even reached 51 °C (124 °F).

I knew I had to accept the offer if I was going to prove myself and get my management career back on track. I told Dhabyah that she and the baby would stay in our house in Dhahran for the time being, until I had a better understanding of my new job. Each department had a few vehicles with air conditioning. I was given a pick-up truck without any air conditioning other than rolling down the windows. I was used to the desert heat so it didn't really bother me.

My new boss was a superintendent named Harry Egy. He told me that the first thing I needed to do was to work with well services to learn what wells were all about. I told him that I had worked with exploratory wells as a geologist. 'Producing wells are different,' he responded. He sent me to work with Johnny Sipe, a great guy with no college education but a hard worker. For the next several months we made the rounds of the oilfields, checking well pressures and temperatures.

One day in the spring of 1969, Sipe said to me that we had a well in Ain Dar, No. 17, which was dry. The engineers had tried the usual steps such as shocking it with hot oil but nothing worked. Did I think I could revive it?

I said I'd give it a try. I discovered that we had a gas injection line passing nearby with 3,000lb of pressure on it, which is a lot. I asked Johnny if he could 'hot tap' the pipe and connect the gas line to the well. He said if you draw me a sketch I can do it. I drew him the sketch he needed and he tapped into the gas line while the gas was still flowing, inserting a valve, and we connected that to the dead well. To my knowledge, that was the first time such a procedure was used at Aramco.

Now all we could do was wait and see if the pressurized gas could unplug the well pipe. I told Sipe to go home for the night. My producing foreman, a Saudi named Ahmed, and I stayed with the well all night. Because of all the snakes in the area we slept in the back of my pick-up truck in sleeping bags.

At about three o'clock in the morning we heard a low, thundering sound. The well had revived. It came in and was blowing smoke, gas, steam and rocks out of the pipe. Every oil well has an emergency flare that can be lit to burn off associated gases that can erupt suddenly from active wells. Ahmed got the flare lit and the plume of flame could be seen for miles around. We got the flow of oil under control, getting covered in it in the process.

By five o'clock in the morning it was getting light and we could see Sipe was driving rapidly toward us across the desert in his truck. He hopped out with a big grin on his face. 'I saw the flare,' he shouted over the roar of the flame as he walked up. 'You did it!' He offered us a box of sweet rolls for breakfast.

I said that we'd all done it. It was Ahmed's turn to grin this time. Sipe didn't appreciate what I was saying about my fellow Saudi deserving to share in the credit. 'I am going to see my manager and tell him what you did,' he said. I asked him what he was talking about. 'This was your test,' he said. So after that test, on 1 April 1969, I was appointed superintendent of Abqaiq producing, the first Saudi to hold a superintendent position. Until that point, we had only had Saudi foremen.

One of the first jobs I had was to teach the Saudis who now reported to me how to set their own department budgets and monitor spending. In the past the superintendent had been in charge of budgets. Then maintenance departments would add on projects that weren't included in the budget because there was not enough monitoring of expenses. That resulted in what were called 'gold-plated' projects that unnecessarily took money away from more worthy enterprises.

Around this time I was placed on temporary assignment in charge of our giant gas turbine plants. Going through invoices at the end of the day, as was my habit, I thought I had found a clear-cut case of fraud. The turbine maintenance group was ordering rice by the pallet. Imagining their lavish lunches at the company's expense, I called the manager into my office and slapped the invoice down in front of him. 'What about this?' I asked. 'How do you explain ordering this much rice?'

That was easily explained, he said with a look of relief. He pointed out that turbine blades, despite their large size, are actually very delicate. If you use too abrasive a material to clean them you can pit or damage the edges and degrade

87

their performance. The team had discovered that raw rice provided the perfect solution: sturdy enough to act as a cleanser but soft enough not to damage the blades. I congratulated him and his team for their ingenuity.

After a time, though, I felt that once again my career had hit a plateau. Ali Baluchi was a boyhood friend who had attended the Jebel School with me and was also rising through the ranks at Aramco. He was in charge of community services in Abqaiq at the time and would later hold the same position in Dhahran. I used to complain to Ali that I was frustrated by the slow pace of promotions. He urged patience. It was good advice. Of course, I never said anything outside my close circle of Saudi friends.

No American or other Westerner ever actively tried to obstruct my career, but I and many Saudis had a sense that old habits died hard among some of the Americans, usually those with modest educations. They still saw Saudis as natives who weren't up to the job. Years later Ali showed me a picture one of these 'rednecks' had taken of me in Abqaiq wearing a coat that was several sizes too big. The intent of taking the picture and circulating it was clearly to show me as a man who wasn't big enough for the job, Ali and I agreed. It was relatively harmless in the context of discrimination against workers from Gulf countries that was experienced by others in the oil industry, I am sure, but it made me mad. It also made me more determined to show everyone that I was a leader.

In 1970 my second daughter, Nada, joined our lives. She was a fun little girl and these were happy times at home, despite my occasional frustrations at work. But things were picking up. In 1972 I was promoted to assistant manager of oil operations in Abqaiq. A year later I became manager. That made me only the third Saudi to reach that level. Mustaffa Abuahmad, my friend from the scholarship course at AUB who had joined Aramco in 1944, moved into my position in public relations when I left the department in 1968. He was named department manager in 1969.

I was very busy during this period of my life, but I tried to make time for our family. I used to enjoy taking the kids fishing and swimming at Half Moon Bay on the Gulf, and for nature walks in the desert. Reem was particularly intrigued by the lizards that skittered away from us and buried themselves in the sand to hide.

We had a small garden in front of the house in Abqaiq. We grew some vegetables and flowers, nothing fancy. One day I thought I would teach Reem and Rami a little something about geology. I had a piece of charcoal from our backyard grill and showed it to the kids. 'You see this?' I asked. 'If it is buried in the earth for millions and millions of years, it will turn into a beautiful shiny diamond.' Reem was particularly intrigued. They helped me dig a hole and in went the piece of charcoal. It wasn't too many days later that I came out on the front porch and there was Reem, checking to see if her diamond was ready yet.

Abqaiq was generally pretty quiet, but now and then we had some excitement. It was a Friday, and my brother and his family were visiting. We were all having a nap after lunch when we heard sirens. We went out to see what was happening and the recreation hall next to the housing area was on fire. So three of us rushed over, grabbed a hose and started trying to put the fire out. The other two men couldn't hold on, leaving just me on the end of this high-pressure hose, bouncing around, up and down, too afraid to let go of the end for fear that it would flick around and hit me. Eventually someone turned off the hose, but the effort cost me a hernia.

One of my unofficial roles was as a mediator in labour discussions at different facilities. Saudis learned that I was being promoted, so they often came to me with their problems. I always made it a habit to listen closely to their complaints. Often I discovered that someone's problem went beyond just that individual. It was a broader issue impacting Saudi workers in general. When I later spoke with American managers and supervisors, I would try to put such complaints within this bigger picture. Senior American managers would later tell me that they appreciated my thinking, saying that providing such fact-based context helped produce broader improvements in labour relations.

Aramco's oilfield development and processing and the expatriate community living in Dhahran had often been the subject of Western media attention in the postwar decades. In 1972 they came for a visit once again, this time in the form of the CBS television programme *60 Minutes*.

The CBS producers wanted to compare the life of American expatriates in Saudi Arabia working for the oil company with those of a Saudi family. My family, which now numbered three children, Reem, Rami and Nada, was chosen to represent the Saudis and one of our neighbours in Abqaiq, Bob Luttrell and his family, were the Americans. Our PR people were worried that the CBS team would try their best to show that Saudis weren't being treated as well as the Americans.

In fact, they found that there wasn't much difference in our lives. Our children went to the same schools and our wives socialized with each other as well as with other Saudi and American mothers. Bob and I saw each other at work, though we didn't work together. The segment that they eventually included on *60 Minutes* was very flattering to everyone at Aramco. We had no way of knowing at the time, but we would be hearing from *60 Minutes* again in little more than a year.

By 1973 Israeli–Arab tensions had again reached boiling point. That October, Egypt and Syria launched a surprise attack on Israel during the Jewish holy day of Yom Kippur. In the midst of the conflict, the OPEC countries dramatically increased the price of oil to match the 'spot' price that reflected the panic buying that occurred as hostilities continued. And when the US, several European countries and Japan provided aid to Israel during the war, Arab members of OPEC declared an oil embargo. Shipments were totally cut off to the US and the Netherlands, and sharply curtailed to the other countries that had aided Israel.

When King Faisal announced the embargo, Frank Jungers, who had been named Aramco CEO earlier in 1973, had the difficult job of assisting its implementation or risk having the entire company nationalized. His actions drew a lot of criticism in America because Aramco was controlled by four American oil companies. Since 1973 the Saudi government had assumed a 25 per cent 'participation' in Aramco, and the ownership stakes of the four oil companies had been reduced proportionately. After several months the embargo was quietly wound down.

We felt little direct impact of the war or the embargo in Abqaiq. But, like the 1967 war, it inflamed the passions of many Saudis and other Arabs. The Arab press and radio expressed considerable anti-American sentiment, but we didn't see any anti-American actions at our oil facilities.

In 1974, *60 Minutes* returned. The programme's lead reporter, Mike Wallace, wanted to visit Dhahran and interview Frank Jungers about the embargo. Our PR people were keen to ensure that Wallace and his team got a broad view of life at Aramco and of how well Saudis and Americans got along. I didn't know anything about the visit until I got a call from the PR department in Dhahran telling us to expect Wallace and some of his team for dinner in Abqaiq.

Our PR people didn't know what an independent thinker my wife had become. She may have been just finishing high school when we were married, but in the following years she had become a well-rounded person with strong opinions of her own. During the 1972 visit from *60 Minutes* she had seen no reason to speak up. Two years later, with Mike Wallace coming to report on the embargo, things were different.

As is the custom in Arab homes, we willingly extended hospitality to visitors. Dhabyah couldn't have been more gracious as the official hostess. But when the talk turned to politics she let Wallace know where she stood. She accused him of being biased against Arabs and said that most of the US media agreed with him. He was clearly not prepared to be challenged by a Saudi woman. I admired her of course, but I also remember thinking, 'Uh-oh.'

Wallace handled the criticism like a professional. He told our PR people back in Dhahran that he was impressed with the Saudi housewife in the middle of the desert who spoke her mind. And when the interview with Jungers finally appeared on *60 Minutes* it was much more even-handed than any of us had hoped.

While I was still in Abqaiq my friend Ali Baluchi and a group of other relatively senior Saudi employees of Aramco asked for and were granted a meeting with Minister Yamani.

At the top of their agenda was the standing complaint that the Americans for whatever reason were not promoting Saudis fast enough. Yamani was very supportive and assured the group that he would act on their concerns sooner rather than later.

In the autumn of 1974 I was promoted to manager of Northern Area producing, and we moved back to the residential community in Dhahran. I had operating responsibility for eleven of Aramco's fifteen producing oilfields. These fields were responsible for the vast majority of the oil revenue Aramco generated for the shareholders and the Kingdom. It was one of the most important operating positions in the company.

That same year Faisal Al-Bassam, who was more than a decade older, was named the first Saudi vice-president of Aramco, overseeing public affairs. Once again, I and other younger Saudis were proud that one of our own had attained this new, senior rank. With my new promotion and operating responsibilities I was certain that it would be years before I would be in line for another significant advance in rank.

Little did I know.

8. On the Rise – the 1970s

We took pride in our work ethic at Aramco. We walked into the Dhahran camp canteen for breakfast shortly after 5 a.m. We would finish our coffee and make the short walk to our offices so that we were at our desks by 6 a.m., and often didn't return home until five or six in the evening.

Once in a while other Saudis referred to us as 'worker bees' or 'drones' because of the long hours. As far as I am concerned they were just jealous. Most of us at Aramco who were rising through the ranks – and most oil company employees today, I am sure – felt like we were working to build our country, not just finding and producing more oil and gas.

Our business was booming even before the price of oil tripled as a result of the oil embargo. Demand for oil from the US, Europe and Japan surged during the early 1970s. Capital spending on oil-processing projects in the late 1960s reached tens of millions of dollars a year. That figure jumped to the billions of dollars by the mid-1970s. We were buying all the steel and concrete and hiring all the drilling rigs we could find. By 1975, our payroll had risen to 19,500, double that of just five years before.

Our office facilities hardly reflected our good fortune. The company was expanding rapidly and space was at a premium. In early 1975, my office was located in a temporary wooden building that we called a 'portable', wedged in next to the fire station by the south entrance to the camp complex. We dropped in portable offices wherever there was open ground. My office building was torn down years ago but the fire station, much improved and enlarged, still stands.

I was working on several projects at once, which was typical, when one day I heard a knock on my flimsy office door. It was our CEO, Frank Jungers, wearing his standard work clothes, which consisted of boots, khaki trousers and a short-sleeved shirt. No tie. Not surprisingly, we all tended to dress like the boss. 'Ali, let's go for a ride,' he said.

I remember thinking to myself, 'I have a lot of work to do and I am sure the CEO has even more work than I do, but if he wants to go for a ride, we go for a ride.' We had got to know each other over the years so I wasn't intimidated. But I was curious. I got into his car and we went for a drive around the oil camp. He asked me what was new and generally made small talk for almost an hour. I was beginning to get a little frustrated. Neither the car nor the conversation seemed to be going anywhere.

Finally, Jungers pulled over and parked in front of the main administration building. He turned to me and said, 'Ali, congratulations. You are now an officer of the company.' I was too embarrassed to say that I didn't know what that meant.

Jungers explained that the Aramco board had voted that morning, 1 May 1975, and I was now a vice-president of Aramco. I confessed that I really didn't understand the significance of the board's decision, other than that it meant a big raise for me. He chuckled and said, 'If all the other officers get taken out for some reason, you can legally sign on behalf of the company.'

I was shocked. At age forty I had received a four-grade promotion, from 19 to 23, the first ever in Aramco history.

That was a major promotion for anyone. It was all the more remarkable because I had earned this position as the first Saudi to become a vice-president of an *operating* division, not a supporting department like public relations. I considered the promotion a great honour. I am sure some other Saudis were jealous of my good fortune, but most I spoke with saw my advancement as creating a pathway to success for more to follow. And they had to admit that none of them worked harder than I did.

With my new title came a new office in the main administration building. I was vice-president of producing and water injection, one of fewer than a dozen VPs at the time, responsible for all Aramco's oil and gas wells across the concession.

Since graduating, I had been with the company for little more than a decade. When we came back from America and moved into our first home in Dhahran, I could not have imagined advancing so rapidly. If anything, the pace of change in my career and within Aramco and our country would only accelerate over the coming decade.

My promotion caught the attention of the expanding Saudi business community. Not long after being appointed VP, I received a visit from the prominent Saudi businessman Suliman Olayan. Like many of our business leaders, he got his start with the oil company, being an employee from 1937 to 1947 before starting his own trucking company. He would go on to create or own more than fifty companies, from transportation and consumer goods to finance and insurance, mostly under the umbrella of the Olayan Group, and be worth billions of dollars. Later, in the early 1980s, he would also serve on the board of directors of Mobil.

I was flattered that he had time to meet me, and that he

insisted that I use his given name. Since he was older than I was and a prestigious business executive, he, of course, addressed me as Ali. After exchanging a few pleasantries he got down to business.

Now that I had established myself as a success at Aramco, he had a question. How would I like to join forces with him? He didn't have a specific job in mind, but made it clear that he would double my Aramco salary if I agreed. If I did well, he strongly suggested, I would have the potential to accumulate much more wealth in the years ahead. I didn't hesitate before responding. 'Suliman, you have been successful in your way, but I am going to be successful in mine,' I told him. 'I am interested in people more than money.'

This may sound funny coming from someone who has done well for himself financially, and one who is addressed as 'Your Excellency', but I am not interested in money. I am not interested in prestige. I am interested in results. We parted as friends, with Suliman complimenting me again on my accomplishment. I have never regretted my decision to remain at Aramco. As for Suliman, after a long and successful career and life, he died in 2002 at age eighty-three.

The Saudi economy shifted into overdrive following the spike in oil prices caused by the June 1967 war. King Faisal's first five-year economic plan, developed in the late 1960s with the help of the Stanford Research Institute, had been put in place in 1970. That was the first year in which the Kingdom's annual oil revenues topped $1 billion. The plan was based on fairly modest assumptions about future trends in oil prices and demand. And its government works projects, which included the extensive construction of roads, schools and hospitals, were in addition to the multi-billion-dollar oil facilities building programme under way at Aramco.

The second five-year plan, unveiled in March 1975, reflected the new reality of sharply higher oil prices and revenues that had more than tripled. Massive public works projects included in the plan would within a few years transform the country, and its capital Riyadh in particular. Saudi defence industry spending soared as well. This process of spending oil revenues on goods or projects, many of which were supplied by the West, would become known as recycling petro-dollars.

The cornerstone of the second five-year plan, the largest among many massive projects, was the Master Gas plan. With an estimated price tag of $12–14 billion – more than $40 billion in today's dollars – it was the largest energy development project ever.

The goal of the plan was to transform the country's economy and begin to diversify it from its near total reliance on the oil industry and its affiliated construction and service industries. The natural gas that for the most part was being burned off by flares at our production facilities at the time would be harnessed and used to power the next generation of Saudi industry and commerce.

Gas and oil are both hydrocarbons that are formed, in most cases, within compressed ocean sediments containing ancient marine life. They are often found together in subsurface rock formations, with the gas found in such structures called 'associated gas'. Oil and gas are also found separately, of course, depending on the nature of the rock formations in which they are locked and on other factors.

In the early decades of the oil industry, little demand

existed for this associated gas, and the technology to process and transport it was not very well developed. This was as true in Texas or Venezuela as it was in Saudi Arabia. So the gas was flared off. Even within the past decade the development of the shale oil and gas fields in North Dakota emerged so quickly that the pipeline and related infrastructure was insufficient to transfer the gas for processing. As a result a significant amount of gas there continues to be 'flared off'.

In the mid-1950s, we began capturing some of the associated gas in Abqaiq and reinjecting it back into oil reservoirs to maintain reservoir pressure and keep the oil flowing at a steady rate. A few years later another plant was built to inject gas back into reservoirs at Ain Dar and Shedgum, which were portions of our enormous Ghawar field. But these plants, while advanced for their time, remained the exceptions to the general practice in the Kingdom of flaring the gas.

The *Sun and Flare*. That was an early name for the Aramco in-house newspaper, and that gives you an idea of how much flares were a part of our world, especially at night. When I worked out in the desert at Abqaiq, it was only a slight exaggeration to claim that you could drive your truck at night back to Dhahran without needing to use your headlights. The muffled roar of the flares and the smell of the burning gas were a constant presence.

Since at least the early 1960s there had been calls, including from our first oil minister, Abdullah Al-Tariki, for us to harness the gas and put it to use. Sympathetic oil company executives also used to shake their heads at the obvious waste of a valuable resource. But the government's need for Aramco to focus on producing oil to support our country's growth remained our top priority. By the mid-1970s we suddenly had the billions of dollars needed to realize our dream of harnessing the gas instead of wasting it.

Without question, the move to capture and use the gas was driven mainly by economic concerns. At the same time, even though no one was talking about climate change back then, at least not in our world, many felt that the negative effect of the flares on our lives was becoming too much to put up with. Those of us who were taking on increasing responsibility at Aramco were aware that the oil industry existed to serve our country. As we progressed, our society no longer had to be shaped so dramatically by the needs of the oil industry.

We wanted to breathe clean air. We wanted to see the stars that continued to guide our Bedu tribesmen out in the desert. Change was slow at first, but when I look back, I think the creation of the Master Gas System, whose plants started to come online in 1977 to provide gas to power our industries, was the first significant step on our path toward increased environmental awareness and responsibility.

I don't pretend that our progress has been without some setbacks, but we have made dramatic advances since the days of widespread flaring. I will return to this subject in a later chapter, and I think you will be surprised.

Tragically, King Faisal did not live to witness the benefits of his second five-year plan. Only a few weeks after its announcement he was assassinated in his palace in Riyadh, shot by a twenty-eight-year-old prince who was his nephew. The prince had slipped into the king's presence at the last minute by joining a group of visitors that included the then current Saudi oil minister Ahmed Zaki Yamani, who narrowly escaped death himself. As a member of the royal family, the prince rightly assumed that he would be granted entrance to the meeting.

It later came out in the press that the prince had a long history of problems with drugs and mental illness. He also may have, in his mind at least, been avenging the death of his brother, a religious conservative. King Faisal had championed the opening of the Kingdom's first television station. The brother, deeply opposed to what he felt violated Saudi culture, had been killed while attacking the television facility.

Saudis remember the death of King Faisal the way Americans remember the death of President Kennedy. We all remember where we were. I was in the main administration building. We learned of the death from a radio broadcast, and stopped work to continue to listen for further news. And we called our government relations staff in Riyadh to find out what was going on. As a sign of the respect the royal family had for Aramco, and for CEO Jungers in particular, he was invited to Riyadh the following morning to pay his respects at the funeral for the king and to share his condolences with Faisal's brothers.

Crown Prince Khalid, who had been active in government affairs for years, succeeded Faisal as king and was himself widely respected. Another of our founding king's sons, Fahd, also an astute administrator, was named crown prince. While our kingdom would be well served by these royal leaders, there was a tremendous sense of loss among our people over Faisal's untimely death.

Even though Faisal was nearly seventy when he was fatally attacked, he had been viewed as a dynamic leader who managed to respect Saudi desert traditions while also pushing relentlessly for modernization, thereby dramatically increasing the Kingdom's standing with the outside world. Faisal was also an effective politician. He re-established close relations with the US and other Western powers, bridging the diplomatic gap between his country and much of the West that had been caused by the oil embargo that he himself had backed.

The nation was still adjusting to his loss when we were shocked yet again in the final weeks of 1975. Readers of a certain age will recall that the 1970s were marked by a number of terrorist activities, including the hijacking of airliners. And the most notorious terrorist of the decade was a Venezuelan named Carlos 'the Jackal'.

In mid-December of that year a group of international terrorists led by Carlos attacked OPEC headquarters in Vienna, determined to strike a high-profile blow against global commerce, and took dozens of hostages. Included in the group were Yamani and five other Arab ministers. In fact, Yamani later was quoted in his biography saying that Carlos told him he was the principal hostage.

The pilot of the Aramco plane that had transported Yamani and his assistants to Vienna was among the first to learn of the hostage taking. He had been monitoring the radio chatter from the Vienna airport control tower. Carlos was demanding that an Austrian plane fly the terrorists and hostages to Tripoli. Jungers approved a plan for the Aramco pilot to follow the terrorists' plane from a safe distance, hoping that he would be able to remove Minister Yamani from harm's way as soon as possible.

The flight to Tripoli was followed by others to Algiers, and then back to Tripoli, with many hostages being released at different times, but not Yamani. Ultimately, the crisis was resolved peacefully. Yamani rushed across the runway to the waiting Aramco plane and was flown to safety. Carlos was not captured until 1994, and is now serving a life sentence in France for murdering two French government agents and an informant.

The hostage drama was a reminder to us Saudis that playing a larger role in world affairs had its risks as well as its rewards. From that day forward we have provided our ministers with close protection. I am sure every minister, myself included, remembers what Yamani and his family endured when we start to feel that this ever-present security is a burden.

King Khalid, who was seen as being less focused on centralized governmental control than Faisal, presided over the rollout of the second five-year plan. Spending accelerated at an unprecedented rate, much of it for long-term investments. During this time the cities of Jubail on the Arabian Gulf and Yanbu on the Red Sea were designated as locations for future industrial growth.

Some worried, rightly as it turned out, that the runaway spending would harm the Saudi economy. 'The 1970s were very optimistic,' said Hamad Sayari, the former head of the Saudi Arabian Monetary Agency. 'Government revenues and spending were rising, real estate prices were zooming, people were enriching themselves. But inflation was 30 per cent. It was like overcooking a meal. We were putting too much fire under the pot.' After years of large budget surpluses, the Kingdom actually reported a small deficit for the 1978–1979 budget year and instituted some belt-tightening measures.

At Aramco, we were implementing our own massive expansion. And we were awarding contracts for the expansion of the Master Gas System at the same time. Almost on the side, we were also integrating the Aramco electricity grid with that of the Eastern Province and upgrading power systems as we went.

Significantly, these infrastructure projects were of huge benefit to Saudi contractors. In 1975 Aramco awarded $250 million in gas system contracts to Saudi companies. Just two years later, that amount soared to nearly $2 billion. We were not only laying the groundwork for a new system to power the Kingdom's future prosperity, but also fuelling the growth of its domestic business community at the same time.

During the 1970s, Aramco itself was overseeing the construction of two of the largest projects in its history. The first was a massive, offshore gas oil separation plant in the Zuluf field in the Arabian Gulf. The second was the Qurayyah Seawater Treatment Plant, which remains the largest of its kind in the world.

Sprawling construction worker camps sprang up to house the unprecedented influx of labour needed to build these huge complexes. By 1977 the camps could hold 37,900 unmarried workers and 875 families. When more space was required, we towed in from Singapore and Japan barges containing five-storey-high dormitories, quickly nicknamed floating hotels, to house another 4,500 workers.

Qurayyah was a place especially close to my heart. It was little more than a stone's throw from the trail I used to take barefoot from Thugbah to the Jebel School as a boy thirty years earlier. And it represented another turning point in our company's, and the Kingdom's, focus on the more thoughtful use of our natural resources.

While continuing to experiment with injecting gas into

our oil reservoirs to maintain pressure, our geoscientists also explored the possibilities of injecting seawater. Up to that point it was common industry practice around the world to use well water to maintain reservoir pressure. Faced with a scarcity of well water in the deserts of Saudi Arabia, we had to find another solution. The scientists soon discovered that, after treatment to remove impurities and much of its corrosive oxygen, seawater could be injected along the edges of the reservoirs, a process that proved to be more effective than injecting gas. I was one of the leaders of the team working on seawater injection.

Our team broke down the challenges involved with seawater injection one by one and pushed the project to conclusion. Making sure we were not injecting any foreign matter into the subterranean oilfields was a major concern. To remove much of the oxygen we pumped the water to the top of the plant and brought nitrogen in from the bottom, which bonded with the oxygen, removing it from the water. That in turn greatly reduced corrosion in the pipes and pumps that moved the seawater to the fields.

Drawing water from the Arabian Sea by suction pumps installed at the end of a long custom-built pier, we started on a test basis and quickly moved to full-scale processing. Our initial volume was 4 million barrels a day. The processing plant has since been expanded a number of times, and Aramco is currently processing closer to 14 million barrels of seawater a day.

Once I was a vice-president I had the authority to examine many of our practices in order to identify more economical solutions to our operating problems. With the seawater process now in place, I moved to other issues. I was reviewing invoices one day and thought my eyes were playing tricks on me. Here we were, surrounded by sand dunes, and I was holding an invoice requesting payment for the delivery of sand! Not just any sand, mind you. This was for sand shipped halfway around the world from the state of Wyoming.

The general manager in charge of the project, an American, didn't share my sense of wonder. He said that in fact we had been importing this sand for years. It was known to have certain characteristics concerning the shape of the individual grains that made it perfect for use in specific filters. I told him I was sure it was good sand, but we had a company full of geoscientists and a kingdom full of sand, couldn't they find some sand closer to home that met our needs? As I suspected, once our team started looking at domestic sand types, they found one that met our specifications.

From 1975 onward I was operating in a rarefied atmosphere and was being groomed for ever more senior positions. In 1977, after managing our oil operations for two years and helping launch these major projects, I met Jungers in one of the cramped hallways of the main administration building. We had grown to be good friends since my promotion to vice-president.

'Ali, I think you have been vice-president of oil operations for too long,' he remarked. 'I want to broaden your experience in the company.' With all of the projects currently under way, I felt as if I was already stretched as tight as a tent flap. 'Frank,' I said to him, 'I don't have much space to be broadened. What do you mean?'

He said my first stop would be to run the industrial relations department, which included all of our medical staff and facilities. My response, of course, was to say that I didn't know anything about IR. That was the point, Frank said. I needed to learn about different sectors of Aramco's operations. Once again, I was honoured by the trust Jungers was putting in me. I was also keenly aware that I was being watched closely by supporters and detractors alike. Any mistake and my performance might be used in some quarters of the company as an excuse to set back the promotion of hard-working Saudis, possibly for years to come.

For the next year or so I rotated through different responsibilities so that I could understand how our different departments worked. After four months in IR, I moved over to run community services. The next stop was material supplies. Even though these departments were all part of the same company, each had its own way of doing things and in some ways their own culture. I was getting a crash course in all the strengths required and challenges faced by senior management at Aramco.

The next move included a transfer out of the country, and a new title. 'I want you to go to our company in The Hague, Aramco Overseas Company,' Frank said one day. 'See if you can manage the Dutch office.' I was named president of the subsidiary, known as AOC and established after World War II in part to manage our supply shipments and business transactions in multiple currencies. It was a good experience, especially since I had not worked directly with many Europeans. Most of them were not as naturally open or gregarious as the Americans I had worked with, but I developed some close personal contacts. My wife and children also enjoyed the opportunity to live in Europe for a time and I have an abiding memory of my son Rami, by this time aged eleven, practising the trombone. Fortunately the houses in the Netherlands are on several floors and we encouraged him to play up in the attic!

*

As the 1970s progressed, Frank Jungers was occasionally at odds with the four oil company owner-operators. They questioned his emphasis on the Master Gas System and the electrical grid upgrades, and why Aramco always had to take the lead. Some, who no doubt had their own favourite executives back in the States whom they wanted to rotate through Aramco, may also have questioned the wisdom of accelerating Saudization at the rate advocated by Jungers. In any case, Jungers, who was widely and genuinely respected by virtually every Saudi who worked for him, was pensioned off in January 1978 while still in his fifties and returned to the States. He later acted as a consultant for Bechtel Corporation and advised them on oil company acquisitions.

I was fortunate to have served under Jungers and learned a lot from him. Smart, conscientious and very decisive, he was a model for future Aramco executives. While certainly a hard-nosed manager, Jungers acted with both passion and compassion. He cared about everyone at Aramco, perhaps particularly the Saudis. His deep belief in human development did much to transform the culture within the company. Sadly, it may very well have cost him his job. Jungers was replaced as Aramco chairman and CEO by John Kelberer, an Aramco executive who had most recently been based in the company's New York City office. Hugh H. Goerner, a senior Exxon officer, was named president.

After about six months in The Hague as president of AOC, I returned to the Kingdom and was made a senior vice-president of Aramco in July 1978. Now the most senior Saudi executive in the organization, I was ready to take on my next challenge.

While John Kelberer was not as naturally outgoing as Jungers, the two of us developed a close working relationship.

He clearly backed me in my desire to continue to advance through the Aramco ranks. Lou Noto, former chairman and CEO of Mobil Oil, said in an interview that he and others credited Kelberer, a newcomer to Dhahran, for trusting my judgement regarding the morale and culture of the company. 'John Kelberer had a high regard for Ali,' Noto said. 'To some extent Ali was the mirror by which John got a lot of his insights into what was happening.'

I didn't have the same working relationship with our newly installed president. Hugh Goerner was professional in his dealings with me and other Saudis, but he was not very personable and I'm not sure how genuinely he embraced Saudization. One thing I vividly recall was that during management meetings he insisted on smoking a pipe that always seemed to be filled with noxious-smelling tobacco.

The tremendous amount of time and effort devoted to the large number of projects during the mid-1970s, and the subsequent need to hire thousands of contract workers, had distracted senior management's attention away from Saudization. During one of our first meetings, Kelberer told me that we needed to jump-start that programme, and that I was the one to do it. One of my first duties as a senior vice-president was to serve as vice-chairman of a newly formed Saudi Arab Manpower Committee, or SAMCOM, set up in order to formalize the process that had gained momentum under Jungers.

SAMCOM established a system to track the development of Saudis at all levels, from high-school graduates to those going to college and undertaking professional development courses. I soon discovered that we were not starting from scratch, that there already existed a closely guarded chart within Aramco used by a small number of senior department heads to track the progress of promising Saudi management candidates. Minister Yamani would often take a look when he visited Aramco headquarters in Dhahran. And it was a strange sensation, though hardly a complete surprise, to realize that I was one of the closely tracked candidates.

In what was called the 'greening of Aramco', the chart tracked Saudi candidates for senior management positions. A box representing an executive position held by a Saudi, such as my senior vice-presidency, was coloured green. If within two years a Saudi was expected to be ready to assume a position, it was striped green. Boxes outlined in green represented positions for which there were Saudi candidates but no timeframe for a Saudi to fill it. In Saudi Arabia, when it rains, the arid desert quickly turns green with newly sprouted grass, and I am proud to say that green soon spread across that chart in much the same way.

Our Saudization efforts weren't limited to the management ranks. We also dramatically stepped up the number of Saudi high-school and college graduates hired. I started our programme of hiring Saudi high-school graduates, with the first group in 1970 totalling nearly a hundred students. Despite that promising start, throughout the 1970s, with the focus on building our mega projects, that annual hiring figure remained roughly the same. In 1979 that figure jumped to 796, and in 1980 soared to 1,281.

We also instituted a new college fast-track programme in 1979 to attract top-performing high-school students with college scholarships paid for by Aramco. In its first year fifty-seven high-school graduates met the demanding criteria, including thirteen Saudi women. And we hired more college graduates, bringing on 124 in 1979 and another 203 a year later. Those two years alone exceeded the total number of college graduates hired in the previous two decades since I and my fellow guinea pigs ventured to America in 1959.

My education continued during the 1970s as well. In 1974, for the first time in more than a decade I returned to the US to take advanced management courses at Columbia University in New York, and five years later did similar work at Harvard University in Cambridge, Massachusetts. In each case I found the coursework demanding and rewarding. While I entered the programme with more hands-on leadership experience than many of my fellow students, I greatly appreciated the opportunity to gain a broader understanding of management theory and strategy.

As was the case when I was at Lehigh and Stanford in the late 1950s and early 1960s, some of my most meaningful experiences in America during the 1970s occurred outside of the classroom. When my classes at Columbia were over, Aramco decided it would be a good idea for me to spend some time working with some of our parent oil companies based in the States. Dhabyah and our three children travelled with me. (Our fourth child, Mohammed, would be born in 1978.) My first stop was Texaco, headquartered in New Jersey. After that came Exxon's operations in Texas.

I then flew over to spend some time with Chevron's manager for Texas's Midland Basin, Ed Price. Ed invited me and my family to a lunch of the best barbecued chicken I have ever tasted. At that table I first met Sam White, along with his wife Florence.

Sam White was the founder of Champion Chemicals, which was one of Chevron's contractors. I was impressed with how worldly Sam was. That was not at the time a character trait you would associate with Texans working in

Midland. He had travelled around the world for business and pleasure and was completely at home spending time with our Arab family. He even let our son Rami sit in his lap and turn the steering wheel of his modified M151 US Army jeep (known as a Military Utility Tactical Truck, or MUTT), and he and Flo took our kids to see a movie, *Herbie Goes Bananas.*

Driving with him across the arid plains of West Texas with oil rigs dotting the horizon reminded me a lot of Saudi Arabia, but without the sand dunes. I enjoyed the closest friendship of my adult life with Sam. Even though he was a Texan and more than a foot taller than me, we used to joke that we were both Bedouin at heart.

We had some contact in the following years but rekindled our friendship when I was back in America for the advanced management course at Harvard. Sam not only owned his own corporate jet, he was also a licensed pilot. He flew to New York to meet me when I had some time off from classes for Thanksgiving and flew me back to Midland.

Beginning with that trip, I took up hunting for the first time since my adventures with Uncle Abdullah a decade earlier, and also fishing, with Sam acting as my teacher and tour guide. For much of the next three decades the two of us would travel around the world to hunt or fish, or go on back-country trips closer to home along the Pecos River that flows south of Midland into the Rio Grande. Sam called a tin-sided hunting shelter overlooking the river his Pecos Palace. I was happy to eat the game that we killed. True to my Bedouin roots, I confess I have never developed much taste for fish. Thanks to Sam, however, I now eat it, and have made it a bigger part of my diet as I get older and cut back on red meat.

I suspect some of Aramco's top executives would not have been happy to know the details of some of our farther-flung expeditions. During the late 1970s and early 1980s, like today, drug trafficking made portions of Mexico a dangerous place to be. Nonetheless, Sam and I would take his MUTT into the mountains along some dirt roads that were little more than goat trails. As long as I didn't have to speak I could easily be mistaken for Mexican, as I had learned during my field work in Arizona years earlier.

On one occasion we were driving through a region of steep canyons, or barrancas, on the way back from visiting a friend of Sam's when suddenly we broke an axle. There weren't that many hours of sunlight left, and I was getting a little anxious about how and where we were going to spend the night. Sam put on a pair of overalls that he kept in the back, and he then proceeded to pull out a spare axle. Who travels with a spare axle? Self-sufficient Bedouin of West Texas, apparently. Two and a half hours later we were back on the road. After that incident I said, 'I will travel with you Sam anywhere, even to the moon.'

There is a sad coda. One evening in early March of 2005 I received a call from Flo on my private phone line in Riyadh. I knew Sam had been seriously ill with cancer, and she confirmed my worst fears. Sam had died in Houston that day. She told me that Sam had wanted to be sure I was invited to his funeral. I realized that if I left almost immediately, with a little rearrangement I could both make it to Midland for the funeral and also take in a number of meetings and other commitments in Dhahran that had been planned months in advance. It was a gruelling trip, but the best way I could pay my respects to my truest friend and his family.

Our close friendship over the years meant a tremendous amount to me on a personal level. It also helped me gain a deeper understanding of America and Americans working and living in their own country. My contact with Americans before then had been mostly limited to those working in Saudi Aramco, and of course my college friends. With Sam I developed an understanding of Texans and the independent spirit that makes that state so unique.

Understanding America would prove to be a vital skill for me in the decades to come.

9. Politics and Promotions – 1977–1983

Middle Eastern politics and oil dominated the news in the late 1970s, just as the oil embargo had done earlier in the decade. By late 1977 and into early 1978, demonstrations against the autocratic rule of the Shah of Iran became more prevalent on the streets of Teheran and in other major Iranian cities. Throughout the last half of 1978 the country became increasingly paralysed. As Iran was a major oil producer, we were paying particularly close attention, and so were the major oil-consuming countries. The global impact of the 1973–1974 oil embargo and the recession that followed were still fresh in the minds of millions of consumers around the world.

In the autumn of 1978 Iranian oil production plunged dramatically as the political crisis worsened and labour strikes intensified. From about 4.5 million barrels a day in September, Iran's daily oil exports fell to less than 1 million barrels by November. On Christmas Day, 25 December, Iran effectively turned off the spigots and halted oil exports completely.

The Shah finally fled the country on 16 January 1979. Suffering from cancer, he would receive medical treatment in the US and end up in exile in Egypt, where he died the following year. In February 1979 the Iranian government collapsed. Elections followed, though turmoil increased and in a matter of months the Ayatollah Khomeini, a Shiite, assumed power.

Even though Iranian oil exports gradually resumed in the spring of 1979, global oil markets were thrown into chaos. To make up for at least some of the shortfall, Saudi Arabia very publicly increased its production significantly, boosting daily output to 10.5 million barrels from 8.5 million by year end 1978. We reduced that figure over time as Iranian oil came back on the market. And we intentionally kept our prices stable, initially at $18 a barrel, and well below global spot-market prices offered by oil traders around the world, as well as the official OPEC price. Nevertheless, oil prices rapidly more than doubled on world markets. American television news showed endless images of Americans sitting in their cars in long lines outside gas stations.

As the 1970s had progressed, Minister Yamani had become very vocal about oil embargos. His point was simple: they didn't work. They accomplished three things, all of them bad, at least from the point of view of Saudi Arabia and most other OPEC members: they spurred energy conservation among developed economies, increased the development of alternative energy sources and intensified the search for additional sources of oil outside the Middle East. Indeed, in the wake of the 1973–1974 embargo, oilfield development accelerated on Alaska's North Slope, in the deep waters of the Gulf of Mexico and in the North Sea.

Yamani repeatedly warned other oil producers that the benefits of charging much higher prices for oil in response to the Iranian crisis would only be temporary. In the long run, the actions of OPEC and other producers were going to trigger another round of conservation efforts and additional oil would be found to bring to market, ultimately depressing

prices. It was a valid argument, but for our fellow oil producers the windfall profits were too tempting to resist. And due
to strong demand from the US and other nations and the
outbreak of armed conflict between Iran and Iraq in the
autumn of 1980, the price of oil continued to rise well into
1981 to more than $40 a barrel.

Worries about the oil price were overshadowed in November 1979 by two calamitous events. In Teheran, students and
other radicals stormed the US Embassy on 4 November and
took sixty-three Americans hostage. And in Mecca, a group
of radicals stormed the Grand Mosque during the hajj, also
taking scores of hostages. Their attack was launched on
20 November, the first day of the year 1400 according to the
Islamic calendar.

The well-documented hostage crisis in Iran would last for
more than a year. An American rescue attempt failed in early
1980. The situation by most accounts cost President Jimmy
Carter his chance to win a second term in office, and dam-
aged America's image abroad. The hostages were finally
released on the day President Ronald Reagan took office in
January 1981.

In preparing to oust the radicals from the Grand Mosque,
King Khalid consulted closely with the Kingdom's religious
authorities. After two weeks of often vicious fighting the
remaining radicals finally surrendered and the Grand
Mosque was liberated. The hundreds of dead and injured
included hostages, soldiers and radicals. Muslims around the
world were shocked by the assault on the Grand Mosque and
the tragic loss of life.

In response, Saudi Arabian culture took a much more
conservative turn. Among other things, restrictions on
women's dress and behaviour were enforced more strictly

than in the past. I am proud to say that Aramco, which continues to have a great deal of operational independence, resisted calls from some quarters to restrict the hiring or promoting of qualified women. Nationwide, however, it has only been in recent years that some of the more conservative restrictions put in place in 1979 have gradually been lifted.

The 1980s brought further professionalization of the Saudi workforce and the consolidation of Saudi control over Aramco and its future. My career took another step forward in 1980 when I was elected to the board of directors of Aramco. It was an honour to literally have a seat at the table where corporate power was exercised. A number of Saudis had served on the Aramco board over the years, but they had all been government ministers or other senior government officials. I was the first Saudi to serve on the board as an operating officer of the company. I took it as a sign that the government recognized that our operating expertise, increasingly the result of Saudi leadership, by this point was as good as any of our international competitors.

Also in 1980 the Saudi government officially assumed 100 per cent ownership of Aramco, having agreed the previous year to buy out the remaining shares held by the four oil company owners. In one sense the transfer had been a foregone conclusion. The government had assumed a 25 per cent ownership stake in 1973, and the following year it had increased that holding to 60 per cent. It was just a question of when, not if, the country would take sole possession.

The fact that the transfer didn't involve an overnight nationalization of foreign assets, as happened in several oil-producing countries, was a tribute to sound judgement and good negotiating faith on the part of the country as well as the oil company owners. That relationship had occasionally been tense, but the Saudis and Americans had learned to work together over the years to resolve their differences, and those efforts bore fruit in the transfer of ownership.

The close working relationship did have its lighter moments. As an American diplomat in Saudi Arabia at the time, Brooks Wrampelmeier, recalled in an interview:

> The final Saudi payment was made sometime in 1980. John Kelberer once told me what had happened next. 'I telephoned Oil Minister Ahmed Zaki Yamani and said that we had received the final check and he now had an oil company. Where did he want me to deliver it?' Kelberer said there was a long silence at the other end of the phone and finally Yamani said, 'Why don't you just keep running things the way they are.' This led to a curious arrangement whereby the Saudis legally owned Aramco but the consortium continued to operate it in accordance with its charter issued by the State of Delaware.

From the Saudi point of view there was nothing 'curious' about that arrangement, which would remain in place until 1988 when full operating control transferred to the Saudi government. Yamani and others, again aware of the failures other oil producers had made in nationalizing their foreign assets, wanted to retain close working ties with the original American owners and continue to tap their expertise. To this day, expatriate workers continue to account for approximately 15 per cent of the Saudi Aramco workforce – some years it is more, some years less – in part so that the company can be sure it is getting access to the latest innovations and technical expertise.

*

At the same time as we were negotiating with the overseas oil companies to transfer ownership, we were consolidating and enhancing our domestic technical facilities and capabilities. We cleared some old office complexes near the heart of our Dhahran site and constructed a world-class technology centre that rivalled the best petroleum research and analysis facilities anywhere, including those managed by the world's leading oil companies. Our exploration and petroleum engineering centre, or EXPEC, and adjacent computing centre and engineering buildings were considered an important milestone in Aramco's progress.

The creation of EXPEC and the transfer of related research and IT jobs to Dhahran created an unintended but quite positive side-effect. These jobs had previously been handled by consultants around the world, but as the new facilities came online in 1982, Aramco suddenly had many more positions available for highly trained women. For cultural and other reasons, many field operation positions weren't open to women, but office and laboratory jobs were, and as the 1980s progressed the positions created by EXPEC helped us attract and retain some of the leading Saudi women of their generation.

Several women who joined Aramco during the early 1980s would go on to hold senior leadership positions. Our first female petroleum engineer, Nailah Mousli, was among our trailblazing women employees to climb the ladder. Her accomplishment would have been impressive in virtually any country, in light of the rarity of women petroleum engineers during the 1980s (or, for that matter, today). The fact that she was able to advance so far in the Kingdom's traditional society was a tribute to her skills and determination to succeed.

She wasn't alone. Huda M. Al-Ghosan, who joined in 1981, by 2007 would become the first woman to serve on the board of one of our subsidiaries, Vela International Marine Ltd. She would later be named executive director of human relations for Saudi Aramco. And Nabilah M. Altunisi received a masters degree in electrical engineering from Oregon State University and joined Aramco in late 1982, and in short order was writing code for the IBM mainframe computer in EXPEC. In 2005 she was promoted to manager of the project support and controls department, overseeing more than 380 employees.

Fatema J. Al-Awami returned to Aramco to work in reservoir simulation at the EXPEC complex in 1984 after receiving a degree in petroleum engineering from the University of Southern California. She later served as a supervisor in the reservoir description and simulation department and helped develop Aramco's 'event solution' approach to resolving reservoir management issues.

The official opening of EXPEC was scheduled for 16 May 1983. That day marked the fiftieth anniversary of the signing of the concession agreement granting Standard Oil of California the right to explore for oil across much of eastern Saudi Arabia. Sadly, King Khalid had passed away the previous year, so his brother, King Fahd, accompanied by many Saudi dignitaries, presided at the event. The king made it a point to honour all of the 'Saudis and non-Saudis who have exerted themselves so greatly, and contributed to making Aramco what it is today'.

Minister Yamani, as expected, spoke at the event as well, but his remarks came as a surprise, both to me as well as to most of the audience. 'Aramco is now a Saudi Arabian institution that speaks our language,' he said. 'We hope the sun of this year will not set until a Saudi has become president of this company.' The Saudis in the crowd assumed that the minister would not make such a statement without the king's prior approval.

Aramco chairman and CEO John Kelberer and I were both on the Aramco board and had already planned to fly together that day to our next scheduled board meeting in the States. Kelberer looked at me as we got into the Gulfstream corporate jet for London, the first leg of the trip. 'What do you think, Ali? Should I be worried?' He said it with a laugh, but I think he might have been somewhat serious.

I had been promoted to executive vice-president in 1982. It was a newly created position that didn't really involve any significant change in my responsibilities. Others, including myself, assumed that my title really was president-in-waiting. It wasn't clear what the timing of my next promotion would be, but when I heard Minister Yamani speak, I thought, and hoped, there was a good chance he was talking about me. I turned to Kelberer and said, 'John, don't worry. I think the guy that needs to worry is Hugh Goerner.'

After that board meeting was over Minister Yamani, who was also on the board, took me aside. He said, 'The king has decided that you should be the president of the company.' The board elected me president in November 1983 and I took office the following January. Even though we were 100 per cent owned by the Saudi government, we were still under the operating authority of Aramco, which was registered as a corporation in Delaware, so the board vote was required to ratify my appointment.

In announcing my election as the first Saudi president

of Aramco, Minister Yamani emphasized that I had earned the job solely on merit. I was not Saudi window dressing, selected simply 'because he is Saudi to satisfy national sentiment, but because he earned the office through sweat and hard work, and because he has built himself and helped build others'. I was proud to be recognized, and humbled by the responsibility.

One of the most touching notes of congratulation came from former Aramco chairman and CEO Tom Barger. Though he was battling an advanced case of Parkinson's disease, which would claim his life two years later in 1986, Tom took the time to salute my promotion as a milestone on the long path of Saudization that he had championed two decades earlier. I responded to him with the following note:

> Thank you for the kind congratulatory cable. I am proud and honoured that you were one of the pioneers in shaping many a young Saudi Arab career. You, of all of Aramco's leaders, had the greatest vision when you supported the training effort of Saudi Arab employees during its early days. That visionary support and effort is bearing fruit now and many executive positions are filled by Saudis because of that effort. Thank you again and may God bless you and ease your current affliction, Ali I. Al-Naimi.

In the late 1960s I had a boss named Hal Streaker. He was a kind man, but also represented the mindset that made it so hard for many long-time American Aramcons to envision a time when Saudis would be running the company. One day he showed me my fifteen-year career plan. He pointed out that after fifteen years, I would be a manager! He clearly thought I would be pleased at the thought. I made manager two years later.

Shortly after being named president, I called Streaker into my office. It had been fifteen years, I told him, and now I was his boss. How did he think I had done in my career? We had a good laugh. Then we both went back to work.

10. From Boom to Bust – 1984–1989

The mid-1980s were some of the toughest years of my working life. By the time I moved into the president's office in January 1984, oil prices had been trending lower for over two years, and by 1986 would completely collapse. Our oil production would be severely curtailed, which, of course, caused our revenues to sink, the consequence of which was a drastic reduction in what Aramco could contribute to the Kingdom's revenues.

For the next five years we struggled to respond to challenges both abroad and closer to home. Through it all I was time and again awed by the ability of our people to pull together and do the hard work required to sustain us. Three decades later, as Saudi oil minister, I was still applying the lessons we learned in the 1980s – about our rivals, our customers and ourselves – to the challenges facing us.

Commodity markets often move unpredictably, making it difficult to pinpoint precisely when they take a definitive turn. In October 1981, Saudi Arabia raised the price it charged for a barrel of oil from $32 to $34. The Kingdom also reduced its daily production to 8.5 million barrels, the level that had been in place prior to the Iranian revolution and Iran's sudden cutback in production. Other OPEC members brought their prices down to $34 from $36 to match us. Prices in the so-called spot market offered by oil traders were still more than $40.

In the late 1970s, like virtually every major oil company

worldwide, Aramco had based its strategy and planning on projections of continued strong global demand for oil. Much of that planning, such as aggressive hiring and training targets, was considered essential for future growth. But those levels of demand simply never materialized. As Minister Yamani had predicted, the 1973 oil embargo had triggered a host of changes that, while they took several years to have a demonstrable impact, would dramatically affect the price of oil. Virtually no one predicted the full force of those changes.

In 1975, the United States Congress passed legislation mandating that the average fuel efficiency of vehicles on America's roads must double. Corporations also significantly reduced their oil consumption during this period by, among other measures, improving building insulation, adopting more efficient manufacturing processes and switching to alternative fuels. By the mid-1980s, as a result of these and related efforts, the United States was estimated to be 25 per cent more energy efficient than it had been prior to the 1973 embargo. The impact of conservation was even more pronounced in Japan and a number of European countries.

While consumers and corporations were steadily becoming more energy conscious during the early 1980s, many developed economies were suffering perhaps the worst economic downturn since the Great Depression of the 1930s. Inflation had already been accelerating before the Iranian crisis led to sharply higher oil prices. In America, Ronald Reagan came into the White House determined to address the issue, even at the expense of short-term economic growth. Prime Minister Margaret Thatcher was pursuing similar policies in Great Britain. US interest rates topped 20 per cent and unemployment soared as well. The US economy suffered a punishing downturn in 1980 and again in 1982, resulting in a much reduced demand for oil.

Further changes in the global oil industry during the previous decade began to impact on world supply. Oil prices had more than tripled during the 1970s, which encouraged additional exploration and production of oil in many areas, often with methodologies that wouldn't have been considered when oil was trading in the low teens of dollars per barrel. As a result, non-OPEC oil production was surging. Additional millions of barrels from Alaska's North Slope and the North Sea, as well as Mexico, meant that by 1982 non-OPEC production exceeded OPEC production for the first time since the organization had been created.

By early 1983 Minister Yamani was publicly stating that our price for oil was too high in light of declining global demand. Adding pressure on OPEC's pricing structure was the fact that futures contracts on crude oil, in this case West Texas Intermediate crude, started trading on the New York Mercantile Exchange on 30 March 1983. The futures contract created an alternative benchmark for global pricing.

In May 1983, OPEC cut its official price for a barrel of oil from $34 to $29. OPEC members also agreed to a lower production quota. A statement from the meeting at which that figure was set for the first time identified Saudi Arabia as the 'swing producer' in OPEC. That meant the Kingdom would increase or decrease production as needed to maintain the target price. That would prove to be a momentous and, in many ways, unfortunate decision.

Then as now, the Saudi oil minister sets policy in close consultation with the king and his advisers. The job of Aramco's management is to execute this policy on behalf of the Kingdom. Minister Yamani was at his best, in my opinion,

during the 1970s as he masterminded the Kingdom's participation ownership agreement with Aramco's four oil company
owners. All his skills as a lawyer were brought to bear as he
crafted an equitable, and peaceful, transfer of ownership. It
is hard to overestimate how important that was to both the
Kingdom's and Aramco's success, as well as to the stability
of the global oil industry.

As surprising as it may sound, Minister Yamani was not
an expert on the oil business. He had never worked in the
industry nor did he study the subject at university. The government's willingness during the mid-1980s to have Saudi
Arabia act as OPEC's swing producer and curtail our production to support prices cost us much-needed revenue as
well as market share. When we then boosted production to
regain a bigger share of the market, global oil prices collapsed. That cost the Kingdom dearly. Ultimately, it cost the
minister his job.

Tough times require tough decisions. Whether it be the
high-school apprentices we recruited or my senior leadership
team, I had for years committed myself to developing our
people. But even before I became president I was given the
toughest job of my career: making significant cuts in staff
numbers in order to reduce our costs.

Our revenues were plunging, but in the early years of the
1980s we had still been hiring and training as if oil prices in
the $40 range would continue indefinitely. In fact, coming
into the decade we had estimated that we would need as
many as 75,000 employees by 1985. By 1983 it was clear that
estimate was far too high. To get our head count more in line
with our falling revenues, but at the same time not severely
damage our ability to grow in the future, we determined that

our payroll would need to shrink significantly. From a 1982 peak of 61,227, our employee roster would bottom out at roughly 43,500 in 1987.

These cuts were without question necessary, but they nonetheless were difficult to make. Having grown up in the company, I knew many of those I had to let go. Some, from many nationalities, were friends. But the future of Aramco was at stake.

Our policy of Saudization, with its roots in the original concession agreement, gave us some direction, and ultimately the reduction in staff numbers accelerated its progress. The planned retirement of certain expatriates was pushed forward, and, in the end, more than 14,000 of the jobs lost in the mid-1980s had been held by non-Saudis. While thousands of Saudi jobs were also cut, the larger number of expats leaving Aramco during this period boosted the proportion of Saudis in management positions and in the workforce as a whole to nearly two-thirds. Inevitably, this created hard feelings among some expat employees. They had joined the company knowing that in many cases they would be training and promoting Saudis who would eventually replace them, but the price collapse during the 1980s accelerated this process and forced many expats to leave the company early. The large number of expat employees from this era who continue to attend Aramcon retiree events in the US and around the world, however, attests to the fond memories most of them have concerning their years spent in the Kingdom.

Reducing labour costs wasn't our only issue. Cutting oil output also reduced the amount of associated gas we were producing. The Master Gas System had been designed based on assumptions that oil production would reach 12 to 15 million barrels per day, with a corresponding increase in the production of associated gas. It rapidly became clear that those figures were significantly inflated. Gas powered our economy, and now we faced the possibility that there wouldn't be enough.

The solution to the problem literally lay beneath our feet. As long ago as the late 1940s, Aramco had discovered a large field of gas about 650 metres below that of the Arab Zone of rock strata that contained much of the oil in the Eastern Province. At the time there was no use for this non-associated or free gas in what would later become known as the Kuff formation. In fact the gas, which contained toxic compounds such as hydrogen sulphide, was considered a hazard.

A team reporting to one of our vice-presidents, Ed Price, addressed the issue with ingenuity and perseverance. I had met Ed a decade earlier in Texas when he was still with one of our parent companies, Chevron, and respected his work. His group drafted a programme for extending certain existing oil wells in locations that appeared to have a high probability of finding Kuff formation gas. With the oil company cutting costs wherever possible, the team realized they were not going to get funding for a new programme anytime soon. So they decided that they would request the new drilling depths as part of the ongoing programme of structural delineation, which was our practice of continually gathering information about the rock strata each well was drilling through.

The gas drilling programme was an unqualified success. By 1985 Aramco was able to produce a billion standard cubic feet per day (scfd) of non-associated gas, process it and send it into the Kingdom's Master Gas system. That didn't bring the volume of gas even close to the initial estimates when the system was being designed, but it was enough to keep the system running through years of reduced oil production.

The gas programme was also a tribute to our employees' ability to work under tremendous pressure. They found innovative solutions to problems that, if unsolved, might have derailed our society's development for years.

'When the camel goes down, many knives come out.' That's an old Arabic proverb that came to my mind in my first years as Aramco president. In the mid-1980s, the camel was Aramco. The knives were the vested interests of Saudis who viewed us as a symbol of foreign influence and the era of colonialism.

Even though Aramco had been wholly owned by the Kingdom since 1980, some in Riyadh still thought that we were tainted by our association with our previous owners. In their minds the tough times Aramco was going through were an opportunity to put the destiny of the Kingdom's petroleum resources securely in Saudi hands – even though that's where they already were. I think those taking this position felt threatened. Aramco had been created as a meritocracy. Successive kings endorsed the fact that this institution enabled talented Saudis to rise through the ranks through hard work and ability, rather than family and tribal connections, as had too often been the case among businesses in the Gulf region.

As historian Dr Steffen Hertog noted in a 2008 paper on the subject:

Although Saudi Arabia is not a country most observers immediately associate with lean and clean management, Aramco's role as the Kingdom's greatest modern institution seems unassailable. Hardly a Saudi and practically no foreigner today is aware that Aramco is what it is because of a number of historical decisions which could have been taken differently – and which many contemporaries expected to be taken differently, much to Aramco's detriment. Saudi Arabia was close to taking a course which many other oil exporters took, entrusting its upstream oil assets to an opaque, politicized local institution that was supposed to replace foreign-created Aramco.

Other institutions were being cited as more authentically Saudi Arabian, and hence more worthy replacements for Aramco as the Kingdom's principal guardian and developer of its natural resources. Most frequently mentioned was a government-owned and controlled company called Petromin. Otherwise known as the General Organization of Petroleum and Minerals, Petromin traced its roots to the first flowering of Saudi government reform under Crown Prince Faisal in 1962. Having been championed by our first oil minister, Abdullah Al-Tariki, as well as his successor, Minister Yamani, Petromin was in important ways set up as a mirror to Aramco, operating in the portions of the Kingdom outside of the geographic boundaries of Aramco's concession.

Petromin was initially authorized to develop petrochemical and heavy industry opportunities in the Kingdom. Petromin's success in these areas proved over time to be at best mixed, prompting the government in 1976 to create Saudi Arabian Basic Industries Company, SABIC, to drive development in these sectors. It wisely adopted a lean management structure similar to Aramco's, and the company later sold a 30 per cent interest to the public.

Unlike SABIC, Petromin was known for being top-heavy

with managers who had little operating experience in the field. In that sense it resembled other national oil companies created in the region during the 1970s and 1980s that were similarly plagued with inefficiencies. For whatever reason, those performance issues weren't enough to dampen the enthusiasm in some quarters for a Petromin takeover bid as Aramco's revenues continued to slide. Minister Yamani clearly favoured this option.

For me, this was a battle for the heart and soul of Aramco, the company I had helped to build. It wouldn't be long before things came to a head.

In 1984 Aramco took over operation of one of Petromin's earlier successes, the East–West Pipeline, which had been built in the 1970s by Petroline, a subsidiary of Petromin, and Mobil Oil. The 1,200 kilometre-long pipeline delivered 1.85 million barrels of crude oil per day from the Eastern Province over the range of mountains in the west of the Kingdom to the port of Yanbu on the Red Sea. In short order Aramco embarked on an expansion of the system by building a parallel pipeline tied into the existing pumping stations that increased capacity to 3.2 million barrels per day. By the early 1990s another expansion boosted the pipeline system's capacity to 5 million barrels per day.

So, Aramco in the 1980s was doing battle on several fronts: fighting a hostile takeover attempt while also wrestling with the many painful decisions required to keep the company financially viable during the unprecedented turmoil in the world petroleum market. Aramco may have been down, like the camel in the proverb, but it was clearly not out. In a few cases we actually shelved major projects, but remained determined to move forward with others.

In the early 1980s the company began building a world-class refinery near the ancient province of Qasim. The new refinery was state-of-the art in every respect and was a project everyone at Aramco was proud of, even while still under construction.

But with little oil revenue coming in, the government in Riyadh decided it had to take drastic action. After what I learned later was a stormy Council of Ministers meeting, work on the refinery was halted in 1984, even though it was nearing completion. We had already spent roughly $900 million, so very little was saved. It was a bitter experience for us at Aramco, but one we would also shortly learn from.

My senior management team had its share of tense meetings during this time as well, even if it was not my style to put up with shouting. One of our very able senior vice-presidents at the time was Abdullah Saif, head of our upstream operations. During one of our meetings he was complaining about everything his people were having to do while at the same time cutting costs on every side. At the end of his talk he slammed the conference table with his hand for emphasis. I looked up from my notes. 'So, you're telling me you can't do your job?' I asked. He got the message, and so did the rest of the team. It was our responsibility to get the work done.

I understood the tension. We couldn't continue to abandon facilities like we had the Qasim refinery. That would cripple our ability to produce adequate quantities of oil in the future, as well as crush our morale. There had to be a better way. Drawing on the Aramco tradition of buckling down and thriving under pressure, we found one: mothballing.

Mothballing means shutting down, but not abandoning a

facility, and is a useful strategy in the face of steadily declining demand. A member of the team under the leadership of Sadad Al-Husseini, vice-president of Northern Area operations at the time and another of our rising talents, came up with the idea after reading about US warships being decommissioned after World War II. To implement the strategy on such a massive scale had never been attempted before (or since), but the wisdom behind effectively maintaining spare production capacity through the mothballing process would be underscored within a very few years as another war broke out closer to home.

The huge offshore facilities in the Marjan, Zuluf and Safaniyah fields were among the first to be mothballed. The process involved widespread cleaning to offset corrosion, and a minimal level of ongoing maintenance so that, if necessary, the plant could be brought back online as fast as possible. Diesel fuel was pumped through pipelines to remove corrosive 'sour' crude that contained sulphur and other impurities. And to avoid the corrosive effect of oxygen on instrument panels sitting idle, inert nitrogen was pumped through these systems.

Hardly a region or aspect of our oil operations was spared the mothballing process. Gas oil separation plants in Hawiyah, Haradh and Uthmaniyah were mothballed. So were facilities in Khurais, Abu Safah, Harmaliyah and Mazalij. Even the giant saltwater pipeline running from our Qurayyah Seawater Treatment Plant to the Ghawar oilfield was put in mothballs. While we were able to find other posts for some of the employees working at these facilities, many jobs were eliminated in the mothballing process. Sadly, that created hardships for Saudi families across the Eastern Province, just as industry downturns create hardships wherever facilities are located, in the Gulf or West Texas.

Some aspects of mothballing had to be seen to be believed. The giant rotors and turbines used in numerous facilities were marvels of modern engineering and looked as if they could withstand anything. But our engineers studying the issue alerted us to the fact that these enormous tools would actually warp under their own massive weight if they remained inactive for too long in their horizontal operating positions. That meant enormous cranes had to lift them out of their moorings and stand them on end like huge bowling pins until they were returned to service.

The oil crisis of the 1980s reached a tipping point in 1985. Two years of slashing production to try to prop up oil prices while watching other OPEC members cheat by pumping more oil than they had agreed to became no longer tolerable. At one point in 1985 our production fell as low as 2.2 million barrels a day, compared to 10.5 million during the Iranian crisis. In June 1985 King Fahd took the rare step of publicly rebuking, and warning, other OPEC producers. 'If member countries feel they have a free hand to act,' he said, 'then all should enjoy this situation and Saudi Arabia would certainly secure its own interests.'

The king's anger was understandable. The impact of Saudi Arabia's acting as the swing producer in the mid-1980s was devastating for the country's growth. Saudi oil industry earnings peaked at $119 billion in 1981. That figure plunged by about two-thirds to just $36 billion in 1984. It skidded another $10 billion to a mere $26 billion in 1985.

In addition to our new oil refinery, many development projects across the country were postponed or curtailed, and the Kingdom started running a significant budget deficit. Our debt ballooned to more than 100 per cent of gross domestic product. 'The trouble was that everyone was geared for continuous growth,' said Hamad Sayari, the former head of the Saudi Arabian Monetary Agency. 'Suddenly, there was a cliff.'

To reverse our fortunes, the Kingdom abandoned its role as swing producer. Our new strategy under Minister Yamani's leadership was to recover market share. And that meant pumping more oil. It spelled the end for Yamani. One of our strategies was to create 'net back' contracts with oil buyers. Instead of a standard quoted price, Aramco set the price of oil tied to the value of a particular refined product, after subtracting 'back' refining cost, margins and freight.

We weren't acting alone. Abdullah Al-Attiya, deputy prime minister and former energy minister of Qatar, recalled:

> There was a closed session at OPEC when the ministers agreed to flood the market, get the price down and see the producers from Alaska and the North Sea come begging to OPEC. But they never showed up. One minister said: 'All we have to do is wait and they will come with tears in their eyes.' Well, in a few months, we were the ones with tears in our eyes.

Oil prices actually rose for a time in late 1985. Then the bottom fell out of the market. West Texas Intermediate hit a peak of $31.75 a barrel at the end of November on the New York Mercantile Exchange. By the spring of 1986 it was quoted at about $10, which would be about $20 today after adjusting for inflation. Oil cargoes were quoted in the Arabian Gulf in the single digits per barrel – prices not seen since before the 1973 oil embargo.

'I remember at that time one cargo was sold to Petrobras, 2 million barrels for $3.25 a barrel,' said Esam Trabulsi, former Aramco vice-president of sales and marketing. 'That's the lowest price cargo that ever left Saudi Arabia since the 1970s.'

It was panic pricing, driven by the public acknowledgement by the Kingdom and others that they would compete for market share. But it did not reflect market realities. In fact, OPEC increased its production in the early months of 1986 by less than 10 per cent, as noted by historian and oil industry consultant Daniel Yergin in his Pulitzer Prize-winning *The Prize*, a history of the global oil industry. The damage was very real, however, and would take years to unwind.

As for global consumers, cheap oil helped drive the booming market in the US for vehicles with low fuel economy, such as SUVs and pick-up trucks. More broadly, cheaper oil no doubt contributed to the 1980s economic boom in the US and across much of Europe. At the same time lower oil prices drastically diminished incentives to develop alternative energy sources, including solar and wind power. Government support for alternative energy research dried up in the industrialized world. The sense of urgency around energy conservation and alternative energy created by the 1973 oil embargo and rekindled in many quarters by the 1979 Iranian crisis was gone.

The West's reaction to cheaper pump prices in the mid-1980s in a way reflected Minister Yamani's warnings regarding the spike in oil prices following the 1973 embargo. Alternative energy options were less attractive and consumption swelled over time, thus ensuring healthy demand for OPEC's product going forward. Minister Yamani might have felt vindicated. But he didn't remain in office long enough to celebrate. Things were coming to a head.

Back in the Kingdom, Petromin's ambition to take over Aramco was gaining traction and there was disquiet in the Aramco camp. In early 1986, I called my leadership team together. We agreed that we could not let it happen, and that we were united in our resistance to such a poorly thought out move. I went to see the minister in Riyadh. 'What do you want, Ali?' he asked as I entered his spacious office at the oil ministry. 'We do not agree with your plan to have Petromin take over Aramco,' I told him. 'We do not think the people at Petromin, like those who accompany you to Aramco executive committee meetings, are of high enough calibre to manage us.'

He was clearly shocked by my directness. And he was surprised further when I placed a sealed envelope on the table in the centre of his office. It was a letter of resignation from myself and my entire management team, to take effect immediately upon Petromin's takeover of Aramco. I left the matter with him.

OPEC members met in Geneva in July and August of 1986 with the intention of reinstating a quota system to support oil prices, returning again in October to hopefully complete the task. The king wanted to maintain our production quota as well as set the OPEC price at $18 a barrel. Some felt that Minister Yamani wasn't advocating the Kingdom's position as rigorously as the government in Riyadh might have wanted.

And there were some preliminary warning signs that the minister was falling out of favour. Earlier in 1986 King Fahd cut the ribbon at the inauguration of a new expansion of our

Ras Tanura refining complex. The king thanked the assembled Aramco and government leaders as expected. When he thanked Hisham Nazer, a former Yamani deputy oil minister who then served in various ministerial planning roles, he referred to him as Minister of Petroleum. 'We all thought he'd made a mistake,' recalled Sa'ad Al-Shaifan, a former Aramco senior vice-president. 'This was huge.'

Ahmed Zaki Yamani would learn that after twenty-four years he was no longer the Kingdom's oil minister by hearing it on the evening television news back in Riyadh late that October. No official explanation was offered for his replacement by Hisham Nazer, initially on an interim basis. Nazer would be named permanent minister that December. With Nazer as minister, and new priorities ahead, the Petromin matter was closed, and Aramco continued to operate as before.

Our struggles with low oil prices and the fall of the world's highest-profile oil minister were no doubt being celebrated by many in advanced economies that relied heavily on oil to drive growth. But others realized that it was in the best interests of the global economy if Saudi Arabia could maintain a reasonable return on its energy investment and thus remain a reliable supplier to the world. The United States government was among the concerned.

In 1986 the US vice-president George H. W. Bush visited Crown Prince Abdullah in the Eastern Province. His goal was to convey the message that the Reagan administration believed that the US and the Kingdom had a common interest in stable oil prices. And the US, no doubt in part due to the legacy of the American oil company heritage at Aramco, appreciated that Aramco and the Kingdom could be relied on as long-term partners. I gave the vice-president a tour around Dhahran during his visit. He struck me as a thoughtful man and one who understood our business, based on his earlier career as an independent oil man in West Texas.

'We came to the conclusion that we had a common interest in a stable oil market,' said Bill Ramsay, a career US diplomat whose postings included Riyadh. 'We never agreed upon exactly what we meant by stable in terms of price. They would think higher. We would think lower. But we always had the Saudis on our side in this sort of search for moderate price because they had a longer-term horizon than everybody else.'

America was also on Aramco's agenda in 1986. That's when I, with the support of John Kelberer, began telling anyone who would listen in Riyadh that Aramco had to become more of an integrated oil company in order to boost and diversify our revenue stream. That meant adding more oil refining and marketing, so-called downstream businesses, to complement our upstream exploration and production. The US, where the economy was rebounding strongly by the second half of the 1980s, was an obvious location of choice for our expansion plans.

I made a proposal to the ministry, and they took it to the king. He approved it, and left the implementation of the plan to Aramco. Off we went to America in search of joint-venture partners. Kelberer, though battling health problems, played an active role in negotiating with several of the largest international oil companies.

In 1988 an Aramco subsidiary formed a joint venture in the US with Texaco called Star Enterprise, a name inspired by the star in the Texaco logo. This was hardly a start-up operation. When Star Enterprise began operations on 1 January 1989 its assets included refineries in Port Arthur, Texas (on the Gulf of Mexico), Convent, Louisiana, and Delaware City, Delaware, as well as forty-eight product distribution terminals. Star also had nearly 4,000 employees, more than 11,000 service stations operating under the Texaco brand and four marketing divisions.

In addition to generating added revenue for Aramco, the refineries also provided the oil company with customers. By signing long-term purchase contracts with the joint-venture refineries, Aramco was able to cushion in part the impact of dramatic short-term swings in oil prices. And that gave us added confidence to invest in additional production capacity to meet future global demand.

The downstream business has only grown in importance. In 1998 Star Enterprise was merged with certain assets of Shell Oil to form Motiva Enterprises LLC. Expansion of the refineries operated by Motiva continued, particularly at Port Arthur, which traces its roots back to Texaco's predecessor in 1902 and the landmark Spindletop oil discovery in East Texas. After the most recent round of expansion and improvements, the Port Arthur refinery ranks as the largest crude oil refinery in the US and one of the largest in the world.

By 1987 it was clear that the major industrialized economies were rebounding. Oil prices on world markets recovered as well, bouncing back from the low of about $10 or less in 1986 to the $18 level. OPEC tried to set a basket of prices based on rates for different grades of crude – Arabian Light was set at $17.52 a barrel, for instance – but increased production by some members made it almost impossible to find buyers at the official basket prices.

Aramco's solution, devised by senior economist William Laney Littlejohn, was to link the price of our crude to the

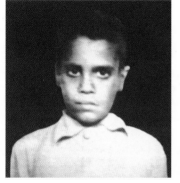

1. The first known picture of me, aged nine or ten. I spent the first eight years of my life travelling around the eastern deserts of Arabia and I still have vivid memories of what was a very different time.

2. This was taken *c*.1946, when I was eleven. I am second from right, holding a ball. The US oil workers taught me baseball and later helped me understand American culture when I took a degree in the States.

3. Aged sixteen, displaying my typing skills to visiting dignitaries. Picking up English and learning to type gave me an advantage, but both took a lot of practice.

4. Here are the four Aramco employees destined to study overseas, in 1959, shortly before leaving for the US to take degree courses. I am on the left, receiving instruction from education supervisor Paul Case. The warning from Aramco was unequivocal: 'Make a mess of it, and no one else will follow.'

5. Aramco's famous 'Flying Camel' that took me to Lehigh University in 1959. When a lady asked me how I'd reached America and I told her I'd come on a flying camel, she was amazed! This was taken in 1967 (*I am fourth from the right*).

6. Joining the board of Aramco in 1982. John Kelberer (*seated middle, blue tie*) was CEO at the time, in what was still a US-run operation. Within six years, Saudi Arabia would take control of Aramco, the culmination of a smooth transition of ownership.

7. Oil minister Ahmed Zaki Yamani (*left*), CEO John Kelberer (*centre*) and me, as Aramco President, pictured in 1985. In 1986 Yamani would be replaced and in 1988 I became CEO of the newly named Saudi Aramco. Kelberer, a good-natured man, would be the company's last American CEO.

8. King Fahd, myself and Hisham Nazer. Nazer became oil minister in 1986 and set about implementing a domestic reform agenda.

9. In 1991 retreating Iraqi troops deliberately created a huge oil slick in the Gulf, polluting the coast and threatening Saudi Arabia's desalination plants. Not only did we halt the slick, we ingeniously recovered and refined nearly a million barrels of the oil it contained. Here's me, pointing, inspecting the damage.

10. As CEO in 1993, doing what I liked most: getting out and about and meeting my fellow employees. I'd already worked for Saudi Aramco for forty-six years and was looking forward to retirement at sixty. It wasn't to be.

11. Pictured here with Abdallah Jum'ah, the man I recommended for the job of Saudi Aramco CEO in 1995. The decision was a surprise, not least to Abdallah, but I knew he was the right man with the sort of intellect, dynamism, work ethic and people skills required for what was, and is, a massive job.

12. In 2009 King Abdullah presented me with a commendation for my involvement in the King Abdullah University of Science and Technology. Building a university was a departure from the usual mega-projects undertaken by Saudi Aramco. In a way, the building was the easy bit. Getting the culture, feel and principles right was a much greater challenge.

13. With Sam White (*centre*) and Garland Paulk. Sam was my best friend. He was from Midland, Texas, but we shared an outlook on the world and spent many a happy time hunting and camping. Garland, who has organized my overseas logistics for many years, has put in thousands of kilometres with me – mostly grumbling!

14. I'm not sure about that hat! Here pictured on a fishing trip off Mexico's Cabo San Lucas in 2000 with energy ministers Alí Rodriguez from Venezuela (*left*) and Luis Téllez from Mexico. We struck up a strong relationship in the late 1990s as we all helped agree and coordinate global oil production cuts.

15. Another day, another mountain. Into my eighties, I'm still an exercise addict, much to the chagrin of my team. It helps me think and lets me work through problems.

16. Sam Bodman was US Energy Secretary from 2005 to 2009, and became a good friend of mine. Sam's background was as a chemical engineer, so he understood the oil business. That wasn't always the case with US energy ministers.

17. Besieged at OPEC, 2009. Sitting alongside Prince Abdulaziz, Saudi Arabia's deputy oil minister, fielding questions during the regular media scrum afforded journalists at every OPEC meeting. The media has its own agenda and is, sadly, increasingly obsessed with the here and now.

18. Talking with Vice-President Dick Cheney as oil prices headed towards a historic high of $147 in 2008. I went hunting with Cheney – he didn't shoot me, either!

19. Prime Minister Gordon Brown (*left*) with King Abdullah in 2008. I'm seated behind the king. For a former finance minister, Brown was surprisingly uninformed about the global oil industry.

20. Khalid Al-Falih, then Saudi Aramco CEO, pulls the ribbon on a sign marking Ali Al-Naimi Road, in S-Oil's Onsan refinery in Ulsan, in the Republic of Korea, in 2015. Saudi Aramco is the majority shareholder of S-Oil and I am a fan of Korea and Koreans. They are good people, and fun-loving like us.

21. Discussing climate-change policy with UN Secretary General Ban Ki-moon at the Paris COP21 talks in 2015.

22. In 2012 I gave the commencement address at Lehigh University, fifty years after graduating. Both my sons, Mohammed (*5th from left*) and Rami (*2nd from right*), were there to see me accept an honorary degree from President Alice Gast.

23. With King Abdullah in Hawaii. The king, who sadly passed away in 2015, was a kind and gentle man.

24. Here I am at home, pictured in the red sands of the Empty Quarter, known in Arabic as the Rub' Al-Khali.

25. This is me, leading a group of visitors down a sand dune in Shaybah. Female visitors would sometimes arrive in heels – that's a mistake when it comes to walking up sand dunes. And don't think you can run up them, either.

26. With my oldest son, Rami, and his son, Ali. I have four children, and now eight grandchildren. Time flies!

price of crude in regional markets, adjusted for various factors, including shipping costs calculated according to distance from the Kingdom. Alaska North Slope was the original basis for sales in the US, later replaced by West Texas Intermediate, while the North Sea's Brent crude was used for European sales and Dubai and Omani quoted prices for sales to the Far East. The success of the new pricing system and the rebounding world economy were reflected in the fact that our crude oil production for 1988 rebounded to 4.93 million barrels a day, the highest since 1982.

After ten years as Aramco chairman and CEO, John Kelberer retired in April 1988. He led our company through some of the most difficult but at the same time transformative periods in our history. I always considered him a mentor and friend. All Saudi employees of Aramco owed him a debt of thanks. He had been ill and underwent several operations during his final years in office. It was a tribute to his endurance that he stayed at the helm until we were clearly on the rebound. John remained as vice-chairman of the board for a time but, sadly, died in 1991.

One of the greatest compliments I could pay John was to demonstrate that the trust and faith he invested in me were not misplaced. I stepped into his shoes as CEO when he retired, though I had assumed many of the executive functions of the post earlier, with his full support. We were still a Delaware corporation at that point, however, and followed the appropriate laws concerning corporate governance. As CEO but not chairman, I could not assume all of John's responsibilities. Minister Nazer was named Aramco's chairman and together we became the first two Saudis to hold the top positions at the company.

The minister and I were not close personally but we had a

good working relationship. We consulted closely to ensure the needs of the ministry and the work of Aramco were aligned. That said, he was more than a little taken aback by the limited role he played as chairman of the oil company.

He asked me if he got to sign Aramco contracts. He was chairman of the board, after all. I told him: 'No, neither the chairman nor CEO signs them. There are procedures.' He then asked about signing cheques. Again, I said: 'No, it's done electronically via banks in the US.' He said, 'So what does the chairman do, apart from run the company?' I said: 'No, I run the company, you just make sure the board meetings are managed. And you get to sign off the minutes.' He wasn't very pleased!

In November 1988, guided by Minister Nazer, the Council of Ministers approved the creation of a new Saudi entity, the Saudi Arabian Oil Company, or Saudi Aramco, to assume the responsibilities that had previous been those of Aramco. There was a certain amount of confusion among the ministers as to just what the name was supposed to mean. If the name Aramco was based on the Arabian American Oil Company originally, and there was no longer any American interest in the entity, why keep the name? Minister Nazer successfully argued that maintaining the continuity of the name was important to the company's future success, and Saudi Aramco it was.

Saudi Aramco prepared for the 1990s with renewed optimism. We were now a Saudi entity in charge of our own destiny. Oil prices were rising and growth accelerating in economies around the globe. Our exploration teams had discovered several new oilfields in the Kingdom in recent years, and now it made economic sense to develop them.

Another event further brightened out prospects for the

future. In August 1988, after eight bloody years, one of the most unsettling regional conflicts of the era, the Iran–Iraq War, finally wound down. As part of a peace agreement brokered by the United Nations, both sides laid down their arms without a declared winner, though there may have been as many as a million losers in terms of casualties among armed forces and civilians alike. But the sporadic disruption to Gulf shipping was finally at an end. This renewed stability provided a more optimistic vision for the region at large as well as its oil producers. Clearly, we had much to look forward to.

How wrong we were.

11. War and Peace – 1990–1994

I began the 1990s proud of the way Saudi Aramco's leadership team had navigated the treacherous markets of the 1980s. I was confident the company was prepared for further success in the decade ahead. But the summer of 1990 proved that I had a lot to learn about geopolitics.

That August I was attending a symposium at the Aspen Institute in Colorado, surrounded by the Rocky Mountains. As a panellist during one of many events celebrating the institute's fortieth anniversary, I was asked my opinion about Iraqi dictator Saddam Hussein. Saddam had captured the world's attention as the year progressed by becoming increasingly hostile toward Kuwait in both word and deed, including mobilizing tens of thousands of troops at that country's northern border. Saddam audaciously claimed that Kuwait was not an independent country but rather, based on his reading of regional history during Ottoman times, a province of Iraq. In his mind that meant Kuwait's oil was rightfully his. To us in Saudi Arabia, we thought this was classic Saddam gamesmanship.

I was fresh from an OPEC meeting in Geneva. There I witnessed representatives of Iraq, Kuwait and other Gulf countries air their grievances peacefully, if a bit raucously. No violence was threatened. Based on those observations, I told my Aspen audience not to worry. 'This is really just a summer storm cloud that will come and go.' A few hours later a friend who had been at the meeting knocked on my hotel room door. 'You better turn on CNN,' he said.

The network was endlessly repeating videotape of Iraqi tanks rolling into Kuwait on 2 August. Kuwait shared its opposite, southern border with Saudi Arabia. Given that it is a fairly small country, this was of compelling interest to me and Saudis everywhere, not to mention the thousands of expats still working at Saudi Aramco facilities, some of which were very close to Kuwait. Like most Saudis, I hadn't expected Saddam to carry out his threat.

I received an insight into future events the next day. I was walking around the institute's campus before heading back to the Kingdom when, perhaps bizarrely, I crossed paths with Margaret Thatcher, Britain's prime minister, who, along with the US president, George H. W. Bush, was scheduled to speak at the institute later that day. Thatcher was, like me, out for an unaccompanied morning walk. As we fell into step, she said hello and asked where I was from. When I told her Saudi Arabia and that I was CEO of Saudi Aramco, she offered me her firm assurance. 'Don't worry,' she said, 'this invasion will not stand.' Later that day she stood next to President Bush as he made the same assurance and I've admired Thatcher for her guts and determination ever since. She gave Bush the backing he needed.

For the first time since World War II, our oilfields and production facilities, as well as part of the Kingdom itself, faced the imminent threat of being overrun or destroyed by a hostile foreign power. That meant a significant portion of the world's oil supply was threatened as well. If Saddam were to succeed in annexing Kuwait and treating its vast oil reserves as his own, it was likely he would threaten us next.

The United Nations condemned the invasion within a few days and later set a 15 January 1991 deadline for Saddam to withdraw his troops and armaments from Kuwait. In the meantime, the Dhahran airbase adjacent to Saudi Aramco's headquarters and its residential compound became a centre of round-the-clock activity. A multinational force began to assemble and war materiel amassed during the months leading up to the deadline. The airbase, as well as our facilities and homes, stood less than 320 kilometres from Kuwait, and thus we were well aware that we could become targets.

The US would lead the global response to Saddam's aggression, forming a 'coalition of the willing' including Saudi Arabia and more than thirty other countries. But it was Prime Minister Thatcher who first made the clear case for international action during her speech in Aspen: 'Iraq's invasion of Kuwait defies every principle for which the United Nations stands. If we let it succeed, no small country can ever feel safe again. The law of the jungle would take over from the rule of law.' Within a few days President Bush would publicly echo Thatcher's defiance. Thatcher also privately appealed to Bush to be resolute in the face of this violation of international law and not 'go all wobbly on us'.

While our government coordinated our defence, Saudi Aramco had its own marching orders. In the wake of Iraq's invasion of Kuwait, leading industrialized nations had agreed to an embargo against buying any oil produced by Iraq or occupied Kuwait. That effectively removed 4.8 million barrels per day from world markets, causing oil prices to soar from $16 to more than $35 a barrel within a few months. Our job was to replace as much of that supply as quickly as we could. In addition to being responsible for keeping global oil supply in balance, we were also tasked with meeting the aviation and diesel fuel needs of the coalition forces.

Nassir Al-Ajmi, our executive vice-president, had been at the Saudi Aramco helm in my absence. He and the rest of our leadership team also hadn't anticipated the timing of the invasion. This was not a matter of naivety or negligence, but common sense. At that very moment, representatives of the Gulf nations were meeting in Jeddah by the Red Sea. 'I took a call from Harry Alter [in our Riyadh office] at 4 a.m.,' Al-Ajmi said. 'He said Saddam had invaded Kuwait. The Iraqi delegation was in talks in Jeddah, so we never thought it would happen then.'

In the first four days after the invasion I had been in almost constant contact with our leadership team in Dhahran, and Minister Nazer in Riyadh, while making my return trip from the States. I arrived in Dhahran on 6 August. My first obligation, however, was personal. I went straight to the hospital to see my wife and daughter Nada and lay my eyes upon my first grandchild. Welcoming the next generation into the world helped me stay focused on the fact that the conflict we were in was about more than oil. It was about maintaining our freedom to live the lives we choose. I gave everyone a kiss and a hug and then went to work.

The atmosphere in the Saudi Aramco headquarters compound and residential camp was electric, with rumours flying everywhere. Information about Saddam's intentions or the battle plans being developed by the Kingdom and the coalition was hard to come by. So naturally everyone assumed the worst. As Al-Ajmi said, 'We didn't think they would stop at Kuwait.'

In this moment, my most important job as a leader was to set an example. I was concerned, but I was not afraid. I knew that our team was extremely well prepared for what we were called on to do: run our oil company and dramatically increase production as fast as possible. Others trained in warfare would protect us and the Saudi people, and force Saddam out of Kuwait if he refused to leave on his own.

It may seem unbelievable to those who have never led during a crisis, but our clarity of purpose gave me a sense of inner calm. Others understood my approach. Abdallah Jum'ah, one of our then senior vice-presidents who provided exemplary leadership during this critical period, said to me later that he appreciated my own calmness under pressure and that it certainly helped the team. We were all in it together.

It was important for us to show the outside world that we were in control. Even though Jum'ah was in charge of making public comments, I made it a point to be available to any diplomatic or other high-level representative passing through Dhahran. Alan Munro, the former British ambassador to Saudi Arabia, appreciated the effort. 'Al-Naimi was very calm when I saw him during the Gulf War,' he said. 'He was very much in charge and well aware of his, and the Saudis', critical role. He gave you confidence. There was no question of him faltering.'

I created a leadership structure for both dealing with the crisis and threats to our people and facilities as well as boosting production. We used our existing operational control centre for monitoring all facilities and critical communications, with a senior company officer in charge of the control

centre at all times. I took the day shift, from 7 a.m. to 7 p.m.
I felt it was important that people knew I was there and that
our leadership team was in charge.

I also called a number of 'town hall' meetings with our
employees to tell them of our plans. The 3,000 or so expatriates on the payroll were especially concerned. We had already
given the green light for dependants to be evacuated at company expense for an indefinite period if that was what they
wanted. Since it was August and many expats were out of the
Kingdom on vacation, we agreed to extend vacations rather
than require employees to return immediately to the Kingdom and what might turn out to be a war zone.

But beyond these important company matters lay an even
more critical task. The world's eyes were on Saudi Arabia,
and Saudi Aramco. If a line was to be drawn in the sand to
halt Saddam's advance, it would be drawn in Saudi sand at
the Kuwait border. And it was our Dhahran airbase as well
as temporary bases built closer to Kuwait that were the sta-
ging grounds for the coalition troops assigned to drive the
Iraqis from Kuwait if Saddam didn't heed the UN's demands.
Meanwhile Saudi Aramco, with the world's highest sustainable production capacity, was to fuel the global fight against
Iraqi aggression, and at the same time meet the rest of the
world's energy needs.

I told expats as calmly and as clearly as I could the stakes
involved. We understood their situation. We would not prevent anyone from leaving. However, if employees we deemed
essential to our efforts did leave, we couldn't guarantee that
they would have the same job prospects or benefits if they
wanted to return after the conflict ceased. Inevitably, some
people saw this as a form of blackmail. I saw it as reality. We

Saudis were staying on the job. Yes, it was our country, but that didn't mean we were any less at risk if we should come under attack.

I put Jum'ah in charge of external communications. An expert communicator, he was the obvious choice for the role, and performed flawlessly. He explained our position during the crisis to veteran *New York Times* war reporter Philip Shenon, 'We are not holding anybody against his will. All we are saying to our employees is, look, you are here because we need you, and we need you now. If you leave, you will have to forfeit certain things that you otherwise would have.'

While a relatively small number of expats did leave and received plenty of media attention doing so, the vast majority stayed with us and worked side by side with their Saudi co-workers to help us deliver on our promises. Many kept 'grab bags' by the door loaded with maps, money, essential papers and clothing should they need to evacuate at short notice. No doubt many also had relatives in the US and Europe telling them they were out of their minds to stay. All Saudis continue to owe these people a debt of gratitude.

The military build-up started within twenty-four hours of my return to Dhahran. Advance troops from the US started arriving at the Dhahran airbase on 7 August, where many were greeted by Saudi Aramco workers offering coffee and doughnuts. That began a months-long relationship between the Western expats in Dhahran and the troops. With our blessing, of course, but little if any involvement by the oil company leadership, expats began hosting troops in their homes for much-appreciated breaks from the harsh desert conditions they were coping with in their forward bases.

Soldiers were offered home-cooked meals, a chance to social-
ize with fellow citizens and, in that pre-internet era, phone
calls to family and friends back home.

The build-up was a truly massive endeavour. On 6 August,
US vice-president Dick Cheney met in Riyadh with King
Fahd, Crown Prince Abdullah, our ambassador to the US
Prince Bandar bin Sultan and others. All agreed that the situation was grave, and shared the conviction that Saudi
Arabia didn't have the luxury of waiting for Saddam to make
his next move if we were going to defend our country. Convinced that such extreme circumstances warranted extreme
measures, the king said that temporary bases could be established on Saudi soil to support the allied troop build-up, in
addition to the use of the existing Dhahran airbase and other
bases in the Kingdom.

Dick Cheney described that key meeting with King Fahd:

> The king was very business-like and very direct, no small
> talk. After we'd been through a presentation I led the dis-
> cussion and then had General Schwarzkopf [leader of the
> coalition] brief on the kind of forces we were prepared to
> send. At that point, Prince Bandar stopped translating and
> the king turned to his colleagues and spoke in Arabic.
> Crown Prince Abdullah was certainly a key figure in the
> discussion. Later, one of my team recounted the Arabic
> conversation. Some wanted to act, some suggested to the
> king that they should wait. At this point the king responded.
> He said, 'The Kuwaitis waited and now they are living in
> our hotel rooms.' He turned back to me and said, 'OK.' The
> decision was made.

In little more than a month the allies would have roughly
200,000 troops positioned within striking distance of Iraqi

forces in Kuwait. And more were arriving by the day. By early 1991 the allied military build-up would total about 700,000 troops, with 540,000 coming from the US and nearly 100,000 from Saudi Arabia. About 43,000 came from Britain, the largest contributor among European nations. Together they faced a force of roughly 600,000 Iraqi soldiers.

With Jum'ah as our spokesman, I was free to help drive the effort to ramp up production capacity. Minister Nazer and a group of dignitaries visited Dhahran in September to show support. Privately, he wanted to be sure we were going to be able to deliver on our, and his, promise to the king to fulfil our country's commitments. We named Mohammad Yusof Rafie, vice-president of petroleum engineering, to head a committee charged with 'de-mothballing' our huge facilities that had been taken out of service a half-decade earlier.

This massive and complex project was hampered by insufficient manpower. While most essential employees stayed with us, I was annoyed by the departure of many highly trained technicians, analysts and diagnosticians vital to the de-mothballing effort.

To meet our short-term needs, I thought the best way to replace them would be to borrow talent from our four former owners until we could bring our plants back online. I flew to the US and met with senior management in all four in turn. Each was considerate and said they wished they could help, but were struggling to fill such positions in their own companies. They simply didn't have any technicians to spare.

I remember sitting in my hotel room in Los Angeles toward the end of the trip, feeling about as low as I had been since the invasion began. Then the phone rang next to my bed. It was Rafie, our de-mothballing expert, and he had good news. 'Abu Rami [father of Rami],' he said excitedly, 'you can come back. We have solved the problem.' I asked how. 'We have taken the people who have finished three to four years of courses in our advanced maintenance training academies and put them to work.'

I don't think I have ever been more proud of our people. These Saudi students, numbering in the hundreds, demonstrated that they had been well trained, and were able to learn on the job as well. We mixed them in with our existing labour force to work as teams dedicated to bringing key installations back up to fully functioning status. It helped that among our senior Saudi technicians there had been little turnover since the 1980s. As a result, many of our present workers had actually participated in mothballing our plants in the 1980s, which helped us expedite the reversal of the process.

By the year's end, these crews were able to recommission an astounding 146 oil wells and a dozen gas oil separation plants in our Harmaliyah, Khurais and Ghawar fields, as well as the saltwater treatment pipeline. From our average daily production of 5.4 million barrels per day in July, we were producing 8.5 million barrels by December. No other country in the world would have been remotely capable of bringing that much additional capacity to market in that length of time. (Venezuela and a handful of other countries also increased production, but at much lower volumes.) When we assured Minister Nazer in September that we could de-mothball all the plants and wells, I thought it was going to take at least twice as long.

Al-Ajmi later said with pride that the fact that we could de-mothball oil-producing facilities and go from 5.4 to

8.5 million barrels in three months was a sign of the tremendous progress made by Saudis.

Our work was completed just in time. As the deadline set by the UN for an Iraqi withdrawal from Kuwait neared, Saddam showed no sign of backing down. On 29 November 1990, the UN Security Council authorized the use of 'all means necessary' to force Iraqi troops out of Kuwait. On the following 12 January, the US Congress narrowly approved the use of force in the region after an extended debate. It was a much closer vote than we had been hoping for. I'm not sure any of us in Saudi Arabia followed the broadcasts of the US Congress on the C-SPAN cable channel more closely before or since.

The 15 January deadline came and went, setting the stage for the first phase of the war. Allied air strikes on Iraqi positions began in the early morning of 17 January, local time. And within a matter of hours, the Iraqis began firing back, lobbing Scud missiles at Saudi Arabia as well as Israel. Our Dhahran facilities appeared to be among their main targets.

We had been preparing for such attacks for months. With neither the US nor Saudi authorities sure whether Iraq had or would use chemical weapons, we had issued gas masks to essential personnel. When word spread that certain workers were getting gas masks, it was understandable that everyone would want one, including maids and janitors, so rush orders were issued to buy as many gas masks as needed.

When we heard the air-raid sirens, we were supposed to go to safe rooms in our homes or workplaces, where the windows and any other air vents had been sealed. Warning of an imminent attack would be sent in Arabic and English on the Saudi Aramco cable TV channel. At our home we prepared the garage as our safe room.

During one of the first attacks the sirens went off one evening as I was sitting outdoors on our patio. Our maid Josie came running with a gas mask for me. 'Boss, you hear the siren, put the mask on.' I told her to put the mask on herself and go to the safe room. I would be there later. Truth be told, I never believed there would be a chemical attack, and never wore a mask. But it was important for me to be seen carrying one in public. When Josie later pointed to a dead bird on the patio as possible evidence of a chemical attack, I pointed out to her that birds die all the time of natural causes. Or from flying into patio doors.

A portion of one of the Scuds, which may have been intercepted by a Patriot missile from one of the many defensive batteries in the area, fell near our old house in the residential compound. I laughed when I heard that. 'Saddam must not realize that I don't live there any more,' I told my son Rami.

A few days later, part of a Scud missile, or perhaps a portion of one of the Patriot interceptors, landed near our refuelling station on camp. Fortunately, in these and other incidents in the residential camp, no one was injured. Rami picked up a piece of the missile and called me excitedly to tell me the news. 'Throw it away,' I told him. 'Leave it where it is for security to pick up.' As much as I hadn't expected a chemical weapons attack, we still couldn't be certain what sort of volatile fuel or other compounds could be on the missile wreckage.

Scores of residents meantime gathered to view the remains of a missile that tore into the pavement of one of Al-Khobar's streets. And in one of the hotels nearby, where many members of the foreign media were staying, the wreckage of a Patriot missile was propped up in the lobby and quickly became one of the most photographed objects in the Eastern Province.

I saw it as my role to continue to keep our people focused on doing their jobs during the attacks. This included my family as well as our company. As my son Rami later recalled at a family gathering, 'I remember waking up early in the morning when an attack on Dhahran happened. It was 4 a.m. My father was having breakfast. I asked him: "What's the deal today?" He said: "I don't know about you, but I have to go to work."'

I don't mean to minimize the effect the attacks had on our employees, Saudis as well as expatriates. It was a nerve-wracking experience for many, including members of our leadership team. One of my senior vice-presidents was such a nervous wreck that I told him to take his family and leave the country on vacation for a few weeks. He was no use to us in such a condition. I wouldn't even let him work in the control room. Another fellow would walk around the compound all night and sleep only in the daytime. So there were some tensions.

Many of our workers in onshore as well as offshore facilities were much closer to the front lines. Iraqi forces attacked Khafji, on the Saudi border with Kuwait, on 29 January. Two days of battle followed before they were repulsed. Workers in our onshore Safaniyah plant, only ninety-six kilometres south of the Kuwait border, were understandably anxious, as were those in our Tanajib desalination plant another twenty-four kilometres to the south. The same went for our nearby offshore plants, where starting in late December three floating mines released by the Iraqis had exploded under some of our offshore platforms. While we were thankful that no one was injured, those explosions nonetheless resulted in $700,000 worth of damage.

Despite the wartime conditions, the sense of purpose that had been forged among the company operators and plant managers shone through. At the Safaniyah plant, for example, operators had been working in shifts of fourteen days on, seven days off. When the air war started, every single operator, Saudi and expatriate, reported for work. And those who had been on their week off rotation returned to work as scheduled. Their performance and commitment was repeated at virtually all of our facilities during the crisis.

The mood in the residential compound became more sombre a week or so after the first attacks when a Scud missile landed in Riyadh, killing one Saudi man and injuring twenty-three others. The darkest moment of the war for those of us of all nationalities in the Dhahran area came on 25 February, when a Scud missile scored a direct hit on a US army barracks in Al-Khobar, killing twenty-eight American soldiers and wounding ninety-nine. It was a sobering reminder of the sacrifices the allied forces were making in the war against Saddam.

James B. Smith, a US fighter pilot, recalled the attack on Dhahran and the relentless allied air assault: 'We were doing twenty-four hour operations. We slept in an underground bunker and there were thirty-two of us living in this room. Because half were always flying and half always sleeping, the lights did not come on for three months. At the end of it we woke up to see who was there!' Eighteen years later, Smith returned to Saudi Arabia as US ambassador.

The direct hit on the barracks at Al-Khobar came shortly after the war entered its final phase. After more than a month of allied bombing sorties, Saddam still refused to withdraw.

On 24 February the allied ground attack began. There were a few minor setbacks, but the assault, which included Saudi tank units and other troops, began to rapidly disrupt Iraq's offensive strategy and ultimately decimated their defensive positions from the Kuwaiti border to downtown Baghdad. Four days later, on 28 February, a cease-fire took effect at 8 a.m.

Oil, a prime reason for Saddam's invasion of Kuwait, became one of his major weapons against the allies. No one knows exactly when, but the Iraqis started deliberately pumping massive amounts of Kuwaiti crude oil into the Arabian Gulf within days of the start of the air war. One of the rationales for releasing the oil may have been to prevent or at least hinder an amphibious assault on Kuwait by allied forces.

Much of the oil appeared to come from Kuwait's Al-Ahmadi Sea Island loading terminal thirty-three kilometres offshore. Abdulla Zaindin, who went on to become Saudi Aramco's global oil spill coordinator, learned of it in the early hours of 25 January when he received a call from a security officer who said that there was 'a lot of oil in the water in the Kuwait-Khafji area'. A study of prevailing winds and currents revealed a grim conclusion: the oil was headed our way.

An environmental disaster in its own right, the oil spill also seriously threatened the safety of our people and the war effort as a whole. We faced the stark possibility of having to shut down all of our offshore crude oil production. And it could force us to shut down our desalination and seawater-cooled power plants that were for both civilian and military use. All it would take to trigger a shutdown would be less than one part per million of crude oil in the water. The desalination plant at Tanajib was especially crucial because it supplied 1.8 million litres of water a day for the allied military forces, in addition to being the chief source of drinking water for Saudi Aramco personnel.

Such tactics didn't come as a complete surprise to Dhaifallah Al-Utaibi, chairman of the oil spill committee. As he told *Saudi Aramco World* magazine in 1991, 'We knew the Iraqi government had been threatening to "turn the Gulf into flame". They planned to release oil and ignite it in an attempt to stop any amphibious landings. We had met about that threat and were getting prepared for such an event.'

I designated another of our senior vice-presidents, Abdelaziz M. Al-Hokail, as the spokesman for our containment and clean-up efforts. We called a 27 January news conference at the Dhahran International Hotel, where most of the foreign news media were staying, to convey the message that we were on top of the evolving situation.

'We feel quite confident at this time that we will be able to emerge from this incident without any effects on our oil production, processing or exporting capability,' Al-Hokail said at the press conference. Al-Hokail didn't understate the likelihood of 'serious' environmental consequences. That said, he assured the media in the room that 'critical industrial facilities that use seawater for cooling purposes or as a desalination source have already been well protected and will, therefore, not be affected'.

This was easier said than done. Our teams worked heroically in the face of rapidly shifting wind and weather conditions. Others joined the fight. Two international oil spill cooperatives, one comprising Gulf oil-producing countries and the other a global group based in Southampton in England, added nearly seventy tons of protective booms and oil skimmers to the clean-up effort. At its peak in February, more than 450 men and women were committed to the containment. The international effort to supply us with equipment included gear from Japan, Germany, New Zealand, France, the UK, Canada, the US and the Netherlands. Even Russia provided support. One of its huge Antonov-124 cargo planes coordinated with other cargo aircraft from several nations to deliver crucial booms and other containment materials directly to Dhahran.

Working in treacherous seas with highly toxic oil residues wasn't the only hazard. At one point the crews came under fire from the Iraqis. As Mike Erspamer, part of the oil spill response team, told *Saudi Aramco World*, 'I remember the Thursday morning we were out getting some booms deployed off Safaniyah pier. Three rockets flew over our heads and exploded in the water about 300 metres off the pier. That got everyone's attention.' It turned out to be an isolated episode, thank goodness, and didn't slow the containment effort.

At one point, I recall Minister Nazer asked me to send some of our people to advise the allied commander-in-chief General Schwarzkopf about where his planes could strike certain polluting refineries in a way that might stem the leaks. He wasn't altogether impressed when two short Saudis in thobes from Aramco turned up. But, after studying the maps and using their knowledge, they suggested targets for the general and the strikes did indeed have the desired effect.

Fortunately, our work was made easier by two natural features of the Saudi coastline in the Gulf south of Tanajib. Manifa Bay and Dawhat Al-Dafi, a large shallow bay, served as natural containment ponds. By directing the oil into these bays and containing it there for treatment and removal, we were able to lessen dramatically the environmental impact on much of the rest of Saudi Arabia's Gulf coast. However, we should not understate the significant amount of environmental remediation that would continue for the next few years, led by Saudi Aramco and the government. An equally intense clean-up effort was required in Kuwait to contain and repair damage caused by the Iraqis' torching of hundreds of Kuwaiti oil wells as they retreated in late February.

By early May 1991, Saudi Aramco had recovered roughly 900,000 barrels of oil from the Gulf. After the oil had been de-salted and further cleaned of impurities we were actually able to sell it on the open market. An additional million barrels is estimated to have evaporated. No one knows the total volume of oil the Iraqis dumped into the Gulf. International groups later estimated that it may have been as much as 4 million barrels, which is roughly equal to the amount of oil estimated to have been spilled in the Gulf of Mexico during the 2010 Deepwater Horizon disaster. That would rank the Iraqi spill as one of the worst environmental catastrophes of all time.

International cooperation was key to the successful response to Saddam's aggression. And both Saudi Arabia and Saudi Aramco were proud to play pivotal roles in the Gulf War. I also learned valuable lessons about my responsibilities as the company's CEO. We sit on top of the world's largest known oil reserves, and thus everything this company did under my leadership has a global impact.

We were once again actors on the world stage, but this time, unlike during the oil embargos of the 1970s, the eyes of much of the developed world saw us as the good guys, on the right side of history. Saudi Aramco kept the world supplied with oil, and the Kingdom served as the major base of operations through which an international alliance thwarted a vicious dictator's attempt to seize a nation unable to defend itself. Even before the Gulf War ended, as my team and I prepared for the future, we were already applying what we had learned about international cooperation and partnership with our allies in the West.

Now it was time to look to the East.

12. Eastern Promise – early 1990s

While the Gulf region was being rocked by conflict, we started looking at longer-term opportunities in Asia. Saudi Aramco had some experience with a limited number of crude oil sales in Japan, the Republic of Korea, Thailand, Singapore and the Philippines, but not much given the region's potential. Asia clearly represented the growth opportunity of the decade and beyond. As we mapped opportunities for growth, there sat China, a virtually untouched blank space. So in 1989 I sent two of our people, our Marco Polos, off to explore that possibility.

Unlike the famous Italian explorer who is forever associated with the Silk Road, our crew, one American and one Saudi, said the opportunity for us in China resembled little more than a cycle path. They described a country filled with bicycles, hundreds and thousands of bicycles. Millions of people were still uniformed in drab grey and black suits, and they seemed to confine their travel to what could be reached by riding bikes. Our team didn't think there was much future for cars there, or much growth potential in consumer spending.

They were reporting what they saw, to be fair, but, to me at least, it didn't seem right. I am an avid reader. Every month there was another book or magazine article predicting that China, whose economy had grown dramatically during much of the 1980s, was the market of the future. And not only for cars but for just about everything. The twenty-first century was going to belong to China, just as the nineteenth had belonged to Europe and the twentieth to America. Business and strategy consultants were telling us the same story.

We agreed that we would send another team. But this time, I wasn't willing to have someone else do the exploring. During the bitterly cold winter of 1989–1990, I accompanied oil minister Hisham Nazer on a trade tour of Asia. We went to Indonesia on an official ministerial visit and then added Korea, Japan and China to our itinerary. Trade and energy ministry representatives in each country received us warmly, despite the minus 20 °C (minus 4 °F) air temperature at one point in Korea. We saw plenty of potential in Indonesia, Korea and Japan, leaving no question in my mind that they would be an important focus for us as we expanded into Asia.

Our arrival in China seemed to confirm what our first team had reported. The two-lane road from Beijing airport into the city was jammed with hundreds and hundreds of bicycles and rickshaws. Plus all the utilities were burning coal, resulting, as it does still today, in horrible smog, especially in the winter. Who was going to buy our oil?

Back in Saudi Arabia I retuned our Asia strategy over the next several months, eventually determining not to be unduly influenced by our first impressions of China. We would pursue business there as a long-term opportunity. For the moment, we would focus on the Asian countries that, for business and cultural reasons, appeared most able and anxious to reach agreements.

I knew that some failures along the way were likely, but I was determined that, with our expertise and size, we could achieve our share of successes as well. Sooner or later, we would secure long-term markets for our oil and become the major energy supplier to this vast and vital continent. If we were going to be a truly world-class company, run by citizens of the world, we had to expand into Asia. It seemed obvious. Well, to me it did.

I would like to report here that my enthusiasm for doing business in Asia was widely shared within Saudi Aramco. While that eventually became the case, I met a lot of resistance at first. Some felt that culturally, because of our previous American owners, we were better off sticking with the US. We had just made the Star Enterprise joint venture in the States in 1988, after all, and we all saw tremendous potential for growth there. And dozens of us among the company leadership had been educated in the US and were sending our children there for their college educations.

Many people said to me, 'Why bother with Asia? We like it more in the US.' It is easy to appreciate it now, but in the 1990s many characterized Asia as a group of underdeveloped, poor countries, with bad governance. Not me. I saw the potential.

Saddam Hussein's invasion of Kuwait in August 1990 drew focus even further away from Asia. Our self-preservation rightly took precedence. We were consumed with demothballing our facilities to replace much of the crude oil produced by Iraq and occupied Kuwait, at that time boycotted by the rest of the world. And as charter members of the 'coalition of the willing', our nation's goals were closely aligned with those of our allies, led by the Americans and Europeans.

I wasn't going to let a war stop us from acting on what clearly was going to be vital to our long-term success. That made me a 'coalition of one' in the early days of our shift toward Asia. People wondered, quite vocally, 'While the

Middle East is mired in war, why are you looking 3,000 miles away to Asia?' It's called foresight.

Korea was the obvious first choice for us as we looked for Asian business partners. They had been buying crude oil from the Iranians since the early 1970s. For various reasons, they told us, that business relationship had soured. Here was the opening I was looking for. We also had other links with Korea since it was Korean labourers who had, over the previous few decades, helped build some of the infrastructure in modern-day Saudi Arabia.

Even as we were racing to finish the de-mothballing process back home, we announced an agreement on 26 November 1990 to set up a joint oil refinery in Korea. The agreement was with the Ssangyong Oil Refining Company, Korea's third largest refining operation. The joint company would use Ssangyong's facilities to refine up to 175,000 barrels of Saudi crude oil a day, destined for markets throughout Asia. It would also own and operate Ssangyong's Onsan coastal refining complex at Ulsan, more than 300 kilometres south of the capital Seoul.

The joint venture deal was just our foot in the door, at least in my mind. The real goal was acquiring an equity interest in the refining company itself. In January 1991, as the air war with Iraq was about to begin, we started talks with the Koreans. I immediately felt that I had good chemistry with their negotiators.

Our internal chemistry was not so good. Most of our team discouraged pursuing the deal. The volumes were too small, they said, and Korea was of no strategic interest to our company or Saudi Arabia itself. But I followed my instincts, and within six months we had come to an agreement. I found the Koreans to be very businesslike and professional. In

August 1991 a Saudi Aramco affiliate bought a 35 per cent interest in Ssangyong Oil Refining, which was later renamed S-Oil.

In addition to the pleasant business environment, Korea's mountainous terrain offered me an excellent opportunity to indulge my love of hiking. Our regular meetings also created an opportunity to witness all four seasons, a particular pleasure to those of us raised in the desert. To get a better understanding of our new partners, I asked them at one of our first meetings, 'What do you do in your spare time?' They said they liked to hike. So we formed a trekking club. That helped us understand the Koreans and their mentality, their drive and their sincerity.

It also helped us overcome some language barriers. We didn't speak Korean and they didn't speak Arabic, so our business language was English. But we didn't need any spoken language to share a deep appreciation of Korea's beautiful natural landscape. Words often were not needed and this helped create a strong bond between us.

One Friday every quarter was reserved for our executive committee meeting, and then Saturdays we would hike together. Then chairman Dr S. W. Lee and I, who were ten to fifteen years older than most of the Saudi and Korean executives involved in the project, would take turns leading the trekking group. We were conscious of setting the leadership approach for the others, of course, but I also think we were in better physical condition than most of the rest of the team. Dr Lee saw our trekking adventures as a means of 'promoting harmony' among the teams. Our outings most definitely served that purpose.

Not sure of our abilities on our first outing, and not wanting to embarrass us, the Koreans proposed a one-hour hike not far outside Seoul. At the end of the hour I looked over a few ridges and saw hikers on top of a mountain. 'Why don't we keep going to the top?' I asked. Two hours later we reached our destination, celebrated with tea and sandwiches the Koreans had in their backpacks and then started our descent. Since then we have gone trekking in all types of weather, and even have strapped on spikes to trek through the ice and snow during the winter.

After a day of hiking, Saturday evenings were reserved for celebration. The Koreans like to party, and we would join them. Despite our hosts' love of karaoke, it's not my thing. I recall one time they insisted I take a turn so I went for Frank Sinatra's 'My Way'. That was my first and last foray into singing!

Over the years our business and personal relationships with the Koreans have only deepened. We are the largest provider of crude oil to Korea, in recent years delivering more than 820,000 barrels per day of Saudi crude to the country, including more than half a million barrels per day to S-Oil. The capacity of the Onsan refinery has been increased a number of times and now exceeds some 650,000 barrels a day, or nearly four times its capacity when we made our investment.

In 2013 we opened a Saudi Aramco office in Seoul so that we could be closer to our Korean corporate customers. And in 2014 Saudi Aramco paid $2 billion to increase our stake in the Onsan refinery to 65 per cent from 35 per cent. The company's investment in Korea remains one of the most profitable refining investments the company has ever made.

I have met many Korean officials over the years, including a number of their presidents. President Lee on one occasion allowed us to hike in the mountainous area directly behind the country's Blue House (equivalent to America's White House), to which access is usually restricted, and even invited our team in for an elaborate luncheon afterwards. That was a rare honour.

On another occasion I met Ban Ki-moon, Korea's foreign minister at the time, who went on to become secretary general of the United Nations. We first met in Riyadh while he was on an official visit to Saudi Arabia with the Korean energy minister, and I learned that he too loved to hike. On my next trip to Korea the future UN head joined our trekking group, and we have talked about hiking together many times since then.

After he joined the UN in 2007, we occasionally met at UN headquarters in Manhattan. During one of our meetings there he gestured at the array of midtown skyscrapers, lamenting, 'In New York City, we can only climb these high-rises.' While we haven't gone trekking in recent years, we have been fellow travellers of a different sort on issues relating to global climate change, as we shall see.

Dr Lee and I have remained close as well, and often host each other while on business trips. He said of me, 'Even if he is from Saudi and we are from this part of the world, if I have had one of the closest friends that I can recall in connection with business, I should say it is him.' I would agree with that. As I like to tell people, I have acquaintances in the other Asian countries where we have done business, but in Korea, I have good friends. Why? Ahmed Subaey, our executive director for marketing, says, 'Koreans are the Bedouin of the East.' That's a compliment, by the way.

In addition to an honorary degree from Seoul National University, the Koreans recently gave me an unusual accolade. Following our 2014 acquisition of a controlling stake in the Onsan refining complex, I visited the facilities at the invitation of the Korean government. To find myself walking down A. I. Naimi Road, in the midst of the soaring distillation towers and condensing units, was both a surprise and a delight. I am proud of the role I have played in bringing our countries together, and am confident that future generations of Saudis and Koreans will continue to join hands in other successful ventures.

To support these new international refining and sales and marketing relationships, we greatly expanded our fleet of oil tankers. We had formed our own shipping company, Vela International Marine Ltd, in 1984, with an initial fleet of four used tankers. Given the depressed price of oil at the time and the ongoing Iran–Iraq War, we did not invest much in the business in its first several Years. And much of the work was carried out by expatriates working outside the Kingdom, although the shipping subsidiary was based in our Dhahran headquarters. That changed dramatically as the 1990s progressed.

In 1992 the then executive vice-president Nassir Al-Ajmi and I asked one of our top-performing vice-presidents, Dhaifallah Al-Utaibi, to serve as president of Vela International. As the head of our supply and transportation operations, Al-Utaibi's appointment made sense. But he admitted to being surprised, saying, 'I don't have a clue about the shipping business.' And like many Saudis of his generation, he added, 'I don't even know how to swim!'

Al-Utaibi took over a business that was in the midst of a major transformation. At the time Vela had eight supertankers: four that could carry up to 2 million barrels of oil, called very large crude carriers (VLCCs), and four that could carry more than 2 million barrels each, called ultra-large crude carriers (ULCCs). We also had four smaller product tankers.

That may sound like a lot of shipping capacity, but we were just getting started. Over the next three years Vela would take delivery of an additional fifteen VLCCs, built in shipyards in Japan, Korea and Denmark. By mid-decade our Vela International fleet, now managed out of an office more strategically located overlooking the Gulf in Dubai, would rank among the largest in the world. Under Al-Utaibi's leadership, Vela International also established a safety and efficiency record that has become the envy of the industry. I know for a fact that Saudi Aramco's approach, particularly in terms of hiring and retaining predominantly Filipino sailors, was second to none. And, indeed, our terms and conditions, the way we trained and treated people, had ramifications for industrial relations more widely in the Philippines, and we are rightly proud of the role we played in that legacy. Ownership of Vela International passed to the Saudi National Shipping Company (known as Bahri) in 2012, with Saudi Aramco retaining a minority stake. The aim was to create a national shipping champion and it's working well.

Japan and Saudi Arabia have a history of relationships, in energy, business and culturally, dating back six decades. In terms of energy, this kicked off in the late 1950s when a Japanese company came in to develop hydrocarbon resources in the Neutral Zone between Saudi Arabia and Kuwait. The Japanese-owned Arabia Oil Company signed a concession agreement with the Saudi government in 1957, and with Kuwait in 1958. The concession ended, in somewhat bizarre circumstances, when I had become minister. I'll get to that later.

At the same time as we were negotiating our refining partnership with Korea in 1990, we began offering to sell our crude oil directly to Japanese oil companies, rather than through our previous American owners. Our plan was to follow our successful investment in Korea with a similar partnership in Japan. Given Japan's decades of experience in the Neutral Zone, we had reason to expect that one success would follow another.

Our talks started excellently. Or so I thought. I had a meeting with key Japanese officials and at the end of it I asked them if we had a deal. To a man, they all smiled and said yes. With a spring in my step, I went off to see the Japanese energy minister to break the news to him. 'Everyone agreed,' I told him. He raised an eyebrow. 'Did you get it in writing?' he asked. 'Er, no,' I told him. Not to worry, I would get it in writing the following day. The next day I saw the same officials and asked them to sign an agreement along the lines we'd discussed. There was a lot of smiling and nodding, but no one actually signed. While Japan and Korea are, geographically, only some 200 kilometres apart in places, I had a lot to learn about their differing approaches toward negotiating. I discovered that, in Japan, on this occasion at least, that 'yes' meant 'I hear you'!

Some of it I attribute to personal chemistry. It just wasn't right. From my point of view, the Japanese officials involved in the talks, particularly the lead negotiator, were unusually stubborn. It may have been because Japan as a whole had dramatically expanded its economy and its global economic reach during the 1980s. Maybe the refining officials didn't think they had to give much ground to representatives from a one-product economy like Saudi Arabia. For whatever reasons, our meetings were going nowhere.

Because of my rising frustration with our discussions, at the next meeting I brought along a Saudi student who was studying in Japan. His Japanese was excellent, but I told him not to speak, just sit at the back and listen. And I told him not to listen to the folks across the table from me, but to the people behind them. While our counterparts were saying 'yes', our student could hear the people at the back saying 'no way'. It was a fascinating insight.

Our executive VP at the time, Abdallah Jum'ah, and I were sitting side by side across the conference table in Tokyo at our final meeting with the Japanese during this period. We had been negotiating on and off for two years to try to acquire an equity stake in Nippon Oil's Shin-Kudamatsu refinery. Finally, Yasuoki Takeuchi, chairman and CEO of Nippon Oil, pounded the table and said that he would never sell us a stake in Shin-Kudamatsu. He got an absolute mauling for his approach in the Japanese press, which can be remarkably hostile considering how polite and charming most Japanese people are.

We left Japan in August 1993 after two years of negotiating with nothing to show for our efforts. I later received a letter from Takeuchi. He was apologetic and said he felt as if Nippon Oil had left Saudi Aramco at the altar, adding, 'Better left at the altar than left with a bad marriage.'

Later though, in the 2000s, our countries would form lasting partnerships: with a Saudi investment in refining in Japan; in a joint venture partnership, Showa Shell, with Royal Dutch Shell Group that made us the largest crude oil supplier to Japan; and our massive strategic crude oil storage facility on Okinawa which holds some 6 million barrels. The relationship would be strengthened further by Japanese corporate participation in developing our massive Petro Rabigh petrochemicals complex on the Red Sea coast north of Jeddah.

Our relationship with Japan is not motivated purely by business, energy or self-interest. In the aftermath of the devastating earthquake of 2011 in eastern Japan, Saudi Arabia, spearheaded by Saudi Aramco, provided support worth $20 million to the Japanese authorities in the form of critical liquified natural gas supplies. The Japanese people showed remarkable fortitude and bravery in the face of this overwhelming natural disaster and I'm pleased we were able to play a small role helping our friends.

Petron Corp., the largest crude oil refiner in the Philippines, was another of our Asian export targets. Like Saudi Aramco, Petron traced its roots to American oil companies, in this case Standard Oil of New Jersey and Socony-Vacuum Oil Company of New York. Similar to our experience in Japan, we again were involved in nearly two years of negotiations. This time it was a very competitive process undertaken as part of a broader privatization campaign by the Philippine government.

Sa'ad Al-Shaifan, a former senior vice-president of refining, supply and distribution, led the effort from our side. 'We spent two years negotiating on the Petron deal. We were up against two other companies and it fell to me to put in our final offer,' he recalls. I told him not to worry, that our offer was well conceived and financially reasonable. The negotiations had gone well and were very businesslike. I told him that if we get it, we get it, if not, he shouldn't let it bother him. Well, we got it. In early 1994 we acquired a 40 per cent equity interest in Petron.

Since I'd had such a wonderful experience hiking in Korea, I suggested that our team and the Petron executives form a trekking club to get to know each other. The only enthusiast among the Filipinos was the vice-president of finance, who was very fit. The hot, humid weather was an excuse for many to avoid hiking. We formed a base camp for trekking, and only the VP of finance joined our team while the rest stayed at the base camp and ate. (All the Filipinos I met loved to eat.)

Khalid Al-Falih later served as president of the Petron joint venture. He recalled a song that suggested my trekking legacy wasn't embraced by everyone. 'You'd go and you'd get tired and you'd stop,' Al-Falih said. 'Then somebody would start singing the Petron song, which included a line: "Oh, it's because of you, Al-Naimi."'

Not everyone on the Saudi Aramco team was quite as enthusiastic as I was about trekking. On the other hand, they knew that I wouldn't take no for an answer. Khalid Abu-bshait, a former executive director of affairs at Saudi Aramco who was then my assistant, admitted that one time he was looking for an excuse not to join our trek. He claimed he had forgotten his walking shoes, so I told him to buy some new ones. 'It was hot, humid and there we were, climbing a mountain and me with new shoes that didn't fit,' Abubshait said. 'Do you think Al-Naimi would wait? No.' He wasn't the first to grumble at my exercise regime and he wouldn't be the last.

Shortly after we bought our stake in Petron, the company offered shares of stock to the public. We had a good relationship with Petron and the Philippine government. And our investment did well. But after more than a dozen years the government decided to open up the domestic refining market to foreign competition. We determined that increased competition would likely shrink Petron's profit margins. Therefore, it would not make sense for us to invest in additional refineries in the country, an option we had been considering. In 2008 we sold our 40 per cent stake in Petron to Ashmore Group, a London investment fund, for $550 million, generating a healthy profit for Saudi Aramco. Meanwhile, we continued to supply Petron with Saudi oil under existing long-term contracts.

It's timely now to include another of our overseas efforts – this one not in Asia but in Europe – since it occurred around the same time. In 1996, we saw an opportunity in Greece that represented our first European refining venture. This was a more controversial arrangement than those in Asia because the refining company, Motor Oil (Hellas) Corinth Refineries, S.A., and its marketing affiliate, were controlled by a private investor, the Vardinoyannis family. Also, some of the folk in Aramco, most notably Laney Littlejohn, a senior economist in our corporate planning department, were, in his words 'vehemently opposed'. He was forthright with his views, as ever. He didn't think it made sense from an economic point of view. 'It was like hauling coals to Newcastle,' he remarked.

Greek magnates more broadly, the most famous being Aristotle Onassis, had long played an important role in the global oil business, principally by controlling fleets of oil tankers. But their finances and financial practices were, to be diplomatic, opaque at best. We eventually decided this was not a long-term investment we were comfortable with or one that was aligned with our corporate values and sold our interest back to our partners in 2006.

Based on an earlier personal experience with Athens-style business practices, I should have been more vigilant approaching that deal. I think the phrase 'beware of Greeks bearing gifts' applies. I received a call one day from our oil minister saying that the Greek billionaire tycoon and financier John Latsis was coming to see me and that he wanted to buy some crude oil. Latsis, who passed away in 2003, arrived at midday on a Friday, our weekend, and proceeded to talk about his great relationship with King Fahd. I stopped listening after four hours and finally asked him what he wanted. He announced that he wanted to buy 2 million barrels of Saudi crude. 'OK,' I said, 'but why are you talking to me? Talk to the marketing guys.'

Latsis made it clear that he was talking to me because he expected the CEO to give him a discount, hence the four-hour diatribe about his close friendship with King Fahd. He was proposing an eye-watering discount of about $10 a barrel. With oil then trading at around $18 to $20 a barrel, that would have been some deal. Implicit in his comments was the expectation that I might request a commission for helping him land such a bargain. I told him he could have the same terms as everyone else placing such an order, which would have been a fraction of that amount. And, of course, I made no mention of a commission.

'Forget about 2 million,' he said, pulling out his chequebook with a flourish. He said that he would buy 1 million barrels, and pay then and there with a cheque drawn on his own bank. I gently reminded him that Saudi Aramco only transacts via four major global banks. 'As far as I remember, your bank is not on the list,' I said, suggesting instead that he arrange a line of credit through one of the four. You could almost see the steam coming out of his ears.

No cheque? Fine, he said. He would buy 100,000 barrels and he would pay cash! I said that was fine, and that Saudi Aramco would reimburse him for the interest on the funds covering the time it would take for the trade to be processed. Possibly to demonstrate his disdain for the way I had treated him, he later returned the interest cheque to Minister Nazer, who forwarded it to my department. And yes, we accepted it.

Asia remained a better hunting ground. I'd travelled widely throughout much of the continent by this point, but not in mainland China, except for some brief business trips. I did once spend part of a family holiday in Hong Kong in 1981. It was memorable for two reasons. First, I recall walking by a jewellery shop which had a $35,000 diamond necklace in the window. The sales guy dragged me in and we started haggling. I wasn't really serious about buying it, but haggling is fun. And while I am sometimes mercilessly ribbed by my friends for the odd time I get ripped off, I'm pretty good at it. I said I'd consider giving him $25,000 and he put on a look of horror. He eventually said he needed to speak with his boss before accepting such a low price. Two minutes later, he was back. 'OK, yours for $25,000.' At this point I said I'd changed my mind, but might take it for $15,000. More histrionics and another call to the boss. It was probably his wife. This went on until he agreed to sell it to me for $5,000. I told him, 'If you're prepared to sell that $35,000 diamond necklace for $5,000 – then they are not diamonds. Thanks, but no thanks.' And off I went back to my hotel. But the guy didn't give up. He started chasing me down the street, almost in tears, saying something like it was bad luck for the first customer of the day to walk away without buying something. Bad luck for him.

The second reason Hong Kong is memorable was thanks to my daughter, Nada. We were staying in the Peninsula Hotel, overlooking Victoria Harbour, and one day Nada, who was then eleven, came rushing in saying she'd just seen the great American boxer Muhammad Ali. Yeah, yeah, we thought. Unbeknown to us, she then went and found his room and knocked on the door for a signed photo. I'm not sure what his entourage made of this feisty young girl, but they politely told her he was sleeping. The next morning at breakfast, there he was. He came over to our table with a signed photo for Nada and shook my hand. (His own were huge, by the way!) 'Hi, I'm Muhammad Ali.' Now my name is Ali Ibrahim Al-Naimi. The Ibrahim part is the name of my father. That's how we do it in Saudi. My youngest son, who was then aged about three, is therefore called Mohammed Ali Al-Naimi. I said to the boxer, 'My son is also called Mohammed Ali.' He smiled, picked up my son, and gave him a kiss.

Anyway, back to business. China remained on our radar from the early 1990s onward, throughout the ups and occasional downs of our other Asian ventures. On my second trip there, in 1992, I saw more cars on the road, and further indications of accelerating economic growth everywhere. That year we signed our first marketing agreement with the Chinese. We also began negotiations to invest in the country's refining sector, through a joint venture based in Qingdao, with the aim of ensuring continuity of oil supply to this important market. Little did I know they would go on for some fifteen years. It was a good thing I had stamina.

Having made a few relatively small purchases from us, the Chinese had proven themselves very shrewd and opportunistic buyers. Now they were indicating that they were ready to buy in bulk. Very early in the 1990s they came to see us, saying they wanted as much as a million barrels per day.

The source of their renewed interest was obvious: China's economic growth was accelerating at a staggering rate. Its oil imports would grow by about 2.6 million barrels a day by the end of the 1990s, making China responsible for an amazing 37 per cent of all of Asia's increase in oil consumption during the decade. And Asia by far accounted for most of the world's increased oil consumption during the same period. Despite the fact that we relished this opportunity to have China as a customer, providing a million barrels a day was a serious commitment of our resources; we didn't reach that mark until just a few years ago.

In my opinion, the reason it took so long to ultimately consummate our first refinery deal in China was their cumbersome bureaucracy, which seemed to be undergoing continual reorganization, including the consolidation of their various energy agencies. There was no animosity on either side; it's just the way business is done there. Plus I never felt like I saw the same people twice. There was a constant churn of people.

Again, we tried the hiking approach. During one of our first meetings in Beijing in 1992, I expressed interest in hiking along the Great Wall. One of the members of the Chinese team made a comment that was translated as something along the lines of only 'real men' make that kind of hike. I protested that my team were certainly real men and up to the challenge. They then changed course, this time claiming that my proposal would disrupt the schedule. Our schedule the following day was to begin with lunch at noon, followed by the meeting at 1 p.m. Considering that it was a ninety-minute drive each way, they strongly felt that we wouldn't have time to reach the wall, climb and return. I countered that we would have plenty of time if we left the guesthouses at 7 a.m.

There we were, boots and backpacks on, ready to go at 6.45 a.m., somewhat to the surprise of our hosts. With a police escort clearing the way we made the drive to the trail in less than one hour. Our guide said that there are two ways to go. The tourist route or the hard route, for which you receive a certificate from the mayor of Beijing if you reach the top. By this point in our story it will probably come as no surprise that I said our group would take the hard route.

One of the Chinese vice-presidents from the day before had come with us, wearing a suit and nicely shined shoes. He clearly had not been expecting us to take the hard route. After he had managed about 200 metres, slipping with almost every step, I suggested he wait there for us. We made it to the top of the trail on the Great Wall, collected our certificates and brought one back for him as well. Compared to the Korean mountain trails we had traversed, it was a long but not especially difficult hike. We made it back to the guesthouses by 11 a.m. and had plenty of time to shower and change into suits for our lunch at noon.

It was clear that our hosts' impression of this bunch of Saudis had changed. The manager with the slippery shoes made a point of telling his compatriots that we were indeed real men, and had climbed the hard trail with ease. I don't think he shared the part about his sitting out most of the climb.

At the meeting, the Saudi delegation was a party of five, including a representative from our joint venture in Korea. The Chinese side numbered thirty. I felt that negotiating with thirty people was both ridiculous and impossible. So I suggested that the chief negotiator join me in my suite, where we could finalize the deal and then present it to the full assembly. China's negotiator and I agreed to the terms of the deal almost immediately, and the bigger group approved it as a matter of course.

Nothing eventually came of that agreement. I like to think that our performance on the trail and around the negotiating table, however, demonstrated to the Chinese that we had staying power and were committed to making a deal work. In 1998 we raised the stakes further. Crown Prince Abdullah led a Saudi delegation to China, and the visit included marking the opening of Saudi Aramco's first marketing office in Beijing. But the Chinese remained difficult to budge. By the start of the next decade I had made six trips to China, but still no refining deal.

Finally, in 2007, our efforts paid off. On 25 February of that year, in a ceremony held in the Great Hall of the People in Beijing, our Saudi Aramco Sino Company subsidiary signed a pioneering agreement with our Chinese partners Sinopec Corp., the provincial government of Fujian and Exxon-Mobil. We launched the first fully integrated Sino-foreign projects that included crude oil refining, petrochemical production and the marketing of fuels and chemicals. Fujian Refining and Petrochemicals Co. Ltd began operations that June and the marketing joint venture opened for business the following month.

Our new Silk Road runs both ways. Recently, Saudi

Aramco has been pursuing strategic investment opportunities in south-west China that will boost development in that region and provide additional markets for our oil terminals on the Indian Ocean. And within Saudi Arabia in 2015, working with Sinopec, we commissioned on the Red Sea the world's most advanced and environmentally friendly refining complex. In all, Chinese companies have won $25 billion worth of business in Saudi Arabia in recent years. And there is more to come.

From what was essentially a standing start in 1990, we now provide roughly 70 per cent of all crude oil sales to Asia. Most years, we are the largest importer to each of the major Asian economies. And without a doubt, we are the trusted provider of choice of crude oil to Asia and, frankly, to the world.

Saudi Aramco's domestic refining capacity increased greatly in 1993 with the addition of Samarec (the Saudi Arabian Marketing and Refining Company). Founded in 1988 as the domestic refining arm of Petromin, Samarec was folded into Saudi Aramco by royal decree. What corporate entity oversees our refining business may seem pretty esoteric. And it is. But it also was one of the factors that likely set in motion the next, and largest, promotion in my career.

Echoing the long-running Petromin–Saudi Aramco disputes of the previous decade, some senior government officials, including Minister Nazer, continued to advocate for an independent Samarec. In fact, he had approached me as the CEO of Saudi Aramco to strongly suggest that we make an equity investment in Samarec of up to 5 per cent in order to pump some life into the flagging operation. As with

Petromin earlier, my team and I remained unimpressed with the quality of the leadership at Samarec and some of the transactions they had engaged in. I turned him down.

Later in 1993 I received a call from Riyadh. King Fahd wanted to see me. Apparently, he was concerned about whether Saudi Aramco was providing enough mosques at our work facilities for employees to pray in, as well as the condition of the mosques themselves. Someone must have complained, I assumed. I ordered a quick review and subsequently documented the site of each of our mosques – traditionally in Islam, one is never supposed to be more than a ten-minute walk from a mosque – and described their condition. I even included photographs. I concluded we were more than meeting our obligations.

Bulging file under my arm, I entered his palace in Riyadh at 6.50 p.m. for my 7 p.m. scheduled meeting. As I waited, I was offered the traditional Arabian coffee followed by tea. Two hours later food appeared, but still no meeting. At around midnight I saw Yasser Arafat walk into the palace. I thought, 'Well, if the king is meeting with the Palestinian leader tonight he certainly isn't going to have time for me.' And it was well past my bedtime. But it is not a good idea to leave a royal palace without being dismissed, so I waited.

Around 1.15 a.m. I was told the king was ready to see me. I entered the receiving room and King Fahd was sitting comfortably in a chair, no ghutra headgear, no bisht robe, very casual. I came, kissed him on the head as is customary and shook hands. 'Ali, sit,' he said, gesturing at the chair next to his.

I had rehearsed many statements about the condition and location of our mosques, depending on how he wanted to begin the conversation. I might as well have left the file in my office. The king wanted to talk about oil policy and related issues. So we talked.

The king was gifted with both determination and stamina. We talked for three hours and never once touched on mosques. He made it clear that he was unhappy with Minister Nazer in connection with Samarec. I was careful not to criticize the minister's performance, or comment on OPEC when the talk turned in that direction. I realized that the king was sizing me up to see what my responses would be.

I told him, 'I am managing your company,' and that was all I was focusing on. He said, 'Yes, we know that you are doing a great job.' I left the palace after 4 a.m. in a daze, flew back to Dhahran, took a shower and went to work.

The minister and I continued to work closely together and maintained a cordial relationship. Like most people in our industry, we even gossiped about who would succeed him, neither of us coming up with a suitable name.

I didn't include myself among the eligible candidates because in 1993 I had decided that I wanted to retire when I turned sixty. I had friends and family around the world I wanted to spend more time with, and I felt I had a strong team of senior executives working for me who could take our oil company into the future.

I sent my letter to Minister Nazer in 1993, requesting permission to retire in two years' time. He forwarded the letter to King Fahd. The king rejected my request, with no explanation, which is his right. I thought, 'Oh well, back to selling oil, at least for a few more years.' I had no idea that he had other plans for me.

In June 1995 I made another trip to the Philippines for a Saudi Aramco/Petron Executive Committee meeting.

Immediately afterwards, I flew to Alaska to join a salmon fishing trip sponsored by Bechtel Corp., one of the main contractors helping to develop our mega construction projects in the Gulf. I was looking forward to some world-class fishing and an opportunity to decompress.

Fat chance.

13. The World Stage – late 1990s

My visit to the Philippines over, I was packing my briefcase and about to leave for Manila airport when my mobile phone alerted me that I had received a message. It was from the governor of the Eastern Province, Prince Mohammed bin Fahd, one of the king's sons, asking me to call his office. I assumed it had something to do with our oil operations in the province. Since Minister Nazer and my management team knew I was off for a week of fishing in Alaska, I decided to let someone else handle the problem.

I flew to Anchorage, and then on a small plane to King Salmon City, south-west of Anchorage on the way to the Aleutian Islands. As I was walking through the small airport I heard a message over the PA system: 'Would Mr Ali Naimi please call this number.' A telephone number from Jeddah followed. More operational details, no doubt.

I ignored the call and set off for our remote fishing lodge on an even smaller plane that was equipped with floats for landing on water. I had been told there was no phone service there, and was looking forward to some peace and quiet in a natural environment.

The setting was spectacular: crystal clear rivers flowing between grass-covered banks, with Alaska's rugged mountains as a backdrop. With the sun near its summer solstice, we could fish well into the evening if we wanted to. This was a catch-and-release fishing trip, which was fine with me since, as I mentioned, like most Bedouin I really don't enjoy eating fish. Once we got used to the mosquitoes, there were only the bears to worry about. None of the guides had guns, but they assured us brown bears were huge but harmless, unless we got between them and their cubs.

At breakfast the next morning a man came in and asked for me. He said someone needed to talk to me and it sounded urgent. I figured if someone needed me enough to send a messenger to this remote location, it must be important. So, I jumped back on the seaplane and went to the nearest outpost with a phone. I called the number, which belonged to Ibrahim Al-Angary, special adviser to King Fahd, in Jeddah.

'Sheikh Ibrahim, what is it that you want?' I asked. 'I'm in Alaska trying to fish for salmon.' He said, 'You have been appointed Minister of Petroleum and Mineral Resources. Please return to the Kingdom on Wednesday, when it will be announced.'

It was Monday. I asked if I had a choice in the matter. He said no. So, I did what anyone in my position would do on hearing that momentous news: I went fishing. I returned to the lodge and went out again as I waited for the Saudi Aramco plane to fly from its US base in Houston to Anchorage to pick me up. I was with Harold 'Bill' Haynes, then a Saudi Aramco board member and previously CEO and chairman of Chevron. I had a lot to think through.

I was genuinely shocked. This was the second time I had been taken completely by surprise by a job promotion. (The first was when I was named a vice-president at age forty.) I had assumed I had a few more years to work at Saudi Aramco before retiring. Now, at age sixty, I was about to start an entirely new phase in my career without any clear sense of what I needed, or wanted, to accomplish.

As I was standing mid-stream in my waders, trying to refocus on the extraordinary nature surrounding me, I suddenly caught sight of this monstrous bear rearing up on its hind legs on the river bank in front of me. It was looking straight at me, and didn't seem at all pleased. I dropped my rod and backed away as quickly as I could. And there, behind me on the other bank, was Bill, calmly taking photos! It turns out the bear was hungry for fish, not Bedouin.

If I thought jinns travelled as far north as Alaska, I might have seen the bear as an omen, like the desert wolf of my youth. Omen or not, I realized I had no choice but to go back to Saudi Arabia. The salmon and the bears belonged in their natural environment, and I belonged in mine.

We left Anchorage on the company plane and flew east halfway around the world to Saudi Arabia. I soon discovered that my appointment was part of a reorganization of the government ranks, with several ministers being replaced. Minister Nazer was removed, but not given the sort of public dismissal to which Yamani had been subjected. After a brief stop in my office, I headed for the king's summer diwan in Jeddah with the other new ministers to swear our allegiance to the king in his presence, as is our country's custom.

My appointment as oil minister also marked the first time that an oil company executive, rather than a political appointee, would hold the office. Veteran Libyan politician Abdalla el-Badri, who would be named OPEC secretary general in 2007, approved, saying, 'Naimi is a very rare case in OPEC. Nobody went up the ladder from a well site geologist and became the chairman of Aramco, nobody. Unfortunately not too many OPEC ministers have this knowledge.' David J. O'Reilly, former chairman and CEO of Chevron, agreed. 'Naimi was a contrast to a lot of other oil ministers around the world who were typically political appointees without a lot of expertise.'

Closer to home, Khalid Al-Falih spoke for past and present Saudi Aramco personnel when he said, 'Many people probably never thought it would happen. We had this picture of politicians in Riyadh as completely different creatures.' On the other hand, Nassir Al-Ajmi thought that my appointment was about more than me as an individual. 'Al-Naimi becoming minister was recognition, not of the man, but what he represented. The government was looking at capability, not loyalty,' he said.

I said in the Introduction that, when people ask me the secret of my success, I tell them hard work, good fortune and making the boss look good. Of course, now that my boss was the king, I didn't have to worry about that third one.

After swearing allegiance, I had a private meeting with him, something I had done often as CEO of Saudi Aramco but the first in my role as minister. It signalled the beginning of a closer relationship not only with the king but also with the royal family as a whole.

One of my first big tests as minister was in appointing my replacement as Saudi Aramco CEO. My recommendation would inevitably make one executive happy and disappoint the rest but I had to make the decision.

After Al-Ajmi retired as executive vice-president in 1993, I had elevated four of our promising leaders to that rank the following year. My intention, and that of our board, was that my successor as CEO would be chosen from among this quartet. I, as oil minister, would now serve as chairman.

I knew it was going to be a difficult and contentious decision. When I had been elevated to CEO it had been clear for a number of years that I was basically the only Saudi candidate for the job. Now, thanks to our focus on Saudization over the years, we had a group of talented Saudi executives in line for promotion at many levels in the company. But only one of these four would become the next CEO.

The four executive VPs in line for the job were Nabil Al-Bassam (finance), Sadad Al-Husseini (exploration and development), Abdelaziz Al-Hokail (industrial relations), and Abdallah Jum'ah, (international operations). I knew every one of them. I had been responsible for their development and promotion. I knew their capabilities, how they worked with others, how they behaved under pressure. I sat down with a piece of paper and wrote down their attributes, their strengths on one side, their weaknesses on the other.

As difficult as it was to make the decision, in the end after weighing all the considerations my decision seemed obvious to me. But it came as a shock to many, including the man himself, when I picked Abdallah Jum'ah. I knew that some would find this a strange choice. He wasn't an engineer, nor a geologist, nor a physical scientist. He was a political scientist and a historian and a literary man. In nominating a published poet to lead a global oil firm, I knew I had some explaining to do.

I chose him because he had always seemed above the entanglements or agendas of one division or discipline within the company. I believed that his forward-looking vision would allow him to sit atop the company and make decisions with the greater good of Saudi Aramco in mind. He also was a natural 'people person', with a knack for getting the best out of whatever group of employees or executives he was working with. When we were travelling together to meetings in Asia or Europe over the previous few years I had been encouraging him to learn as much about the oil company's operating businesses as he could, so that he would be prepared for such a move.

The succession race was closely tracked by Saudi Aramco watchers around the world. John Hamre, president and CEO of US policy think-tank CSIS, said, 'Jum'ah taking over certainly wrong-footed a few people at Aramco. I think what Al-Naimi was doing at that stage was saying, "I need a guy who is going to help broaden the bench and the personnel depth for Aramco."' Quite right.

Rightly or wrongly, Jum'ah was initially named acting CEO. I didn't see a reason for the delay, but on the positive side, I thought it would give him time to prove himself. Some in the government wanted me to submit two names and then leave the final decision to be made in Riyadh. I said, no, this is my choice, since I wanted to keep politics out of the process. So that probably played an important role in his being elevated on an acting basis.

That December, the king's approval came through and Jum'ah became the permanent CEO. As soon as I heard the news I reached him by phone on the company plane while he was flying from Cairo to Dhahran and congratulated him. Now he was fully in charge. What followed was not an easy transition. There was a lot of dirt thrown at both me and him by many people who simply didn't agree with the appointment for various reasons. But I stuck to my guns.

As a member of the government, I gave Jum'ah the authority to run the company the way he wanted to. When we had senior management promotions he would check with me just to see if I was comfortable with the choice. But I never told him not to do something.

Now and then Jum'ah did make it clear who was CEO, and I respected him for it. As he said about me, 'Of course, sometimes we joked and when he asked me to do something I would tell him that if when he was CEO he had received these instructions from the Ministry of Petroleum he would have hit the ceiling and he would not like it. Then he would look at me and smile and say, "But I am no longer the CEO." '

King Fahd had indicated in one of our early meetings that he wanted to take a more active interest in our oil policy. He had done so with Minister Nazer and suggested that he looked forward to a similar working relationship with me. In fact, a matter of months after I became oil minister I was all set to have my first big oil policy meeting with King Fahd when he was cruelly, and severely, debilitated by a stroke. We never did have that discussion and, while he remained king, many of his duties were assumed by his half-brother, Crown Prince Abdullah.

Crown Prince Abdullah and I had met numerous times over the years. I found him to be very attentive and personable. He was a kind and caring man. When I became minister, we developed a close working relationship that would only grow stronger over time. But, unlike King Fahd, he preferred not to get deeply involved in the details of oil policy. Nonetheless, I would make sure I kept him posted about what was going on in my world.

King Abdullah told me one thing early on that has stuck with me to this day. He said, 'Ali, fear no Prince. Only fear God.'

I have always strived to do the right thing, either for Saudi Aramco or for the Kingdom. I'm not in it for myself, I'm here to make a positive difference. And I am always straight and, I think, honest with people. Perhaps that's partly why I remained in the position for so long. Also, I have never sought power or influence, and never been desperate to cling on to the job. This is also a source of strength.

Being appointed oil minister was my first return to government employment since my early failure to fit in at the Ministry of Agriculture in the 1960s. This time, I was able to influence the culture of the office and the department. Staff got the message that if the minister is showing up to work on time, like the managers at Saudi Aramco, then they had better be prompt as well.

By comparison, OPEC made the ministry look like a model of efficiency. The first OPEC meeting I attended was in 1995. I arrived for the 10 a.m. meeting at 9.55. The first minister arrived at 11 a.m. and the rest had all turned up by noon. Remarkable. When I spoke, I got straight to the point. 'At future meetings, if we say we're meeting at ten, we should come at ten.' Next meeting, everyone came on time. I don't think they liked me for that.

Indeed, OPEC's problems went beyond punctuality. Because of its lack of focus and discipline, the group had lost the respect of many in the rest of the world. As Abdullah Al-Attiya, Qatar's former Minister of Energy and Industry, candidly admitted, 'We used to spend weeks at OPEC meetings in Geneva doing nothing. People liked the winter sports and the shopping. Even when they set a quota, no one respected it. Everyone was cheating.' As veteran Lebanese journalist Walid Khadduri said, 'Before Al-Naimi, OPEC was all in-fighting.'

I was determined to change that. Representing the largest oil producer in OPEC and holder of the largest proven reserves, I wanted the organization to reorient itself, to focus on the oil business rather than politics. It was not a popular position and many scoffed at the idea then – and now.

Suleiman Al-Herbish, director general of the OPEC Fund for International Development, recalled my first meeting. 'Al-Naimi said something like, "Let's not politicize our work. Let us separate politics from our discussions." This is impossible! Outside the meeting I told him that this kind of statement does not fit here.' We'd see about that.

Abdalla el-Badri, the future OPEC secretary general, was more supportive of my efforts. 'He tried to detour OPEC from the political discussion to the economic side. He was always interested in what benefits the group,' el-Badri said.

Nat Kern, president of the Washington DC-based consultancy Foreign Reports, and the first non-Arab to attend university in Saudi Arabia, added, 'He made OPEC businesslike. Mr Nazer would sometimes be about Saudi Arabia teaching a lesson to the rest of OPEC. I don't think Mr Al-Naimi is into teaching lessons that are very expensive for the teacher and the students don't learn anyway.' As it turned out, the Asian economic crisis of the late 1990s was about to teach all of us in the global oil and financial markets some very expensive lessons – and nearly cost me my job.

Our problems began when we tried to address issues around supply quotas. Sadly, as Abdullah Al-Attiya had already noted, cheating on production quotas was the rule rather than the exception for many OPEC countries. But some were worse than others. As 1997 progressed Venezuela in particular stood out as not even pretending to abide by the quotas in place at the time. Their taps were wide open, producing at a rate of about 3.6 million barrels a day when they were supposed to be under 3 million. Their state coffers were filling with the proceeds from their extra oil sales at the expense of the rest of us.

At an OPEC meeting I confronted the Venezuelan energy

minister Erwin Arrieta. 'Look,' I told him, 'because of your actions we in OPEC are violating the ceiling that we agreed to. If you want to continue that way I suggest we allocate this increase among all the members.' The Iranians, OPEC members with whom we have had profound disagreements over the years, independently delivered much the same message. When the Venezuelans showed no sign of curbing their production, the rest of us in OPEC no longer felt bound by the tighter production limits either. So total OPEC production started increasing toward the end of 1997 and into 1998.

This additional supply would soon have global consequences. Due to what was then being termed the Asian financial crisis, demand was about to plummet. As I noted in the previous chapter, many Asian economies grew enormously during the 1990s. Yet too often regulations and other financial controls didn't keep pace with this growth. As a result, excessive use of leverage, or borrowed funds, fuelled speculative bubbles in financial assets as well as real estate across the region. In addition, many currencies were unofficially pegged to the US dollar, which served the countries well during good economic times but proved burdensome as growth cooled and exchange rates weakened.

By 1997 it was increasingly clear that economic growth rates and asset prices were unsustainable across much of Asia. Thailand appeared to be the weakest. By mid-year the baht had lost half its value and the nation's stock market valuation had plunged 75 per cent. That August, the International Monetary Fund stepped in with a bailout package totalling more than $20 billion. We all hoped the contagion had been contained and that Thailand's neighbours would learn from that country's mistakes.

Unfortunately, however, the financial crisis quickly infected others. Countries closest to Thailand were hit first, but within a few months the calamity spread, both throughout the continent and around the world. Indonesia was the next to face a run on its currency and plunging stock and real asset prices. The Philippines followed, as did the Republic of Korea. Japan's economy and that of Hong Kong also suffered significant downturns. Economies from Russia to Latin American were also caught in the downward spiral. For months to come, the IMF and the US took turns offering financial aid to one swooning economy after the next.

American growth, slowed by a crisis in its savings and loan industry in the early 1990s, was soaring by the second half of the decade. The Clinton administration and the Republican-controlled House of Representatives had agreed on spending constraints, and the so-called dot.com boom was driving economic growth and stock prices higher. Nevertheless, the Asian crisis sent shock waves even along Wall Street, where fears arose that this prolonged ordeal would derail the US economy as well.

On 27 October 1997 the Dow Jones Industrial Average plunged 554 points, or 7.2 per cent – its largest one-day point drop ever. The slump would continue to plague the world's largest economy for months to come. Nearly a year later the US Federal Reserve would prod a group of Wall Street bankers to provide $3.5 billion to bail out a single American hedge fund, Long Term Capital Management, whose pending failure triggered by the crisis threatened global financial stability.

Crude oil had been trading at roughly $18 a barrel for the previous few years. Prices briefly touched $21 in October 1997, and then started heading south as supplies increased and demand lessened. The International Energy Agency estimated OPEC's daily production at 25.84 million barrels in 1996. According to the IEA, that figure increased in 1997 and again in the first quarter of 1998 until it was roughly 28.55 million barrels a day, a rise of more than 10 per cent, or 2.5 million barrels a day, above 1996 levels.

The next scheduled OPEC meeting was in Jakarta, Indonesia, in November 1997. OPEC was in disarray and largely unaware of the scope of the crisis enveloping us. Everyone knew that our production was increasing rapidly, but the official production ceiling did not reflect this fact. So we sought to rectify that disparity and, at the conclusion of the meeting, OPEC issued a statement confirming a more accurate – and higher – production figure. All hell broke loose.

Veteran journalist and seasoned OPEC watcher Walid Khadduri explains. 'I remember Jakarta very well. We were sitting in the lobby as journalists and we were all shocked by the decision. I mean really shocked. I remember the faces of oil company people turned white when they heard the news.' For many, the announcement was portrayed as yet another instance of OPEC being out of step with reality. Here we were in Jakarta, in the midst of a global economic crisis, and OPEC was increasing production! Global media reaction was predictably damning and I was singled out for particular criticism. But OPEC wasn't increasing production, it was simply being honest. Prices collapsed.

A sense of panic was spreading through the capitals of major oil-producing countries. By March 1998, Brent crude had crashed to $11 a barrel on world markets. And for certain countries the price was much lower. In Mexico, which is not a member of OPEC, the economy had slowly but steadily recovered from the forced devaluation of the peso in 1994. A pro-business administration led by President Ernesto Zedillo was working to inject renewed economic vigour. But that recovery was suddenly threatened by the slump in oil prices. For a number of reasons, Mexican oil was trading during this period at a significant discount to global benchmarks, with prices during the first few months of 1998 quoted as low as roughly $6 a barrel.

Before this time there had never been any coordinated action between OPEC and non-OPEC oil producers. Our diplomats would talk, of course, and the talk as often as not turned to our countries' most valuable export. But there was little formal communication at company or ministerial level. A handful of my counterparts among oil-producing countries and I concluded at roughly the same time that this lack of communication and coordination had to change if we were going to spare our economies further pain.

First, I asked the widely respected Algerian politician Youcef Yousfi, who would later serve as that country's energy minister as well as prime minister, to travel to Caracas in February to meet with the Venezuelans on behalf of all of us in OPEC. It was a cordial meeting, but the Venezuelans, at least according to their public comments, were not yet prepared to budge. Venezuelan energy minister Arrieta issued a statement that month saying that his country was not prepared to reduce output 'by even one barrel'. Behind the scenes, when not trying to please their domestic audiences, Venezuela and other oil producers were indicating they might be open to production cutbacks, if the pain was shared widely by OPEC and non-OPEC producers alike. I kept pressing.

My counterpart in Mexico, Luis Téllez, a highly regarded

government technocrat, started serving as oil minister in October 1997, just as the oil markets in many developing economies were heading into freefall. Worried about Mexico's economic fragility, he met with President Zedillo and his finance minister in early 1998. 'We were basically saying, look, the only way we can avoid any collapse is if OPEC does something and we join them,' he said. It was a revolutionary statement coming from a well-known advocate of deregulation and free markets, and the subject of the meeting remained a closely guarded secret among those at the top of the Mexican government.

Drawing on his close ties to the Clinton administration formed during the 1994 bailout of the peso, Téllez visited the White House during this period to give Washington a heads-up about Mexico's intentions. He met with former chief of staff 'Mack' McLarty and Sandy Berger, the national security adviser. 'I told them what was going on with our public finances and the effect of the decrease in prices and that I was going to talk to OPEC,' he said. 'Of course, we were going to do it with or without their agreement.' The Clinton administration members said that the US had similar worries about the impact of sustained low oil prices. 'They didn't encourage our meeting' with OPEC, Téllez said. But 'they didn't discourage it', either.

Throughout these months Saudi Arabia was also letting American officials know of our interest in trying to coordinate a cutback in OPEC production, as well as our insistence that the major non-OPEC producers had to participate as well. American officials were careful not to make any public statement that might suggest they wanted American consumers to pay more at the pumps. But they understood that our exploration and production, as well as that of the major

American oil companies, wasn't sustainable indefinitely at such low prices.

The next step for Mexico was to reach out to Venezuela. At a previously scheduled event in Miami early that year, Téllez met discreetly with Petróleos de Venezuela's Luis Giusti. The two had developed a close personal relationship during previous negotiations and meetings. Their idea was, 'Let's get OPEC back on track and it would be very helpful if you, Mexico, can help us out being an outsider,' Téllez said.

By mid-March oil producers were willing to make at least some positive public comments about coordinated production cutbacks. Téllez flew to Oslo to meet representatives from Norway's government. They issued a statement on 19 March saying they had discussed 'bilateral problems in oil policy' and 'the current oil market situation and possible future developments'. Publicly, the government said, 'At this time Norway is not prepared to take a position on reduction of production; we are awaiting further developments.' Privately, Téllez called President Zedillo from Oslo to report that 'they basically said they would accompany us on this, and that created a sense of comfort for the Mexican government'. This, Téllez said, was 'so that we wouldn't be alone' as the only non-OPEC country working with OPEC.

I said to the Venezuelans, 'You are hurting and we are hurting. If you want to improve the price, you bring the Mexicans with you to me in Riyadh. And we'll have a meeting. We'll have an agreement.' So I secretly invited the Mexican and Venezuelan delegations to talks with me and our negotiators on 21–22 March in Riyadh. It was time to develop the specifics of the first-ever coordinated cutback in crude oil production that went beyond OPEC members.

We did not want news of our meeting to influence oil

markets until we had a deal. The two groups flew to Spain separately, and met privately with Algeria's oil minister at the airport in Madrid to get his input. I'm told the minister wasn't altogether pleased that the Mexicans were playing the 'honest broker' role that he coveted. It wouldn't be the first or last time that egos, personal ambition and domestic political priorities tried to muscle in on our aspirations for a greater good. Anyway, the Mexicans and Venezuelans secretly flew together to Riyadh on the Venezuelans' plane to avoid arousing suspicion.

We were successful, up to a point, but that didn't stop the media speculating. The weekly *Middle East Economic Survey* reported in its 23 March issue that Erwin Arrieta had left Caracas for Europe on 19 March for 'an unidentified destination on unidentified business and has been lost track of since then'.

I met the Mexican and Venezuelan delegations at Riyadh airport with their respective ambassadors to Saudi Arabia at my side. On their flight from Spain, the Venezuelans and Mexicans had decided that the Mexican delegation should speak first, possibly because they realized I had already shared some pretty pointed remarks with Venezuela's Minister Arrieta. Téllez said that Mexico wanted to cooperate with Venezuela and the rest of OPEC, and based on his talks in Oslo he was confident that Norway would agree to cut back on production as well.

Lourdes Melgar, a highly regarded official who would go on to be a minister but who was then an adviser to the Mexican oil minister, said, 'At that moment we were not quite aware of how difficult the relationship between Saudi Arabia and Venezuela was, but Mexico became a bridge because, for some reason, I guess the Saudis saw us as being able to keep the Venezuelans honest. We did have a close relationship with Venezuela at the time.' I made it clear we appreciated the role Mexico was playing in this historic gathering.

The next morning we got down to business. I went straight to the point, 'I will take off a barrel of oil and each one of you take a barrel off.' Well they didn't like that deal. So I said, 'Take it or leave it. You want an improved price, that's the deal.' After several meetings they eventually agreed.

I contacted the rest of the members of OPEC to inform them of what we were doing, and that they would be expected to make production cuts as well. To demonstrate Saudi Arabia's intent to be as transparent as possible in dealing with OPEC and non-OPEC producers alike, the Mexican and Venezuelan ministers were present when I was phoning most of the OPEC members. Téllez said, 'It was a relationship between the three countries that were in that meeting that was very transparent, open. We saw what he was negotiating with the others.' I also said I would go to meet with Norway and Russia to bring them into the agreement as well. Saudi Arabia, Venezuela and Mexico publicly announced our agreement on 22 March. As the statement read: '[We] decided to undertake an effort together with the rest of OPEC members as well as non-OPEC producers to withdraw from the market an amount of 1.6–2mn b/d.' As per the so-called Riyadh Accord, Saudi Arabia reduced its production by 300,000 barrels per day.

We'd done a good job keeping our talks secret, based on the fact that crude oil prices shot up $1.50 to $2 a barrel almost immediately after the announcement. The news was applauded in the capitals of most oil-producing countries, though there were some reservations expressed in local newspapers about non-OPEC countries getting too closely involved with OPEC. Minister Téllez was referred to as 'Sheikh' Téllez by the Mexican press, for instance, and was criticized for appearing to backtrack on his earlier free-market philosophy.

Marit Arnstad was Norway's energy minister from October 1997 until 2000. She says:

> I found that through different kinds of meetings during that period in '98/'99 we were able to create a trust also between the countries within OPEC and outside OPEC. That also made it possible for Norway to make that decision. I think Mr Al-Naimi was a very important part of that because his way of having a dialogue with the other countries was a very wise one. Very open-minded, but also very wise with respect for the different decisions of the other countries.

The balance of 1998 seemed like one meeting after another aimed at trying to ensure that agreed-upon cuts were actually taking place.

Even though prices had recovered initially after the announced agreements, they again slumped as the Asian financial crisis wore on. Additional unease arose from indications that not everyone was keeping their promises. Russia, Iran and Venezuela in particular didn't appear to be even close to cutting their output to the agreed-upon levels. Adding to the oversupply problem was the fact that Iraq was significantly increasing its crude oil production. To help relieve the hardships suffered by the Iraqi people but not enhance the strength of Saddam Hussein's rule, the UN allowed Iraq to export oil under an oil-for-food programme put in place in the aftermath of the 1990–1991 Gulf War.

Government spending was impacted around the world. Mexico had to revise its budget three times during 1998 to reflect reduced oil income, which had slumped from 37 per cent to 28 per cent of their total federal revenues over the last year. Our own budget was feeling the pinch as well. In 1998, Saudi Arabia's oil revenues dropped by 30 per cent compared to 1997, and once again government debt soared to more than 100 per cent of GDP, twice the level it had been during the Gulf War. Of course, most global oil consumers enjoyed the low prices.

As the anniversary of our landmark agreement in Riyadh announcing coordinated cutbacks approached, the world was again facing crude oil prices in the very low double digits, and, in the case of Mexico, less than $10 a barrel. Diplomatic efforts were stepped up a notch. In early March 1999, Crown Prince Abdullah held a telephone conversation with Iran's President Mohammad Khatami in which they agreed 'to combat the collapse in oil prices'. On 8 March, I met the Iranian oil minister Bijan Zanganeh in Riyadh. After further meetings with the oil ministers of Kuwait, Qatar and Oman, we committed to 'take all the necessary measures, in close consultation with OPEC and non-OPEC producing coun-tries, the most important of which is a considerable reduction in current production, sufficient to remove excess inven-tories from the market, thus leading to higher oil prices'.

Next up was a key meeting hosted by Youcef Yousfi at the Algerian Embassy in The Hague on 11–12 March. Present were representatives of Saudi Arabia, Venezuela, Mexico, Algeria and Iran. I was not happy that Minister Téllez of Mexico was not there, but he felt obliged to stay at home to support a government programme being unveiled President Zedillo at the same time. So while the ministers would nego-tiate, groups of officials would be hammering out a text that everyone could sign off on.

One of the Mexican delegation was Lourdes Melgar. She recounts the particular challenge she faced:

> At that time I was the only woman. The negotiators were squabbling about what should be in it and what shouldn't. Finally, I got really fed up because they would not allow me to do or say anything. So I stood up and declared: 'Look, I'm here representing the Mexican state. If you don't want me to be here, that's fine I'll just get up. If I walk out, Mexico walks out.' You should have seen their faces. The Iranian guy understood and he's like, 'No, no, no, no! Please stay! What does Mexico have to say?'

The meetings, held in the spacious living room of the ambassador's quarters, were gruelling. Standing in for Téllez was the then head of Mexico's state oil firm Pemex, Adrian Lajous. When it came to signing the final production cut agreement, Lajous admitted it was above his pay grade. I went into the kitchen and spoke with Lourdes Melgar and asked her to call Minister Téllez in Mexico City so I could negotiate directly with him. It was well before dawn but she called and got him on the phone. Téllez admitted that only the Mexican president could give the OK, so he waited until Zedillo woke up, called him and got his blessing.

As I left the embassy I flashed a peace sign to the press waiting outside the gate. I then called Crown Prince Abdullah with the news and made my way back to the hotel for some much-needed sleep.

The agreement, announced on 12 March 1999, committed OPEC plus Mexico, Norway and Oman to further cuts in crude oil production of 2.1 million barrels a day. That was on top of the OPEC agreement to cut 2 million barrels a day. As the *Middle East Economic Survey* put it, 'There is no question that Saudi Arabia, the major OPEC producer, is putting its full weight behind the proposed agreement, which is an element critical to the success of the deal.' By June 1999, OPEC met in Vienna and members ratified their reductions. This time we were determined to make the cuts stick.

Lord Browne, the former CEO of BP, summed up how difficult the negotiations had been. 'There was a lot of mismanagement in OPEC,' he said, 'of course mostly on behalf of Venezuela not actually on behalf of Saudi Arabia – quite the reverse.' He could see we were trying to make a difference. He added:

> Naimi was realistic about the limits to decision making. He was also clear about what the objectives were. He never told an untruth, although he sometimes withheld all the truth! Of course, he would because it's part of the negotiation, but he was very clear about the purpose, what was needed and how the crisis was to be solved. It seems to me that he pulled off an extraordinary set of negotiations, which allowed Saudi Arabia to control the price of oil without actually squeezing Saudi Arabia into a corner, which happened to Zaki Yamani.

The US and other industrialized nations were mostly in support of the agreement. 'We feel that lower oil prices are good for consumers,' US energy secretary Bill Richardson told *New York Times* energy reporter Youssef Ibrahim on 22 March, 'but we recognize they can have a negative impact domestically and on some of our friends like Venezuela and Mexico.' He added, 'So far, OPEC's response has been responsible and restrained.'

We followed through on our agreement to reduce production. Oil prices responded by trading higher for much of the year. That November the 'Riyadh Trio' – ourselves, Venezuela and Mexico – reconfirmed that the cuts would stay in place at least until late March 2000. That month crude oil prices hit a high of $25, a level not seen since the Gulf War, and for all of 1999 averaged about $18 a barrel, which had been a level OPEC had targeted that spring during our negotiations. By the summer of 2000, Saudi Arabia was once again increasing production to help moderate crude oil prices, which had topped $30 a barrel thanks in part to rebounding economic growth in Asia.

My first five years as oil minister had been a trial by fire, but I had survived. More importantly, Saudi Arabia had established itself as the undisputed leader among oil producers, not just within OPEC, but around the world. I was confident that the alliances and understandings we had formed during the crisis we had just put behind us would serve us well as we planned for the future.

Maybe that was wishful thinking.

14. Out of the Desert – 1995–1998

While the international oil price was collapsing in 1997 and 1998, I faced some major challenges at home.

The first was a great test for Saudi Aramco as a company, but which had much wider significance for Saudi Arabia as a nation. It was an ambitious project that would test the company's technical prowess, the will of its management and the skills of its workforce. It was, in a word, Shaybah.

Outside of Arabia, and maybe the oil industry, little is known about Shaybah. The reason is simple. It is located in the south-eastern corner of the country, in the Rub' Al-Khali desert; the English meaning of which is the Empty Quarter. The name is apt.

The largest sand desert in the world, it covers 650,000 square kilometres and is an awesome natural wonder. Famed British explorers Bertram Thomas and St John Philby traversed the region in the early 1930s and, between 1946 and 1950, Wilfred Thesiger mapped and described the Shaybah region of the Rub' Al-Khali in his book *Arabian Sands*.

He recalled the sensation of traversing the seemingly endless sand dunes: 'I looked round, seeking instinctively for some escape. There was no limit to my vision. Somewhere in the ultimate distance the sands merged into the sky, but in that infinity of space I could see no living thing, not even a withered plant to give me hope.'

Daytime temperatures can exceed 50 °C (120 °F), they can drop to freezing at night, and annual rainfall is less than three centimetres. The vast sand dunes that characterize the Shaybah portion of the Empty Quarter tower up to 300 metres high. It goes without saying that life here – such as it exists at all – is harsh. I learned that first hand when I fell ill while working in the area as a young man. Of course, the hardy and industrious Bedouin have criss-crossed the region for centuries, transporting goods on camel trains from the south, but it's a dangerous place and not one to be taken lightly. Even today, with all our GPS technology and mobile phones, people get lost and perish there. It is also a region steeped in myth and folklore.

And here we were, pondering oil exploration.

Oil company geologists had surveyed the edges of the Rub' Al-Khali as early as 1938 and would return in 1948. They didn't venture into the sabkhas or salt flats in the heart of Shaybah to conduct exploratory drilling until the late 1950s. And it wasn't until 1968 that we struck oil at Shaybah Well No. 1. Over time we determined that the Shaybah oil-field, in the north-east portion of the Rub' Al-Khali near our border with the United Arab Emirates, is approximately sixty-four kilometres long and thirteen kilometres wide. It contained a staggering amount of oil, more than 14 billion barrels, which was equal to the entire oil reserves in the North Sea, as well as 25 trillion cubic feet of natural gas, which was roughly 10 per cent of our total gas reserves.

But for all the positives, this is hostile terrain. It is some 800 kilometres from the oil company HQ. There were no roads.

By the time I became manager of production in our Northern Area in 1974 we had drilled fifty exploratory wells in Shaybah. We were limited to drilling these vertical wells on the salt flats between the giant dunes. By the way, we have been tracking these dunes by satellite since the 1960s and determined that they don't drift over time like most dunes. Sand blows off the surface, of course, but the essential shape of the dunes remains intact, probably due to the moisture leaching up into the base of the dunes from the surrounding sabkhas. This was particularly interesting to me since, as I mentioned, I had studied the dunes in the Dhana sands between Riyadh and Dhahran and they travelled as much as four metres a year.

I tested the wells to gauge how much oil they could produce. Each was drilled to the relatively shallow depth of 2,000 or so metres, the depth at which we were producing oil in our giant Ghawar field to the north-west. They could all produce oil, but only about 2,000 to 2,500 barrels a day. That would be an adequate rate of production for the fields around Midland, Texas, for instance, but it wasn't enough to make them economically viable for us, given the remote location and harsh desert conditions and the fact that similar wells in the easily accessible Ghawar field were producing three to five times that amount a day. Adding to the level of difficulty in extracting the oil was that it was sandwiched between a layer of water below and a layer of gas above the oil-bearing rock. Based on those well test results, we decided not to develop the Shaybah field at that time.

The Soviets had drilled rudimentary horizontal oil wells – wells that started as vertical wells then turned at a certain depth to continue drilling horizontally to target strata of oil-bearing rock – as early as the 1930s. The technology wasn't widely disseminated in the rest of the world or, frankly, thought necessary for several decades. Fifty years later horizontal drilling enjoyed a renaissance after several horizontal wells were drilled in Texas in 1985 in what is known as the

Austin Chalk trend. The technological know-how quickly spread around the world.

We had already been drilling at an angle, rather than straight down, to reach hard-to-tap reservoirs in some of our offshore fields. As of April 1991, Saudi Aramco drilled its first successful horizontal wells in our offshore Berri oilfield. By using this new technology these horizontal wells were producing three times the oil vertical wells in the same field were yielding.

Once we adopted horizontal drilling, its potential for helping us to exploit the Shaybah field was obvious. We paired this technique with three-dimensional seismic imaging, which we had been using in early, more primitive forms since the late 1970s to produce detailed plans of underground reservoirs. Suddenly we had a means to locate and tap oil located beneath Shaybah's giant mountains of sand, not just the oil reachable directly below the salt flats.

But did the projected payoff justify the costs? Beginning in 1989, the Saudi Aramco management committee looked several times at developing Shaybah. On each occasion we concluded that the technological advances, as impressive as they were, didn't justify the time, effort and money involved. Our cost estimates at the time were roughly $5 billion for a projected five-year project. Despite the repeated shelving of proposals, however, I wasn't willing to give up on Shaybah.

In early 1995, while I was still CEO, we took another look. Drilling and imaging technologies were continuing to improve. We also conducted an environmental impact study and determined that we could move portions of the giant dunes to build oil-processing facilities, a worker community and an airport without damaging adjacent dunes or salt flats. And oil prices were holding in the upper teens a barrel, which was an attractive price that could justify the cost of developing Shaybah.

Another factor put added pressure on us. I had recently learned that foreign oil companies had approached the Saudi government, Minister Nazer in particular, about developing Shaybah. Representatives of Shell Oil and Mobil Oil separately reached out to him and said in effect, 'You have this beautiful oilfield in Shaybah. We don't think Aramco is up to developing it. They keep rejecting the idea. We can do it for you. It will take five years and cost $5 billion.'

The more I looked into the issue, the more concerned I became. Shell and Mobil weren't alone. I read that Total S.A. of France had discussed a swap of upstream Saudi Aramco assets, notably Shaybah, for downstream refining and other processing assets. It later came out in the press that associates of President François Mitterrand were convinced that King Fahd or those in his inner circle had promised such a deal in return for France's participation in the Gulf War. (I suspect this was a case of a European mistaking words of praise and support from an Arab leader as a specific quid pro quo, but I was not a party to the conversations.) In fact, if France's other major oil company, Elf Aquitaine, which later merged into Total, had not learned of the potential deal and tried to get in on it, thereby complicating the negotiations, we might have been presented with what the French call a fait accompli and lost control of Shaybah.

These foreign companies threatening what I saw as our national interest wasn't the only issue. I admit I was still frustrated by our inability to conclude a refining deal with the Japanese in 1993. The Shin-Kudamatsu refinery would always be for me, an avid fisherman, the one that got away. There are times when we need to work with foreign partners – developing refining and processing assets in their home markets is an obvious example – and be willing to accommodate their practices and goals that are sometimes at odds with ours. There are other times when we need to go it alone.

When it came to developing Shaybah, there was no question in my mind that we needed to go it alone.

Abdallah Jum'ah and I were sitting across the conference table from each other in a Saudi Aramco management committee meeting on 15 February 1995, at which we were to vote yet again on whether to develop Shaybah. It was a long meeting and all the pro and con arguments were brought out and discussed. I made the argument that this was a case of national pride and that we could no longer afford to push this project into the future. I finally called for a vote. It was unanimous in favour of recommending to the Saudi Aramco board of directors that we develop Shaybah. I picked up a legal pad and scrawled a message for Jum'ah and slid the piece of paper across the table. It said, 'Shaybah is my Kudamatsu.'

Nadhmi Al-Nasr is a third-generation Aramcon from the Eastern Province. His father and I came up through the Aramco ranks together and knew each other well. The day Nadhmi graduated from King Fahd University of Petroleum and Minerals in 1978 with a degree in chemical engineering, he walked from the campus adjacent to our headquarters compound straight to the Aramco employment office. Our limited security then reflected simpler times.

Al-Nasr started with Aramco as an engineer in June of that year. He worked on the Master Gas System, as well as production, refining and pipeline projects, both in the

Kingdom and overseas, and had been promoted to manager in 1993 while based in Abqaiq. It was a broad range of assignments that prepared him for his next, life-changing career move. He was the young manager I wanted to spearhead the development of Shaybah.

We put Al-Nasr in charge of the Shaybah taskforce. He was given two weeks to make a presentation on the project to the management committee in March 1995. Like a good engineer he did his homework. He had access to the four earlier proposals on Shaybah, costed between $5 billion and $6 billion and taking an estimated five to six years to complete. His taskforce proposed that through fast-tracking some procedures and eliminating others, we could cut the cost of building Shaybah to less than $4 billion. But we would still need five years, with 2000 as the target for completing the facilities.

I told him the presentation was impressive, but we had to have Shaybah completed before the turn of the century. The foreign oil companies were projecting a five-year project. This was our country, our oil and our expertise on the line. We had to do it faster. The management committee debated the details and timelines while Al-Nasr looked on. We finally settled on a mid-1999 completion. Al-Nasr was ready to commit to that date, but we insisted that he and his team take three months to confirm it, because I was determined that we should announce the project to the world, and deliver it on time.

While this was going on I went on my fishing trip in Alaska and learned that I would be named oil minister. Jum'ah took over as CEO of Saudi Aramco, and that meant that he took over responsibility for developing Shaybah as well. But I wasn't about to let go of this high-profile project.

Jum'ah and his team flew to Los Angeles, where Al-Nasr was working with the contractor Parsons Corporation in nearby Pasadena to begin the design of the mammoth project, to confirm that mid-1999 was an achievable completion date. Al-Nasr not only said that mid-1999 was achievable, but confirmed that his team could do it for less than $4 billion. All systems were go.

Back in Dhahran, where I kept my office as chairman of Saudi Aramco, Jum'ah and I met to discuss the project. The more time I had to think about Shaybah, the more I realized that I wanted more. It was no longer enough for us simply to show incremental improvements in our ability to deliver a major construction project.

I was viewing the world differently as oil minister. If we were going to achieve the prominence on the world stage that I thought we were capable of as the world's most prolific and most trusted oil-producing nation, we had to rethink the way we conducted our business. We needed to be bold and confident of our abilities.

I wanted us to complete Shaybah one whole year sooner, and at significantly less cost. Our team re-examined every step of their plan, and every alternative they could come up with. They came back with an audacious proposal. Mid-1998 delivery, or in three years, for $2.5 billion. That was the new reality for the development of a world-class oilfield in a remote location. All Al-Nasr and his team had to do was deliver.

It was up to Jum'ah, as CEO of Saudi Aramco, to do the worrying and apply the pressure. Indeed, Jum'ah once joked that the development of Shaybah was a kind of 'Mission Impossible'. For my part, I saw my role more as chief motivation officer.

I visited the Shaybah team often to offer encouragement. I would spend the day and night with them if I could, even when they were housed in temporary accommodation in the remote desert. These men were heroes. I used to go there to motivate them. I would come and highlight only the positive aspects of what they were doing. I knew they were nervous, I knew they were scared, I knew they were shaking.

The Shaybah team, others in the company, and the global oil industry understood the stakes involved. We were doing something that had never been done, at a time when I and Saudi Aramco were meeting pretty stiff resistance on multiple fronts — some I have mentioned earlier and some I will address shortly. In many ways Shaybah was the highlight of my first term as a minister because I was really challenged by the world to show that Aramco was up to the job. Shaybah was the toughest, harshest place to develop a field. We boasted that we could do so, and for less than any oilfield had ever cost before.

Shaybah's remote location and harsh environment forced our teams to develop new solutions. Small planes could deliver a working group of engineers to within a short drive of the site in a matter of hours, but that wouldn't work for the tens of thousands of tons of equipment and materials that had to be delivered.

To meet our schedule, we couldn't wait for a permanent road to be constructed all the way to the site. While road construction was under way we used contractors' trucks to haul materials two-thirds of the way to Shaybah on existing roads. Then the loads were transferred to Saudi Aramco's deep-desert vehicles with huge wheels that were specially designed for operating in extreme off-road conditions. In 1996 alone more than 3,800 loads weighing a total of 90,000 tonnes were transported through blistering heat and repeated sandstorms using these giant diesel-powered camels.

The permanent, 386-kilometre access road over and around the desert dunes to Shaybah took a year to complete. It was actually completed three months ahead of schedule by dividing the road into three sections and giving each section to a different contractor. Clay-rich soil from marl pits was placed in several layers on the road bed and then watered and compacted to create a solid base on the sand. Then the road was constructed on top of that. Once it was completed, fully laden trucks could make the trip from Dhahran to Shaybah in less than twelve hours. Ten months later we opened a landing strip large enough to accommodate a Boeing 737 by moving around 3 million cubic metres of sand to expand one of the salt flats on site.

The central processing facility in Shaybah consisted of three gas oil separation plants, a gas compression plant and a number of utility plants, including ones for water desalination and generating electric power. Accommodation was constructed for up to 1,000 employees. The initial crew of 750 men worked twelve-hour shifts, and during their leisure time could enjoy amenities including a library, swimming pool and gymnasium. Like many of our remote facilities, this was constructed as a 'bachelor' site. Married men would be able to fly home to their families in the Eastern Province frequently once air service was established, but there were no family facilities on site.

The plans called for us to pump 500,000 barrels per day of the 'extra light' crude oil found at Shaybah. This crude is especially valuable because it can be used for blending with, and lightening, many of the heavier crudes that are found elsewhere in the Kingdom. It is also easier to blend and refine into premium-priced aviation fuel.

To transport oil from Shaybah to the processing centre in Abqaiq, we built a 645-kilometre above-ground pipeline that is 120 centimetres in diameter. Project costs were trimmed by moving the oil at a relatively high pressure. That eliminated the need for building and maintaining a pump station. But at the same time it required the highest standards for pipe fittings and other parts in order to operate at such high pressures in such extreme conditions. We wanted to produce oil from Shaybah as cost effectively as possible, but we weren't willing to compromise when it came to quality. From Abqaiq the Shaybah oil would travel through existing pipeline networks to our export terminals at Ras Tanura or Juaymah on the Gulf.

Beneath ground the work under way was equally impressive. Our first step was to drill seventeen vertical wells in a number of salt flats to further delineate and monitor the underground reservoir. This information was correlated with the results of our 3D seismic findings to identify the best locations and depths for our horizontal production wells. The goal was to have the horizontal wells draw in the oil as efficiently as possible, but without pulling in water from the strata below the oil or gas from above. Four horizontal test wells produced oil at a rate of 12,000 barrels per day – five to six times the production of the vertical wells I had tested twenty years earlier – meeting our predictions. That gave our engineers confidence that we were on track.

In our first phase of production in 1998 we drilled more than a hundred horizontal production wells beneath the surrounding dunes. The typical horizontal well extended for one kilometre into the oil-bearing reservoir. We estimated that if we had used vertical drilling alone it would have cost us six times as much to produce the same volume of oil that our horizontal wells yielded. Within a few years our horizontal drilling technology had progressed so rapidly that our horizontal wells were extending twelve kilometres beneath the dunes and our drill bits were being 'geo-steered' via satellite.

In July 1998, three years after the project got under way and three decades after oil was discovered in Shaybah, the facility was opened for production on schedule. And as impressive as that feat was, the Shaybah team brought the project to conclusion for just $1.7 billion. That was $800 million under an already very aggressive budget target. I would remember that performance in the decade to come when another path-breaking project would land in my lap.

The amazing on-time performance and the pioneering technologies applied to make Shaybah a reality would not have been possible without one key ingredient that came before all others: Saudi teamwork. For the first time in executing major projects, 90 per cent of the team in charge of the Shaybah project was Saudi, in what Saudi Aramco would proudly describe as the 'pinnacle of Saudization'.

Jum'ah gave me a framed presentation as a memento of my commitment to Shaybah. It included the paper note I had handed to him in February 1995 saying 'Shaybah is my Kuda-matsu'. It hangs in my office today.

Shaybah quickly became our destination of choice for showcasing what our engineers, and we as a nation, were capable of to visiting dignitaries and the media. As many times as I have been there, I never get tired of seeing a cross-section of our population hard at work in this remote community, nor of the sheer beauty of the desert.

Crown Prince Abdullah visited Shaybah in March 1999 to officially inaugurate the facility. The technical achievement was a proud moment for Saudi Aramco, but I think the accomplishment had a much more profound psychological impact on the nation.

Fahad Abdulkareem was manager of the Shaybah site from 2007 to 2014. 'I remember learning about the Empty Quarter when I was a young boy,' he said. 'If you wanted to scare someone, you'd threaten to send them to the Empty Quarter. Then along comes Saudi Aramco and we build this facility in three years. And the Empty Quarter isn't empty any more.'

The achievement of Shaybah was all the more impressive considering the oil price collapse that was taking place globally. The depressed oil price in 1999 made the fanfare around the completion slightly muted. But we pushed on with the massive investment because we have a long-term vision and we know that markets and prices are cyclical.

As satisfying as it was finally to develop our resources under the extreme conditions found at Shaybah, I didn't have time to do much celebrating. It turned out to be one of many challenging engineering achievements taken on by Saudi Aramco. More importantly, another domestic battle was looming. And this one would be a fight for the heart and soul of the company I loved.

15. Domestic Pressure – 1998–2003

With the passage of time it is easy to forget how frantic the late 1990s was for our country and the oil industry. And for me. I became minister in 1995 and the oil price collapsed two years later. We were touring the world on a big diplomatic push to forge an agreement on production cuts, plus we were tackling a number of domestic policy areas. These included spinning out our mining assets into what became the state-owned Ma'aden mining company, overhauling the country's mining laws, setting up the Saudi Geological Society and developing major fields in inaccessible regions like Shaybah. It was a hectic time, and it was about to get much more demanding.

It all started innocuously enough. It was autumn 1998, and I was on a trip to the US with Crown Prince Abdullah and our foreign minister, Prince Saud Al-Faisal. On this particular day, we went to the home of our ambassador to the United States, Prince Bandar bin Sultan, in McLean, Virginia, a suburb of Washington DC. When we walked in I was surprised to see the heads of the seven largest American and European oil companies waiting for us in the spacious living room. What I heard next made me even more uncomfortable.

The crown prince started to sound out the oil executives' interest in developing Saudi Arabia's upstream energy resources. I had no idea this was coming and was stunned. I later discovered more of the background from Nat Kern, the president of Foreign Reports, Inc.:

Back in 1997, Prince Bandar asked me how he could use oil to make US–Saudi relations stronger. I suggested he speak with Peter Bijur from Texaco, and Bijur said the best way would be to 'open up Saudi Arabia'. Bandar asked me to write a short paper on the pluses and minuses. I placed a lot of emphasis on how opening up the downstream would make Aramco more competitive. The paper was generally positive about the idea. That was the last I heard of it.

A year later, Kern received a call from one of Prince Bandar's team who asked him to send over that paper again. They also asked Kern to contact the CEOs of the major oil firms and invite them to Washington. Kern recalls it was a Friday evening and the meeting was set for the weekend.

When the meeting came around, the CEOs were there. Prince Saud started talking about the close relationship between the US and Saudi Arabia over the years and how oil formed the basis for these ties. He then moved to talking about ways to 'revitalize' the relationship. At this point, Crown Prince Abdullah said he would be interested in hearing their ideas for investing in Saudi Arabia. Exxon CEO Lee Raymond started talking first, then the others said their piece, including Lou Noto, CEO of Mobil Oil, who was already in talks with Raymond about merging their companies. All were understandably positive about the idea. They talked about oil and gas and the crown prince said he'd like to see their proposals in writing.

I was alarmed. Not only was I in the dark about this major change of strategic direction, there was also a clear implication that Saudi Aramco was not up to the task of developing these resources alone, or at least taking the lead in their development. Journalist Steve Coll recounted the meeting in his 2012 history, *Private Empire: ExxonMobil and American Power.* 'As Raymond, Noto and other chief executives spoke,' he writes, 'Al-Naimi "looked like he had eaten a sour lemon", one person who attended recalled.' Believe me, I felt worse than I apparently looked.

I don't want to suggest that, then or now, we have an antagonistic relationship with ExxonMobil or any of the major international oil companies. On the contrary. They are among the largest customers for our oil. As Raymond's successor Rex Tillerson points out, ExxonMobil is the largest foreign taxpayer in Saudi Arabia. And we continue to work together closely on joint ventures or partnerships in the Kingdom and around the world. ExxonMobil and Saudi Aramco, as mentioned earlier, work closely together in China on the Fujian refining project, for instance. That said, my close personal relationship with Lee Raymond, then head of ExxonMobil, didn't survive these fraught negotiations.

That meeting in suburban Washington began a multi-year odyssey whose outcome was far from certain. If things had turned out differently, international oil companies might have regained nearly as tight a grip on the Kingdom's hydrocarbon resources as they had held during the height of American-owned Aramco's power in the 1950s and 1960s. And I most certainly would not have remained as oil minister. Even though we prevailed, it was a tough few years for me.

The initiative got off to a slow start. Both the foreign ministry and the oil ministry had separate teams working on the project. Both wanted control. I should say that Prince Saud Al-Faisal, who passed away in 2015, and I always maintained cordial relations and shared a great deal of mutual respect.

But the whole idea was slow to get off the ground thanks to these competing factions.

I saw the whole enterprise in clear and simple terms. Saudi Aramco was more than capable enough to develop its own resources. We didn't need US or other international companies to do it for us. It was a matter of national pride, but it was also basic economics. Why on earth would we pass valuable upstream assets to foreign companies and their shareholders to make money?

In 2001 Saudi Aramco brought Khalid Al-Falih back from Manila, where he had been sent less than a year earlier to be president and CEO of the Petron joint venture in the Philippines, to lead our negotiating team. The company promoted him to vice-president at the same time. He had proven leadership skills and he had drafted the Kingdom's first gas strategy and development options before he left for Manila, so he was the obvious choice.

Next, we meticulously studied maps of our natural resources across the Kingdom. Armed with these, Abdallah Jum'ah and I visited Crown Prince Abdullah in Mecca and we outlined our thoughts. Prince Saud was supposed to join us but for some reason he didn't come. In the meantime, we all studied the map and I pointed out what resources we had and where they were. When it came to allowing international companies to explore for new reserves, I stressed the importance of restricting the hunt to areas that were not already known to us – and it would be restricted to gas, not oil. The crown prince understood, winked at us and said 'don't worry'. We also agreed that any investment by these international oil companies (IOCs) had to be tied to vital infrastructure development that the Kingdom badly needed. We felt this was only fair.

So this became the Gas Initiative and in May 2001 Saudi Arabia announced the project and we selected eight companies to participate in three core ventures with a total price tag of $25 billion. There was some grumbling from certain of the companies when we removed oil from the equation, but this was the deal we were offering. ExxonMobil was the lead investor in two of the three projects. Core Venture 1, the largest, focused on the south Ghawar–north Rub' Al-Khali region and involved ExxonMobil, Shell, BP and Phillips. Core Venture 2 was focused on offshore exploration for and development of gas fields in the Red Sea. Here, Exxon had the largest stake, alongside Occidental Petroleum and Marathon Oil. Core Venture 3 was to explore for gas fields and develop gas-processing plants at Shaybah and Kidan, also in the Rub' Al-Khali. Shell and Conoco each had stakes in this venture and Total/Fina the balance.

More than eighteen months of often tense negotiations followed. Al-Falih had a team of ten to fifteen members. They dealt with three separate teams, one for each of the core ventures, that were often twice as large. The IOCs rented much of the commercial space in Riyadh's famous Faisaliyah Tower as their base of operations. I would meet with Al-Falih two to three times a week for briefings, often when we were commuting from Dhahran to Riyadh. It was a high-stress situation for Al-Falih, but it was a good experience for him.

The IOCs started the discussions when oil prices were low and acted as if they had us at a disadvantage as a result. That may have been true initially, but it was a very short-sighted approach to negotiating. As months turned to years, oil prices recovered dramatically, and our revenues with them, which reduced much of the pressure we may have felt to conclude a deal quickly.

From my point of view the IOCs also were unrealistic to the point of being greedy in the terms they were demanding. They wanted guaranteed rates of return on their investments in the Kingdom of between 18 and 20 per cent. We were only willing to offer returns in the 10 to 12 per cent range. And there were continuing disputes regarding what assets should be included in the development plans and the risks they should shoulder in exploring for new gas reserves.

Case in point: in the first expansion of our Master Gas System since the late 1970s, we had already committed to building two massive plants in remote desert locations at Hawiyah and Haradh. These billion-dollar-plus facilities would be our first plants dedicated solely to processing non-associated gas. This gas came from the Kuff limestone formation I mentioned earlier, and an even deeper sandstone reservoir called Jawf, which Saudi Aramco geologists had discovered in 1994. Together these two plants would boost the gas-producing capacity of our Master Gas System by more than one-third to 9.4 billion scfd. Despite the fact we had already done all of this work, the IOCs wanted to include these assets in their development plans, even though developing them involved essentially zero risk.

'We were building the two gas plants, Haradh and Hawiyah, at the time, and they offered to finish building them and take the gas that was supplying them,' CEO Abdallah Jum'ah said. 'We continued telling them that this was discovered gas and that they were not taking any risk. Why should we share something that we have in our hands?'

Exxon also was pushing to include oil exploration and

development in the plan initially. They wanted us to turn over highly restricted information about our Ghawar field, for instance, that isn't even known within the Kingdom outside of the oil ministry and Saudi Aramco. We managed to put an end to that and keep the initiative focused just on natural gas. Or so we thought.

In the early months of the negotiations I was often a lone voice at the ministerial level in our country pushing back against the demands of the IOCs. I had a clear sense that Lee Raymond, for instance, was trying to make the most of his relationship with Prince Saud Al-Faisal to get a better deal for ExxonMobil. Whether it was his intent or not, the result was to isolate me and make me appear to be acting to defend Saudi Aramco's interests. I came in for a lot of criticism in the Saudi media. And a lot of powerful vested interests lined up to question my judgement and motivation.

Over time, I'm pleased to say, others in our government, including Crown Prince Abdullah, realized I was acting on behalf of the Kingdom, not the oil company.

If what was conceived as the core ventures concept had gone through as initially proposed, it would have created a bad precedent and a substantial value drain on the Kingdom. What the IOCs wanted was no taxes due, no royalty payments and a guaranteed rate of return approaching 20 per cent. We disagreed with that. We argued for terms that would be competitive with other deals. We were willing to give them a fair deal, but I think they got greedy. Al-Falih said, 'By holding his ground, Minister Al-Naimi was not necessarily protecting Saudi Aramco, he was protecting the Kingdom from having substantial value drained away in those transactions.'

Abdallah Jum'ah as CEO of Saudi Aramco was also representing the oil company's interests throughout this process. He clearly wanted us to push back against the IOCs. And he made the point that the interests of the Kingdom and Saudi Aramco were one. I would add that, had his efforts not been successful, the Kingdom's control over its natural resources, and possibly its future, would have suffered as a result.

By the spring of 2003 our negotiations boiled over. Prince Saud Al-Faisal asked me and my team to meet with Lee Raymond in California to see if we could resolve our differences. I was convinced that what ExxonMobil and the rest of the IOCs were hoping to get from us on the cheap were reserves known in the oil business as condensate. These are hydrocarbons that in an underground reservoir typically exist as a gas, but then condense — hence the name — into a liquid when they are brought to the surface. This is a very valuable, very light form of oil that appears almost as light as gasoline. My concern was that our initial team under the leadership of the foreign ministry and without any oil industry expertise represented had effectively characterized condensate as gas or left it out of the negotiations completely. Not me. I knew the petroleum business inside out and it was time to take a stand.

It came to a head in California. I told Lee Raymond my views, and that I felt he was trying to gain an unfair advantage. Lee responded in kind, and it got a little ugly. From that point onward our negotiations were over. I haven't seen Lee Raymond since, which is a shame because we were once good friends. For me, it was business.

Despite the challenges, everyone on our team felt badly that, after a number of years, we still hadn't been able to resolve the issue that our crown prince so badly wanted us to accomplish. But we were unwilling to accept what we thought was clearly a bad deal for the Kingdom. Prince Saud Al-Faisal and his team at the same time continued to advocate for moving forward with some form of the three core venture concepts.

The crown prince turned to a long-time friend and adviser, the diplomat and poet Ghazi Abdul Rahman Al-Gosaibi, to get his opinion on the subject. Al-Gosaibi shared an old Arab saying with the crown prince: 'If you want bread, give the dough to the baker, not to someone else.' Al-Gosaibi added, 'This is an oil and gas business venture, you have an oil minister, my advice is assign him full responsibility and let him finish it.'

This decision was key. Saudi Aramco and the senior management, along with me as minister, were certainly the people most qualified to handle the whole process.

In the end, we offered the IOCs pure upstream acreage for gas exploration. Shell and Total, involved in Core Venture 3, were the only ones to take up the offer, in partnership with Saudi Aramco. We offered the rest of the exploration acreage, from Core Venture 1, in three packages that we put out for competitive bidding. In 2004 we formed three additional joint ventures, each with Saudi Aramco holding a 20 per cent stake: with Russia's Lukoil; with China's Sinopec; and with Italy's ENI and Spain's Repsol YPF.

By the time the Gas Initiative had been resolved our government in Riyadh agreed that Saudi Aramco and the oil ministry were our principal instruments for developing our hydrocarbon resources. Crown Prince Abdullah gave us his unconditional support and clearly valued our role in keeping the development of our core Saudi resources in Saudi hands.

We had won the battle. But had we won the war?

16. New Millennium – the 2000s

The new millennium brought new challenges. Initially, things were looking positive. With the Gulf War and the Asian financial crisis behind us, we were looking ahead to brighter days. The oil price had stabilized and the Saudi economy was on a sound footing. Indeed, for the first time in years the Kingdom actually reported a budget surplus, despite a significant increase in spending. It was a trend that would continue in the years ahead.

Higher oil prices, while good for the Saudi economy, were causing some alarm in consumer nations. At $30 a barrel, the oil price was three times what it had been in 1998, and the US government was getting edgy.

Fortunately, our government-to-government communications with the US remained strong as the decade began. President Clinton's energy secretary Bill Richardson came to Riyadh in the autumn of 2000 to discuss oil prices. He said that America was thinking about releasing oil from its strategic petroleum reserve to counteract rising heating-oil prices in the north-eastern US. I said that I hoped the United States wouldn't take that step because it would be disruptive to global oil prices.

He talked at length about the issue of home heating-oil supplies on the East Coast. I remember smiling. 'This doesn't have anything to do with Vice-President Al Gore running for president, does it?' I asked. Democratic presidential candidate Gore had been calling for such a move while campaigning.

Republican candidate George W. Bush criticized the idea as 'playing politics' with energy prices and markets. Secretary Richardson said, 'Well, it's a little bit of that.' We both laughed.

I repeated that I thought releasing the reserves under these circumstances was a bad idea. I also advised him that the issue was a geopolitical one and therefore above my pay grade. He needed to make sure the royal family knew of America's intentions. It wasn't enough for me to just pass along his message. He arranged a meeting with our foreign minister, Prince Saud Al-Faisal, at his home in Beverly Hills to break the news.

Secretary Richardson later recalled their meeting:

> I remember having a meal with the Foreign Minister and I said, 'Well, Mr Minister, I want you to know we are going to release the petroleum reserve and I wanted to give you a heads up, but look it's for home heating oil. We are concerned about scarcity of home heating oil in the north-east. I am going to start a whole effort there to store home heating oil.' He replied: 'Mr Secretary, I know an election's coming up,' and he smiled. Then we had lunch.

We did suffer from a few global cultural miscues during this period. In 2000 Japan's Arabian Oil Company Ltd, AOC, was renegotiating its forty-year drilling concession in the Saudi portion of the Neutral Zone between Saudi Arabia and Kuwait. The negotiations had been going on and off for a few years, but came to a head in February 2000 because the concession expired on the twenty-eighth of the month. Even though our countries had worked on many projects before and since, we were not able to come to terms on this deal.

I wanted them to pay $1 billion for the concession in order

to fund the development of a railway in the north of the Kingdom to act as the transportation backbone of a phosphate industry we were planning to develop. They were suspicious of my motives. I insisted the money was going to build and operate the line.

Unfortunately for both parties, the negotiation was a victim of cultural misunderstanding. Just as we had difficulty understanding when 'yes' meant 'no' when dealing with Nippon Oil during the refinery negotiations in the 1990s, they had trouble understanding the difference between 'God willing' and 'yes'. The Japanese prime minister, Keizo Obuchi, had previously spoken with the king, and left assuming that he had the king's agreement to grant a new concession to Japan's AOC. In fact, the king had used the Arabic term 'Inshallah', which translates as 'God willing'. The Japanese mistakenly took that to mean that they had a definitive agreement.

The Japanese trade minister, Kaoru Yosano, told me, 'Don't worry, we have permission.' I asked him from whom, and he talked about intermediaries and princes. I said, 'I haven't heard from anyone about it, and I'm the man you need to deal with.' Even after I had briefed the crown prince on the subject and he'd repeated our position to him, the Japanese minister still insisted, 'Don't worry, we have the king's blessing.' They didn't seem to understand that in talking with the crown prince they were for all intents and purposes talking to the king.

Days passed and from our point of view they weren't willing to negotiate seriously. We were offering what we considered a gold-plated deal. I flew to Tokyo during the last week in February to demonstrate how committed we were to concluding a deal. I was well received and honoured with various official meetings and dinners. By the twenty-seventh we still didn't have a deal so I flew back to Riyadh. Before I left I said I hope I hear from you immediately because tomorrow is the last day to renegotiate the concession. They didn't seem to take me seriously and let the deadline pass. In so doing they left billions of dollars in oil revenues on the table.

Despite that failure, we parted on good terms. The Kyodo news agency on 29 February 2000 quoted the Japanese prime minister as saying, 'It was a very regrettable result. But there will be no change in good relations between Japan and Saudi Arabia. We would like to work to strengthen friendly relations.' Indeed, the feeling was mutual and we would form important joint ventures going forward.

Our government was on a strong footing in financial terms as the year ended. Even though oil prices did moderate somewhat after the petroleum reserves were opened, we were on track for another strong year economically in 2001. In the meantime we had a new US administration to get to know. Despite releasing the strategic petroleum reserves, Gore lost to Bush in a tightly contested election that ultimately was decided by the US Supreme Court.

I travelled to Washington in April 2001 to meet some of the members of the Bush team. Vice-President Dick Cheney, who had experience in both government and the oil industry as the former US Secretary of Defense and CEO of oil services giant Haliburton, had already taken the lead in forming the new administration's approach to energy issues. We discussed the long-term need for greater supplies of crude oil to meet expected increases in global demand, even if the US economy was already slowing following the collapse of the dot.com boom in 2000. In fact, OPEC announced successive cutbacks in production in response to slowing demand as the year progressed.

I also met with US energy secretary Spencer Abraham. In a press release issued after our meeting he said, 'Saudi Arabia is a strong ally of the United States and a very important OPEC country.' I returned to the Kingdom confident that the Bush administration was going to be a good group for us to work with.

Then, on 11 September 2001, we all heard the terrible news. First one plane and then a second had flown into the World Trade Center in lower Manhattan, and a third had crashed into the Pentagon. I was actually flying from Jeddah to Riyadh when I heard about the attacks. Like the rest of the world, we couldn't take our eyes from the terrible images broadcast on every television channel. We knew our world had changed.

My immediate response was to alert our CEO that we needed to be prepared to respond to any disruption that might occur in global energy markets. In fact there was greater than average volatility in oil and gas prices, as you would expect during a crisis. But in the hours and days that followed none of us knew quite what to expect.

Once the world learned that many of the men on the planes were Saudis, even though they were sworn enemies of their own country as well as America, there were those who wanted to blame Saudi Arabia for the attacks. But, as we would quickly come to appreciate, the US government understood that the terrorists were waging jihad against us as well as the West. 'We looked on it as a problem that had to be dealt with,' Vice-President Cheney said. 'Saudi Arabia has as much to lose obviously as we did. Publicly from a PR standpoint there were those who were suggesting that somehow this was the fault of the Saudi government. That so many of the hijackers had been from Saudi Arabia etc. We never felt that way.' He and others in the administration would coordinate closely with our ambassador to the US, Prince Bandar bin Sultan, who worked tirelessly to ensure that avenues of diplomatic communication remained open.

Complicating our relations with the US during this critical period was the fact that there was no US ambassador to Saudi Arabia when the terror attacks occurred. Career diplomats were in place, of course, but the former ambassador to the Kingdom under President Clinton, Wyche Fowler Jr, had resigned in March and his replacement had not yet been appointed. Robert Jordan, a Texas corporate lawyer, replaced him less than a month after the attacks. I and others in our government made it clear to the new ambassador that we welcomed the chance to work with the US and other nations to present a united front against terrorism.

Jordan recalled our first meeting:

> My recollection is it was fairly early in the situation and he was most gracious in receiving me. We had a very positive conversation. He made it clear that the Saudis in the aftermath of the attacks had offered to make additional oil resources available in the event that world oil supply was disrupted or there were any dislocations in the system. He offered tremendous encouragement and support in bringing any of the terrorists to justice who might have been involved in it. He was a tremendous resource and a tremendous source of strength I would say within the Saudi senior ministry.

After an initial spike in the price of oil following the terrorist attacks, it quickly became clear that the global economy, already weak, was likely to slow further. And that meant oil prices were once again headed sharply lower. By November 2001 crude oil was trading below $20 a barrel.

My fellow OPEC members agreed that we needed to cut our production in order to support prices. But just as we had during the late 1990s, we were insisting that the major non-OPEC producers share the pain and cut their production as well. We would cut our output by 1.5 million barrels a day to 21.7 million if non-OPEC producers together cut their output by 500,000 barrels per day in total.

Mexico once again showed its leadership among non-OPEC member oil producers in being willing to work for the common good. The Norwegians stepped up as well. After many negotiations, even the Russians were on board.

Oman joined in, agreeing to cut its production by 40,000 barrels a day, and Angola cut 22,500. The total non-OPEC cuts fell just short of 500,000, but we in OPEC agreed it was close enough. The cuts were instituted on 1 January 2002 for a six-month period. Monitoring compliance with these cuts, on the part of Russia in particular, just like with the cuts in 1998 and 1999, was a challenge for all of us in the industry.

President George W. Bush and Crown Prince Abdullah met for the first time at the president's ranch in Crawford, Texas, in April 2002. Their stroll hand-in-hand, Saudi fashion, was a very public show of solidarity among the two leaders.

As much as the governments of both our countries cooperated closely in the months and years following the 9/11 attacks, all of us Saudis were aware that there was a certain amount of anti-Saudi sentiment among sectors of the American population. We get most of the cable television channels that are available in the US, and we were hearing the criticisms.

I experienced some of this anger first hand on a hunting trip with Sam White in Texas in 2002. One of the guests made an anti-Arab comment that I was clearly intended to overhear. But Sam and the rest of the group confronted him immediately and asked him to leave. That was a measure of Sam, my best and sorely missed friend.

One of the moments that most clearly sticks in my mind from the Crawford visit didn't involve the meeting of the world leaders but a group of grey-haired Westerners in their seventies and eighties. Rather than protest at our arrival, they greeted the crown prince at the airport with broad smiles and gifts of flowers. They were Aramco retirees who had gathered at relatively short notice to show their support for our country and the crown prince. Ambassador Jordan said, 'It was one of the most heart-warming scenes that I have witnessed. It was a tremendous outpouring of good will that really reflected I think how well they had been treated and how much they enjoyed their time in Aramco.'

Like many countries, Saudi Arabia supported the US decision to invade Afghanistan and rout the Taliban while also searching for Bin Laden. Also like many countries in Europe and the Gulf, however, we did not support the Bush administration's rationale for invading Iraq in the spring of 2003, with British forces fighting alongside. Despite these differences our governments continued to work closely to ensure a continuous flow of crude oil to meet the world's needs and to fight terrorism. We increased our oil production by 1.3 million barrels per day to 8.1 million to make up for the Iraqi production that was taken off the market following the US invasion. We were also offsetting the effect of a strike among

Venezuelan oil industry workers that began in December 2002 and was instigated by opponents to President Chávez.

In 2003 I was reappointed as oil minister to begin my third four-year term in service to our government and people. It was time to look beyond the immediate crises that had seemed to be following one after another over the previous several years and plan for the future. One thing was clear. After the repeated periods of a crude oil surplus in 1998–1999 and again in 2001–2002, global demand was now rapidly catching up with supply. And it was clear also that demand was going to grow significantly as the decade progressed, with much of the increase coming from Asia. That was true even before we increased our output to make up for the loss of Iraqi production.

We realized that in order to ensure that we had roughly 1.5 million to 2 million barrels per day of spare capacity in our system we would need to invest in a significant expansion of our oil-producing capabilities. And we also needed to substantially increase our refining capacity at the same time. In 2004 we added another 500,000 barrels to our daily output. That gave us an average of 8.6 million barrels a day out of a potential total of nearly 10 million. That still left us short of the minimum spare capacity we were comfortable with. And virtually no other oil producer had any spare capacity to keep in reserve in order to soften the impact of sudden supply or demand disruptions.

The tight supply situation was reflected in global oil prices. Crude oil spiked higher, trading above $50 a barrel in 2004, compared to just $20 in late 2001. And there was little on the horizon in terms of supply or demand that suggested that upward trend would change anytime soon.

In the spring of 2005 we forewarned our allies and trading

partners that we had a major announcement coming shortly. We were launching a five-year, $50 billion capital spending programme to boost our production and refining capacity. At the same time we were doubling the number of drilling rigs deployed in the Kingdom. And that price tag would increase as the decade progressed. The goal of the plan was to increase our total daily capacity to 12.5 million barrels.

In late April 2005 I joined a delegation to the US led by Crown Prince Abdullah to brief our allies on our plans. It was clear that the American officials were feeling the pressure of higher prices at the pumps, which at the time were about $2.25 a gallon. The crown prince and President Bush met once again at the Bush ranch in Crawford to discuss the global oil situation and the Kingdom's plans. They issued a joint statement saying, 'Both nations pledge to continue their cooperation, so that the oil supply from Saudi Arabia will be available and secure. The United States appreciates Saudi Arabia's strong commitment to accelerating investment and expanding its production capacity to help provide stability and adequately supply the market.'

In the midst of this geopolitical globetrotting, all of us in Saudi Arabia paused to mourn the passing of King Fahd on 1 August 2005. He had transferred many of his operational roles to the crown prince a decade earlier when he suffered a stroke, but he had remained king. Ten years earlier I had considered retiring. But I knew then that I would remain in office to serve the king as long as I was needed.

The pace of change seemed to accelerate as the weeks passed. The urgent need for additional global crude oil production capacity was brought home to us all late that summer when hurricanes Katrina and Rita slammed into the US

Gulf Coast and disrupted production and refining operations in several locations. Oil prices shot sharply higher to nearly $70 a barrel in the wake of the storms before pulling back. Gas prices hit $4 a gallon in some parts of the US.

New American energy secretary Sam Bodman flew to Saudi Arabia in late 2005 for a look at our existing facilities and to attain a greater understanding of our expansion plans. I personally escorted him around several of our facilities, including Shaybah, during his three-day tour and he enjoyed a dinner of Middle Eastern dishes around the pool at our home in Dhahran along with several Saudi Aramco officials. I was returning the courtesy he'd extended me in May 2005 when I'd visited the US and had dinner at his home in Washington. The guests on that occasion had included Federal Reserve chairman Alan Greenspan.

With his background in engineering, Secretary Bodman impressed our engineers and technicians with his questions. During our tour I overheard them saying in Arabic, 'He understands, he's an engineer, show him and he gets it.' Those were not words we usually associated with political visitors, including his predecessor Secretary Abraham, who visited Saudi Arabia for one day, declining to spend the night.

Secretary Bodman's visit helped put to rest fears in some quarters of Washington that we were not up to the job of meeting global demand for oil in the years to come. As he told *The New York Times* after he returned to Washington, 'I was very impressed, I have to say, by the capability, by the competence, by the enthusiasm displayed. I came back with an increased level of confidence that they would do what they said they would do.' Sam Bodman became a good friend of mine and was one of the few energy ministers I've ever come across who actually understood the industry from a technical, practical point of view.

Our massive projects weren't proceeding in a vacuum. Other oil producers in the Gulf and around the world responded to the soaring demand for crude oil with development initiatives of their own. None of these could compare to the size of our oil and gas expansion programme, but collectively they were competing for the same construction resources and materials that we were, which significantly increased the cost and complexity of many projects. There were times when we used concrete struts to support pipes winding their way through our complexes, for instance, because it would have been too expensive and time-consuming to use the traditional steel supporting racks.

I was proud of the amount of hard work and enterprising leadership and decision making our people demonstrated as Saudi Aramco took on such a tremendous number of massive and complex projects in such a short period of time. We were challenged to provide for the world's future energy needs, and we rose to the occasion. That fact made it especially frustrating to find ourselves in the middle of what quickly became known as the 'peak oil' controversy.

During a visit to our oil-producing facilities in the Eastern Province near mid-decade, American oil industry consultant Matthew Simmons would come up with a theory. Nat Kern, from the Foreign Reports consultancy, was there. He recalls, 'I was in a presentation in Dhahran. Matt Simmons was there. The Saudi engineer giving the presentation was talking about "fuzzy logic". He said we use "fuzzy logic" in our computer programs. On the flight home, Simmons kept going on about this fuzzy logic thing and that's where he got his peak oil theory for Saudi Arabia.'

Reviewing published literature in the field, Simmons was convinced that we weren't going to be able to supply the quantities of oil that we had been saying we would. He then asserted that our reservoirs didn't hold as much oil and weren't as well managed as we maintained. This was incorrect.

Saudi Arabia and its oilfields were in decline, he claimed, and the outlook for the global economy as we shortly reached our 'peak oil' production was dire indeed. His 2005 book on the subject, *Twilight in the Desert: The Coming Saudi Oil Shock and the World Economy*, captured what many of us considered his hysterical tone. That tone, sadly but maybe inevitably, was echoed among conspiracy theorists and crackpots around the world, who seemed to think that a charge was true simply because it was being repeated on the internet.

As much as I and others at Saudi Aramco as well as industry experts around the world did our best to counter these charges, they were a continued distraction at a time when we already had too much to do. Making our job more difficult was the fact that we continue to consider many of the details of our oil and gas reservoir characteristics the equivalent of state secrets. We see ourselves as custodians of our primary natural resource for future generations. Sharing too much proprietary knowledge could very well give other oil producers an advantage in competing with us. We were damned if we did and damned if we didn't. So we went on fighting and we took the fight to the US.

We assembled a team of people to tackle the issue. Senior managers, such as Nansen Saleri and Mahmood Abdulbaqi, were among them. And I also called in one of our rising stars, Muhammad Saggaf. I first noticed Muhammad when he gave a presentation to some of us in London in 2003. I was impressed by his knowledge and enthusiasm. He was just the man we needed to help put our case during a conference dedicated to the subject in Washington DC, hosted by the Center for Strategic and International Studies. 'It was a very widely attended event,' Saggaf recalled later. 'My role was to make a presentation on exploration technologies. My partner and friend Mohammed Qahtani's role was to make a presentation on petroleum engineering technologies. So we were a duo. Other people did presentations but they were extremely boring. I mean, everyone was asleep. Ours was exciting. It was fantastic.' And everyone woke up to the reality about Saudi Arabia.

Our position on the issue has been consistent over the years. Our total proven recoverable reserve is about 261 billion barrels of crude oil. And that is a conservative estimate. The company's goal of raising its recovery rates for most of its fields to 70 per cent could yield significantly more in reserves. Saudi Arabia clearly has plenty of reserves to meet the world's needs for decades to come. And our continued exploration and development of existing fields more than makes up for the oil produced each year in the Kingdom.

Daniel Yergin, Pulitzer Prize-winning author and chairman of Cambridge Energy Research Associates, CERA, noted at the time that Simmons, who passed away in 2010, was the latest in a chain of alarmists who arise every few decades to warn that oil reserves are about to peak. 'This is the fifth time that the world is said to be running out of oil,' Yergin said. 'Each time – whether it was the "gasoline famine" at the end of WWI or the "permanent shortage" of the 1970s – technology and the opening of new frontier areas have banished the spectre of decline. There's no reason to think that technology is finished this time.' In fact, I am happy to point out that the development of shale oil and gas resources in the US in recent years has brought significant additional capacity to world oil and gas markets and proved Yergin's point.

Peak oil proved to be a false threat to our security. Unfortunately, we faced some very real threats. On the afternoon of 24 February 2006 I received a call in my Dhahran office. Terrorists driving two bomb-laden cars had launched a suicide attack on our processing facility at Abqaiq. I quickly made my way to our helipad and took a company helicopter for the short trip to the plant. I was chairman of Saudi Aramco as well as oil minister, and wanted to be near our people in a time of crisis.

As my helicopter approached the plant I could see a small fire. But it was clear there was no damage to the actual oil-processing facilities or mass of intersecting pipelines at the single most important junction in our oil- and gas-processing systems. Our 250-hectare Abqaiq complex alone can process 7 million barrels of oil a day. One of the cars exploded at the outer perimeter gate after guards fired on it. The second car made it through the first gate but also exploded under fire in a parking area. Both of the terrorists were killed. Sadly, two guards were critically wounded as well.

I spoke with the king from the site of the attack and assured him that there was no significant damage to our facilities. He complimented me for rushing to the scene to be with our people. I also spoke to the media to assure everyone that the key facilities at Abqaiq remained untouched. Despite these and other assurances, global oil prices jumped more than $1 a barrel as news of the attack spread.

Because petroleum is so central to our development I haven't talked much about the second half of my ministerial title, which covers mineral resources. I had been in my position as minister for barely two years when in 1997 we formed Ma'aden by royal decree to develop our kingdom's mineral resources.

Initially Ma'aden was primarily focused on developing and expanding the Kingdom's gold-mining operations. But it became clear that Ma'aden, while successful in precious metals, could add even more value by serving as the key to our efforts to expand into new industries that are not based on petroleum products. Barely a decade after we formed Ma'aden we sold 50 per cent of the enterprise to the public on the Saudi stock exchange, Tadawul. As a government minister I stepped off the Ma'aden board once it became publicly owned. But I have been very much involved in helping guide its development.

In 2006 I drove a bulldozer at a remote site called Ras Al-Khair on the Arabian Gulf north of Jubail, one of the industrial cities we built in the 1980s as bases for our expansion into petrochemicals. I scooped up and dumped a load of sand as part of a ground-breaking ceremony. But instead of anchoring another petrochemicals complex, that same location today is the site of our huge plant producing diammonium phosphate (DAP), which is a key ingredient in fertilizers and other products. Next to the DAP plant is an aluminium joint-venture with the American company Alcoa that includes a state-of-the-art alumina refinery, smelter and rolling mill.

The phosphate and bauxite mines and the processing facilities at Ras Al-Khair are all linked by a new rail network built by the state-owned Saudi Arabian Railways. It took a few years, but after the opportunity to use the renegotiation of the Neutral Zone concession with Japan to fund the railway fell through in 2000, we received funding directly from our own Ministry of Finance.

The railway also links these facilities with yet another remote northern desert outpost – Waad Al-Shamal, which means Northern Promise. This $9 billion complex 1,100 kilometres from Riyadh is being built around a phosphate mine linked by rail again to Ras Al-Khair. When completed, this project will include office and residential compounds and a new regional college to train 300 graduate professionals a year to fill the white-collar jobs expected to be created as part of the complex.

All these ventures are part of Saudi Arabia's overall long-term plan to industrialize its economy, diversify away from its reliance on oil and, importantly, create jobs and opportunities for our citizens.

And speaking of jobs, I was about to get a new quite unexpected one directly from King Abdullah that would test the stamina, intellect and abilities of me and my team to the full.

17. Building a University – 2006–2009

Less than a year after King Abdullah officially succeeded his brother in August 2005, he set about realizing a dream he had been nurturing for thirty years. His vision was to build a world-class graduate-level university in Saudi Arabia. It would capture the glory of Islam's Golden Age of science and learning by bringing the world's best technical researchers and students to work and live alongside our top Saudi students. This would soon involve me in one of the most exciting and worthwhile projects I have ever had the privilege to lead.

The topic came up in a meeting in Riyadh but progress to date had been slow. I could tell the king was frustrated that the thing was getting snarled up in committees. Afterwards, I approached him with an offer. Why not let Saudi Aramco take control? We had experience of major projects and the company was staffed by some of the brightest brains in the country. We could deliver the university, I told him. 'OK,' he said.

Since the 1960s, more than a dozen universities have been built in the Kingdom, but they tended to be focused on meeting the general educational needs of our growing population, or, like King Fahd University of Petroleum and Minerals, training engineers for our hydrocarbon-processing industries. They were also strictly segregated by gender, which accords to our tradition in Saudi Arabia.

The king said it was time for us to build a technical

university that could rank among the world's best. It would, he said, be a 'beacon of lasting peace, hope and reconciliation', providing 'a world-class centre for research, exploration, study and learning, open to all on the basis of merit, achievement, and capacity, while further continuing our scientific tradition'. In reality, that meant no gender segregation. And that was controversial to many in the Kingdom.

King Abdullah wanted a modern-day Bayt Al-Hikma (House of Wisdom), like the early form of university in Baghdad that helped define Islam's Golden Age of learning from the eighth to the eleventh century CE. At a time Europe was stumbling through its Dark Ages, the crescent of Islamic civilization stretching from southern Spain through North Africa into the Middle East and south Asia preserved and expanded upon learning in the physical sciences, geometry, medicine, engineering, philosophy and astronomy. The Bayt Al-Hikma was at the centre of that expansion in knowledge. The king felt that our society had progressed to the point where a university open to our own people as well as the rest of the world could look beyond our immediate needs – and once again reach for the stars.

It was a major undertaking. Building facilities was one thing. We could do that. Overcoming local objections was another difficulty, but with the king's blessing this too could be handled. Creating a world-class university? I called Abdallah Jum'ah, the Saudi Aramco CEO, and broke the news to him.

I reached him on his mobile phone in Geneva. He had just left an executive committee meeting of Saudi Aramco and was getting some exercise on the walking trail that leads along the lake with the Swiss Alps in the background. I told him I had a new job for him. I said the king wants

Saudi Aramco to build a new university. He stopped in his tracks.

He pointed out that he had just been talking at the meeting about how stretched Saudi Aramco was with all of the projects already in the works, many aimed at meeting the goal of reaching 12.5 million barrels per day. They had just approved $20 billion in expenditure for 2007 to build new facilities, or refurbish and maintain existing structures across the Kingdom. Even bigger dollar amounts were on the drawing board, we both knew. 'It will be very difficult for us,' he told me, 'but we will reprioritize our work and do it.' It was the answer I was confident I was going to hear. And it represented the can-do Aramco spirit that I would count on to see this project through.

The planning process had been under way since May. A concept paper developed by four senior government officials with backgrounds in international research had been prepared. The expansive site the king had chosen was a barren tract of land on the Red Sea ninety kilometres north of Jeddah near the small fishing village of Thuwal, and an adjacent marine sanctuary incorporating coral reef ecosystems. The campus site covered 16.4 square kilometres on land, the size of a small town, and 19.6 square kilometres offshore. The king wanted work to start immediately and be completed as soon as possible.

The initial team we assembled to lead the project included Nadhmi Al-Nasr, whom we made interim president, based in large part on his success with our Shaybah mega project. I served as chairman. Quite naturally, the team thought Saudi Aramco was going to be in charge of just the construction of the physical campus.

Also on the team was Ahmad Al-Khowaiter, manager of Saudi Aramco's facilities planning department. Al-Khowaiter had not long returned to Saudi Arabia after receiving a masters in business administration from the Massachusetts Institute of Technology, which he thought was a good model for a walkable academic campus.

In fact, thanks to Al-Khowaiter, MIT's Infinite Corridor, or shared passageway running the length of the campus that brings researchers together along a common axis, would ultimately be a major influence on the design of the research core of our university. He quickly started working through the documents with senior facility-planning engineer Abdullah Al-Saleh. To refine their plans, they wanted to meet the team that was planning the academic side of the project, including the scientific disciplines and fields of study, the kinds of labs they would need, what the ratio of faculty to graduate students would be, etc.

We met at my office in Dhahran a few days after I'd spoken with the king. I told them that Saudi Aramco was not only responsible for building the academic campus and surrounding housing and other supporting structures, but also in charge of planning the academics. 'There is no one else. It's you guys. Building is the least concern. That's no big deal. We know we can do that. We are responsible to act as academics,' I told them.

'That was a big wake-up call for us,' Al-Nasr said. 'We knew that this was not going to be business as usual.' In fact, he added, 'We came to find out, this was not like anything that has ever been done.'

That was the beginning of a miraculous three-year journey in the creation of what would soon be known as the

King Abdullah University of Science and Technology, or KAUST. We quickly identified and contacted a number of consulting groups who were vital in our success.

The Washington Advisory Group, something of a club for emeritus university presidents too active to retire, helped us design the academic structure for KAUST; SRI International, the former Stanford Research Institute, helped develop our research focus; and the architects Hellmuth, Obata + Kassabaum, Inc., developed the master plan for the physical campus on the Red Sea coast.

Two of the Washington Advisory Group's leaders who played a major role in developing and advising KAUST were Dr Frank Rhodes, the former president of Cornell University and a highly regarded author, and Dr Frank Press, a former president of the National Academy of Sciences in the US and science adviser to President Jimmy Carter. As Dr Press would later tell *Physics Today*, 'This is a vast experiment. It's nation-changing. It's a sign that Saudi Arabia wants to participate in the international community of research universities.'

The 'two Franks', as we were fond of calling them, were instrumental in opening up to us the doors of university presidents and leading researchers around the world. I lost count of the number of trips I made with them and with Al-Nasr as we engaged in global benchmarking at major research universities in North America, Europe and Asia. I was impressed with the graciousness with which we were greeted almost without exception.

There was, of course, a certain amount of scepticism. Academics we met with said, 'Either you're out of your mind or you don't know what you're up to.' Sometimes it helps not to know the odds against you when you start a project.

One of the team from the Washington Advisory Group

was Dr Bruce Guile, a laid-back Californian with more than twenty years of experience in this field. He recalled the first call he received about KAUST. 'I thought it was a joke and expected it to last six months. But we never looked back. Everything happened incredibly quickly.'

Many of the universities we visited, including Stanford University, the University of California, Berkeley, the University of Texas at Austin, Cambridge University and Imperial College London, agreed early on to partner with us in developing our curriculum and recruiting and preparing professors who were active in research in selected fields. We also launched collaborative research programmes with many universities even while our campus was under construction. That helped us jump-start our academic research.

The truly international reach of our global research effort was indicated by the range of partnerships and alliances we formed in the early stage of the creation of KAUST, including Woods Hole Oceanographic Institution in Falmouth, Massachusetts; Institut Français du Pétrole; National University of Singapore; Indian Institute of Technology; American University in Cairo; and Technische Universität München.

Working with SRI, we developed the first four research institutes at KAUST. Our emphasis was on collaborative work reaching across the intellectual 'silos' created by the traditional discipline-based focus of most universities. Our first institutes focused on energy and environment resources; biosciences and bioengineering; materials science and engineering; and applied mathematics and computational science. It initially offered advanced degrees in nine fields.

Frank Rhodes in particular was instrumental in shaping KAUST's founding document that clearly stated its vision and mission, notably its commitment to academic excellence and freedom. After a few minor tweaks of the team's draft by a lawyer from the oil ministry, and my own review of the document to ensure that it reflected the government policy, the document was approved by the king and the royal court on 11 December 2006.

Perhaps most controversial, in Saudi Arabia anyway, was the aim to 'establish the basis for an ethical, robust, diverse and attractive academic community for men and women of all nationalities built on the highest standards of scholarship and efficiency to contribute to public advancement and posterity'. This was a significant break with Saudi custom and practice, and it was not entered into lightly. The king understood that it was needed, however, if our nation was to create an institution that could truly rank among the best in the world. Experience has shown that the king's faith in his people was well placed.

Teams from Hellmuth, Obata + Kassabaum worked almost around the clock, using the time difference between the Middle East, Europe and the US to refine plans as computer files were passed around the world among their global network of offices. They aligned the core research buildings to maximize the amount of sea breeze pulled into the common areas linking the buildings off the Red Sea via wind towers, a passive cooling technology that has been used in the region since ancient times. Solar panels line a massive common roof and other surfaces that, combined with other passive and active technologies, make the campus one of the most energy-efficient around.

Saudi Aramco broke ground at the KAUST site in October 2007 on the multi-billion-dollar project at a ceremony presided over by King Abdullah and attended by nearly

1,500 dignitaries. In a clear indication that we were not willing to wait for university buildings to be completed for the academic work to begin, to coincide with the ground breaking we convened an academic symposium on the subject of 'The Role of the Research University in the Twenty-First Century'.

In its variety of uses for facilities, and materials used in construction, KAUST in some ways was much more complex than the mammoth processing facilities we were constructing elsewhere in the Kingdom. The price tag included about $1.5 billion for scientific instrumentation in the university's array of world-class laboratories, including one of the fastest supercomputers in the Middle East. Tens of thousands of workers were housed on site during the peak of construction in 2008. Everything they needed on the job or to live was trucked in from Jeddah or elsewhere in the Kingdom.

We had the initial construction cost of KAUST covered, but we knew we needed to create an endowment to fund the university going forward. I was adamant that to remain independent KAUST had to have its own source of funding. We did a quick review of research universities to come up with a figure. I went to the king and told him I needed $10 billion to fund KAUST. He said, 'Ali, that's a lot of money.'

I agreed, but told him I had a plan to raise the funds. Rising oil prices for much of the decade had created a revenue stream that was well in excess of our budgeted expenses year after year, resulting in mounting annual budget surpluses. I wrote a letter for the king to sign that directed Saudi Aramco to put $10 billion into an account for KAUST from our crude oil revenues. He signed the letter and we were all set. At least, that is what I thought.

Our consultants came back and said that $10 billion wasn't enough for an endowment. They said for a fully functional endowment to provide for KAUST as we envisioned the university we would need $17.5 billion.

I went back to the king and decided I would round up to be safe. I said I needed another $10 billion. He said, 'Ali, that is too much!' I explained, 'Believe me, this is what it is going to take to protect the university completely.' He wanted two weeks to think about it. I returned and said, 'I am ready to implement. I need this $10 billion.' He shook his head and said, 'You are difficult. You are insistent.' He signed a second letter and we got our additional $10 billion for the KAUST endowment, which is managed by an independent investment company.

We brought in academics and university leaders from around the world to form in 2007 an International Advisory Council, which would be replaced by a permanent Board of Trustees two years later. One of the members, Shih Choon Fong, president of the National University of Singapore, who had spent thirty years in the US in various research and teaching posts, including at General Electric and Brown University, initially thought he would not be able to make time in his hectic schedule to do justice to KAUST. But the more he looked into our project, the more he realized he wanted to become a part of this unprecedented effort. That was a good thing, since in January 2008 he agreed to become KAUST's founding president.

President Shih helped accelerate the selection of faculty from universities around the world that was already under way. Also in January 2008, KAUST awarded its first 178 scholarships to outstanding male and female undergraduates in engineering and technology from universities around the world. These students were selected using a very demanding set of criteria, and included more than eighty from Saudi Arabia. They formed the core of the first cohort of 400 graduate students who would enter KAUST in September 2009, working closely with a seventy-five-member founding faculty to help build a better future.

Some Saudi families were initially reluctant to have their daughters consider attending a co-educational institution. We understood, and held open days for students and their families. Over time, as they visited and understood what KAUST was about and the opportunities it offered for their daughters, many became very enthusiastic. Now many of the best students in our country, male and female, are anxious to enrol.

At the same time we are maintaining very high academic standards for all students. Some people initially said that KAUST should be 90 per cent Saudi, since it is a Saudi university. We said no, for it to be truly international Saudis should be no more than 50 per cent of the student population. We are at roughly 30 per cent today.

Even as the first class of graduate students was preparing to enter KAUST we were already planning to build another independent institution devoted to research and inspired by the king, the King Abdullah Petroleum Studies & Research Center, or KAPSARC.

Once again Saudi Aramco was tasked with the construction of a research campus, this time on the outskirts of Riyadh. And similar to KAUST, research was under way while the core campus was under construction. The campus is a stunning example of energy efficient, organic design, by renowned Iraqi architect Zaha Hadid, based on six-sided cells that allow for future expansion off the central structure.

KAPSARC's mission today will hopefully help solve some of Saudi Arabia's, and the world's, energy problems of tomorrow. Central to these, in the case of Saudi Arabia, is its worrying over-reliance on fossil fuels.

Like any new venture, KAUST has had a few growing pains. Yet its impact on the creation of knowledge is expanding every year. As is its impact on the future of Saudi society. As Alice Gast, former president of Lehigh University said:

> KAUST is an incredibly significant place. It is a ground-breaking and leading research university attracting talent from all over the world, both faculty and students. It's pursuing really important problems for the Kingdom and for the world; you know, food, water, energy – it doesn't get much more fundamental than that. It's an exciting opportunity to build from scratch a truly world-class institution.

For me, it was a tremendous challenge but also the most rewarding one of my life. So many people contributed to its success – its continuing success – that they are too many to mention here. But Abdallah Jum'ah deserves a lot of credit for his leadership. What other oil company CEO gets a call asking him to build a university and takes it in his stride? It was a great additional strain on him and all of us, but we did it and it will be a lasting testament. We met so many fascinating, intelligent and remarkable people on our mission to create KAUST, and the gift of education is one of the greatest anyone can bestow.

King Abdullah's vision became a reality. Future generations of students will benefit from its facilities. And KAUST has worked closely with other Saudi universities in terms of shared research efforts that are already delivering positive results for the Kingdom. KAUST also works with various

Saudi government agencies, including the Ministry of Agriculture, for instance, providing research on drought- and salt-tolerant strains of wheat. The hope is that this and future research will help mankind overcome scientific and technical challenges to help create a better world for all. That sounds clichéd, I know, but I truly believe in the power of education and, of all people, I personify what can be achieved with some hard work, dedication and good teaching. And some luck!

18. Prices Rise and Fall – 2008–2014

Our previous battles with oil prices were mostly directed at propping them up. From 2008 onward, we struggled to keep a lid on them. It was every bit as challenging, and required global efforts and coordination.

Saudi Aramco was paying an unprecedented price tag for its commitment to providing a spare capacity cushion for the global oil market. What started as a $50 billion capital spending budget in 2005 ballooned to $65 billion by early 2008, as projects were added and expanded and inflation and materials scarcity drove up construction costs. And that was before adding in the multi-billion-dollar cost of building KAUST.

These amounts were impressive in their own right. But they were just a small part of our kingdom's towering, multi-year development budget of $500 billion that took shape as the decade progressed. That huge amount was earmarked for everything from building a number of completely new cities spread across the country to funding new industries that would continue to diversify our economy.

It was an idea that had been around for many years. In addition to developing more than a half-dozen world-class oil- and gas-processing facilities, we had also built up our country's petrochemicals industry. After removing petrochemicals from the earlier Gas Initiative bidding process, we looked at alternatives for using petrochemicals to diversify our economy further. We brought in consultants to help us weigh our options and study the successes in this field achieved by other countries, notably Singapore, Korea and Japan. Saudi Arabia Basic Industries Corp., SABIC, was formed in 1976 to produce some basic petrochemicals and other materials.

A big step in this direction was to form Petro Rabigh, in 2005, a joint venture with Japan's Sumitomo Chemical Co. Across the Kingdom at Jubail on the Arabian Gulf we broke ground in 2011 for another major petrochemical project. This world-class joint venture between Saudi Aramco and Dow Chemical Co., called Sadara Chemical Co., will produce ethylene and polyethylene.

Those new industries, including petrochemicals, fertilizers and aluminium, in turn would provide hundreds of thousands of jobs for our young and rapidly expanding population.

Making all this possible was the escalating price of crude oil. On 3 March 2008 oil contracts on the New York Mercantile Exchange reached an all-time high of $103.95 a barrel. That exceeded by nineteen cents the inflation-adjusted record set in April 1980. And that was four times higher than the average price of just a few years earlier. Prices showed no sign of reversing course. As I looked ahead as oil minister, I felt that we were in uncharted territory.

In many ways Saudi Arabia's spending spree was making up for lost time. The crash in oil prices in the late 1980s and again in the late 1990s had led to chronic under-investment in our infrastructure as our population continued to grow. At the same time we were hoping to avoid the undisciplined spending of the late 1970s that followed spiking oil prices. This time we were focusing on investing in our nation's future. As I told *The New York Times* in January 2008, 'This strategy includes expanding the base of the Saudi economy, diversifying national income sources, attracting international investments and reaping the direct and indirect benefits that these types of projects will accrue to the Saudi citizen.'

Accelerating global demand for crude oil accounted for some of the price increase we experienced during 2007, but demand was flattening out by early 2008. Yet prices continued to climb. A series of isolated events around the world had the combined effect of tightening supplies and building a 'risk premium' into the price of oil.

In February 2008 Venezuela was locked in a legal dispute over nationalizing ExxonMobil's assets in the country, and cut off sales to the giant oil company. A few months later Mexico reported that oil exports were off sharply due to declining production in its huge Cantarell oilfield. In March Iraq's production fell by about 300,000 barrels per day after two export oil pipelines were blown up. ExxonMobil was hit again in April, this time in Nigeria, where union workers went out on strike and the company lost production of 780,000 barrels a day. The total daily reduction in Nigerian output doubled to about 1.6 million barrels by June following militant attacks and sabotage at various oil facilities owned by different oil companies. In the North Sea, Scottish oil workers walked off the job in late April, closing the North Forties pipeline that carried about half of the United Kingdom's North Sea oil production.

We in Saudi Arabia realized that we were facing a crisis as oil prices surged higher. We have consistently argued for stable oil prices that reflect a balance between the costs of maintaining and developing adequate supplies and demand driven by economic growth worldwide. As the weeks passed in the spring of 2008 we felt strongly that oil prices, despite the events listed above, were not in line with the reality of the market. We couldn't find additional buyers for our oil during this period, suggesting the global economy was weaker than many thought. Yet crude oil prices topped $120 a barrel, and then $130, and were closing in on $140. We argued that speculative buying on the futures markets was helping drive prices higher.

'It was a stressful time,' US energy secretary Sam Bodman said. 'Prices were rising and the White House would call and ask what would happen if we did this or that? I tried to explain that these things take time.'

As a result of higher oil prices, in some cities Americans were paying nearly $4 a gallon at the pumps. It didn't help that it was once again a presidential election year. Republicans were using high oil prices as a reason to push for an expansion of exploratory oil drilling. 'Drill, baby, drill!' was being chanted at John McCain campaign rallies. Democratic candidates Hillary Clinton and Barack Obama saw high prices as vindicating the peak oil hypothesis and underscoring the need to develop alternative energy sources.

President Bush and Vice-President Cheney visited the Kingdom in mid-January 2008 as part of a tour of the Middle East. While regional and international security issues were their major concern, energy prices were also near the top of their agenda when they visited us. As President Bush told a group of Saudi entrepreneurs on 15 January:

> I talked to the ambassador, and will again talk to His Majesty tonight about the fact that oil prices are very high, which is tough on our economy, and that I would hope, as OPEC considers different production levels, that they understand that if their — one of their biggest consumers' economy suffers, it will mean less purchases, less oil and gas sold.

I met with the president and vice-president during their brief time in Riyadh. I knew that Dick Cheney understood the oil markets, so I addressed my comments mostly to the president. I walked through the fact that there was no oil shortage, pointing out that the major oil companies, including ExxonMobil, weren't buying our oil. Why would we pump more oil if our biggest customers weren't buying the oil we were already putting on the market?

The president was very attentive and nodded throughout my talk. When I was done he turned to the vice-president and said, 'Dick, remind me when we meet in Sharm el Sheikh with the Egyptians to bring up these points.' Unfortunately, the president's remarks from his meeting the next day in Egypt with President Hosni Mubarak didn't reflect any discussion about the oil market. At least we tried.

Some Europeans didn't display a great understanding of how oil markets worked during this crisis period, either. I remember Gordon Brown, the British prime minister, asking me to pump more oil to bring the price down. I asked him if he was willing to buy it and he said no. I asked if British oil companies would buy it. Again, no. Eventually, I had to explain to him exactly how the oil market works.

I asked Aramco CEO Jum'ah to canvass our customers to see whether they wanted any more crude oil. He did. They didn't. I put it directly to Christophe de Margerie, then CEO of France's Total S.A. I told him, 'You want more oil? Have it. But you cannot swallow it.' He agreed they were not prepared to step up as buyers.

We in Saudi Arabia realized that we would have to be the ones to break the oil market's speculative fever. King Abdullah called for an emergency meeting of both oil-producing and oil-consuming nations in June 2008 in Jeddah. OPEC has long represented oil producers, and major oil-consuming countries formed the Paris-based International Energy Agency, IEA, in response to the 1973–1974 oil embargo. But the two groups rarely communicated effectively. Close coordination among oil producers and consumers in the wake of Saddam Hussein's invasion of Kuwait in 1990 led to the creation of the International Energy Forum, IEF, the following year as a vehicle for continuing producer–consumer dialogue.

Fatih Birol, then chief economist for the IEA, understood what was at stake. 'The Jeddah meeting was crucial. High prices were having significant negative implications for the global economy; however, Saudi Arabia was the only country feeling responsible for taking care of global oil markets.'

The Jeddah meeting was held on 22 June and attended by representatives from a total of thirty-six countries and the major international oil companies. People from OPEC, the IEA and IEF were also in attendance. As much as the king understood our position that there was an adequate supply of oil to meet current demand, he wanted our actions to reinforce our commitment to the long-term stability of oil prices. As a result, we announced that we were increasing our daily output of crude oil by 200,000 barrels a day to 9.7 million barrels. That was our highest level of production since 1981.

The head of the IEA at the time, Maria Van der Hoeven, later said, 'The Jeddah meeting was symbolic. Not all symbolic meetings are important – this one was.' Noé Van Hulst, then secretary general of the IEF, agreed: 'Saudi Arabia made a unilateral announcement to increase production, and stepped up investment to increase production capacity. That was extremely important.'

We were understandably disappointed that the meeting and our announcement didn't have an immediate effect on oil prices. Actually, they shot higher, reaching a peak of $147.02 on 11 July as Iranian missile tests raised geopolitical concerns. Then, as often happens in commodity markets, sentiment and prices turned quickly. Crude oil prices tumbled for the rest of the summer, with a few brief price spikes interrupting the collapse.

As a history of the IEF written a few years later noted, Saudi Arabia's actions 'played a key role in convincing the market to price in a more elastic supply curve. Some of the thrust behind rising prices had come from a perception that key producers were unwilling, or even unable, to increase production to limit oil price rises. That position became untenable when a key producer announced, and then delivered, significant increases in output.'

By August 2008 crude oil prices were back under $120, and they dropped to test the $100 mark just as OPEC held a meeting in Vienna in the second week of September. We were concerned that prices needed to continue to decline to rekindle demand and keep the global economy from tipping into recession. OPEC nevertheless voted to cut production by 500,000 barrels a day. We agreed to the cuts, but at the same time assured our major customers that as much oil as they needed would be available.

When Lehman Brothers declared bankruptcy on 15 September the world changed overnight. The global financial crisis that followed turned a retreat in oil prices into a rout. OPEC responded by cutting crude oil output by an additional 1.5 million barrels in October, but the price kept crashing. Crude oil closed below $60 a barrel in early

November, shortly after Barack Obama was elected president of the United States. By the time OPEC met again in the Algerian coastal resort of Oran in mid-December, crude oil was trading at $40 a barrel. That was more than 70 per cent below its July peak.

I was determined, going into the Oran meeting, that we had to make a dramatic cut in production, and make it stick. King Abdullah had already given a widely quoted newspaper interview a few weeks earlier in which he said that the $75 range was a fair price for oil that would serve the needs of both producers and consumers. Those of us in oil-producing countries were facing a startling new reality as 2008 neared its end. As a result of the global financial crisis, crude oil consumption worldwide was set to decline for the first time in twenty-five years.

Just like during the crisis of 1998–1999, we needed non-OPEC producers to cut production in step with us to have as dramatic an impact on prices as possible. At Oran I met privately with Russia's Igor Sechin, a deputy prime minister and chairman of the state-owned Rosneft oil company. He agreed with me that we would both take off about 300,000 barrels a day in production. We shook hands, and he said he was going to announce Russia's cut in production to the press.

As the Bloomberg news service would later report: 'Mr Sechin said Russia had reduced exports by 350,000 barrels a day the previous month and was prepared to cut an additional 320,000 if prices failed to rise. The reductions never took place, and two months later, the OPEC secretary general, Abdalla el-Badri, said he was "very disappointed".'

The Russians didn't follow through on their promises. Not only would they fail to make their agreed-to cuts in late

2008. In March 2009, while Sechin would claim to be 'decreasing supplies', according to Bloomberg, another Rosneft official, Peter O'Brien, would confirm that they were on target to raise their crude oil production by 2 per cent compared to 2008.

Whether the Russians were with us or not, I wanted the December 2008 OPEC meeting to have as big an impact as possible on oil prices. We announced at the conclusion of the Oran meeting that we were cutting our production by 2.2 million barrels a day – the largest single production cut in the history of OPEC. That made a total of 4.2 million barrels a day taken off the world market in three months. It took a few weeks for the latest cuts to have their full impact on the market, which traded into the mid-to-low $30s a barrel in the meantime.

I am convinced we played an important role in creating a floor for crude oil prices going forward. To ensure that we were having an impact on the market, in January 2009 we reduced Saudi Arabia's output by another 300,000 barrels a day to about 7.7 million. That was a full 2 million barrels a day less than our peak output in mid-2008.

I did my best to remain calm as the price of oil crashed. I knew the $147 price at the top of the market was not real, and I knew $32 for a barrel of oil at the bottom was also unrealistic. Our goal was to remain focused on the business in front of us.

Oil prices quickly rebounded to trade in the $40–50 a barrel range in early 2009, and were back to $60 by June and headed higher. But we realized that even though the worst was behind us, we didn't have much to cheer about as oil producers. Demand was so fragile that as the year progressed we decided not to increase production. And, of course, we were under pressure from the US and other major oil-consuming countries not to take any steps that might damage the economic recovery that was kicking in around the world, country by country. In 2009, for the second year in a row, global oil demand declined.

By the fourth quarter of that year oil prices were back close to the $75 a barrel price King Abdullah had targeted a year earlier. At the time I was quoted as describing this as the 'price that marginal producers need to maintain investments sufficient to provide adequate supplies for future consumption needs'. I felt increasingly confident that we, and the rest of the world, had come out of the worst of the downturn.

In December 2011, British think-tank Chatham House published a report that underscored what many of us in the government already considered a concern. It stated:

> The world's largest exporter of oil is consuming so much energy at home that its ability to play a stabilizing role in world oil markets is at stake. Saudi Arabia's demand for its own oil and gas is growing at around 7 per cent per year. At this rate of growth, national consumption will have doubled in a decade. On a 'business as usual' projection, this would jeopardize the country's ability to export to global markets. Given its dependence on oil export revenues, the inability to expand exports would have a dramatic effect on the economy and the government's ability to spend on domestic welfare and services.

Chatham House estimated that Saudi Arabia consumes about one-quarter of the oil it produces, and that could otherwise be sold to generate export revenues. And we sell the oil to our electricity industry and other utilities for little more than the cost of production. Inefficient air-conditioning units alone account for 65 per cent of our energy use. As then IEA chief economist Fatih Birol said, 'Using oil for electricity doesn't make sense economically when we could be using natural gas. It's like using Chanel perfume to fill your car.'

If that rate of growth of domestic consumption continued unchecked – per capita energy consumption in Saudi Arabia is about twice the world average – we could actually become a net importer of oil by 2038, Chatham House concluded. None of us in government thought our consumption would continue at that rate for so many years into the future. But it was an overdue wakeup call for our society.

The following May our government unveiled an ambitious long-term plan to diversify our energy supplies. We committed billions to alternative energy sources, led by solar power. The goal originally was to have nearly one-third of the country's projected electricity needs, or 41GW, produced by solar power by the year 2032. Wind and geothermal energy would also be integrated into our alternative energy plan and contribute another 21GW. Plans also called for nuclear power to provide 14GW of power in addition to these other renewable sources.

We pushed the target date back to 2040 for a host of reasons, including the need to continue sorting through specific technologies to pursue. We also learned from the experience of Germany and Spain, where overly generous government subsidies in recent years sparked a runaway boom in solar panel installations. But the commitment to alternative energy, solar in particular, remains as strong as ever.

Why should the country sitting on the world's largest proven crude oil reserves make a long-term investment in solar power and other renewables? If you look at maps that show what portions of the earth receive the most intense solar radiation, Saudi Arabia, the north-western portion of the country in particular, ranks right up there with the Sahara Desert. That means that we have tremendous oil reserves to tap underground and we have tremendous solar reserves to tap above ground.

I am committed to solar. I want us to get big in solar, I think that's the future. I believe in science, I believe in technology. And Saudi Arabia is situated right in the solar sweet spot. We have the acreage, we have the silica and we have the sun. We could become a global power in solar.

I have challenged every researcher in this area to succeed. Things are moving very fast in this field. The efficiency of solar panels has risen tremendously in recent years and that is driving down costs, in some cases by as much as 80 per cent. Saudi Aramco has already signed agreements with Saudi Electric Company to produce 300MW of solar power in remote areas of the country to reduce its reliance on diesel fuel to generate power for its facilities.

Saudi Aramco is not acting alone. Saudi solar company ACWA Power ranks among the world's most competitive with its recent pioneering projects in Dubai, Morocco and South Africa.

Prince Turki bin Saud bin Mohammad Al-Saud is the head of the Riyadh-based national research and development agency King Abdulaziz City for Science and Technology, KACST. One of our leading solar proponents, he told the *Atlantic* magazine in mid-2015, 'We have a clear interest in solar energy. And it will soon be expanding exponentially in the Kingdom.'

I don't want us simply to be contracting with solar panel

makers around the world and then have our utilities or Saudi Aramco install them. That's easy. I, Prince Turki and others, including the leaders of the King Abdullah City for Atomic and Renewable Energy, the agency overseeing renewable energy regulation, want us to build our own solar industry. From the silica sand up.

We were experimenting with solar energy at a small site north of Riyadh as far back as 1979 in a joint project with the United States. That was the same year President Jimmy Carter put solar panels on the White House. That facility, like the panels on the White House roof, fell out of favour during the 1980s and 1990s as we and the rest of the world concentrated on developing our fossil fuel resources.

Now we are planning for our eventual entrance into the production of solar panels and equipment on an industrial scale. Decades ago I told Aramco engineers that it didn't make sense to import sand from Wyoming for its filtering properties when we had a country covered with the stuff. So they went out and found a solution to our problem using our own sand. We are taking the same long-term attitude toward solar panels, most of which are based on silica – which we have in abundance.

The thought process driving our renewable efforts is straightforward. If we are going to invest so much in renewable energy technology, we want to be sure to capture the knowledge development, not just pay others for their finished products. We want to get as much as we can out of the entire industrial value chain. That in turn will drive further industrialization and job creation across our country. Our universities, led by KAUST and its Solar & Photovoltaics Engineering Research Center, are coordinating with the government and private sector solar companies to make this goal an eventual reality.

Work on the site north of Riyadh, in Al-Uyaynah, revived in 2010. King Abdulaziz City for Science and Technology built an experimental solar panel assembly line there. The following year they quadrupled capacity. Plans on the drawing board call for the Kingdom to build another solar cell factory that could rival the largest such plants that exist outside China. Due to low labour costs and government subsidies, most of the world's solar cell manufacturing capacity has been developed in China over the past decade. We still have many obstacles to overcome, but I am hopeful that eventually we will rank among the world's most efficient manufacturers of solar panels.

Our embrace of solar will not change our society overnight. That said, I take particular pleasure in the fact that our private sector has taken the lead in solar and renewable energy in general as government agencies sort out oversight and regulatory issues. This is exactly the kind of societal transformation we hope will occur as we open up new business opportunities and career paths for our people, men and, increasingly, women alike.

From producing oil to developing solar resources, we are committed to meeting or exceeding environmental benchmarks that apply to all of our industrial sectors. And let's be clear: we believe in the truth of climate change, full stop. But the problem is not fossil fuels themselves. The problem is the harmful emissions we get from burning coal, oil and gas. The answer is not to leave the world's greatest, most plentiful and most economic energy resource in the ground.

Our particular focus is on carbon capture and storage,

CCS. Saudi Aramco recently launched the Middle East's largest CO_2-enhanced oil recovery research demonstration project. We are collecting 800,000 tons a year of mainly CO_2 from our gas plant in Hawiyah, and transferring it via pipeline to our facilities at our Uthmaniyah field. There we are injecting the gas to maintain pressures in our crude oil reservoir.

In some ways we were going back to the future with this project. Early on we injected natural gas, methane, not waste gas like CO_2, in a few fields to maintain pressure before embracing treated seawater injection in the 1970s, and using the natural gas to spur economic growth. This CCS project is still in its early stages but is already showing promising results.

So from 2008, my life was as busy as ever, handling high prices, economic diversification and increasingly vital climate issues. And I haven't even touched on the Arab Spring, which presented all sorts of additional challenges to the leaders of countries in the region.

But if I thought I was about to enter a period of calm reflection, I was sorely mistaken.

19. The Caravan Rolls On – 2014

People have extracted oil from the ground since prehistoric times. It has been used for construction, heating and lighting for thousands of years. Yet it was really the nineteenth and twentieth centuries that saw the dramatic impact of the modern petroleum industry, driven in part by the invention of the internal combustion engine, and then by the switch from coal to oil in terms of mass transportation. Since then, oil – and the increasingly valuable array of products that can be derived from it – has become a vital part of all modern economies. In many ways, fossil fuels helped build the successful Western economies we see today. And they will play a vital role in the future growth of developing nations. And that makes oil valuable.

If you have read up to this point in the book, it must be clear by now that efforts to control and manage the oil price over the decades have been mixed at best. Oil is a commodity. Demand rises and falls. The price rises and falls. It was ever thus.

Yet, by 2014, there was a new dimension to the global oil market and it came in the form of something called shale oil.

Although viewed as a recent phenomenon, Europeans were documenting research on shale oil in the Middle Ages. Commercial production of such oil, which is tightly bound in very dense rock compared to the relatively porous rock formations where conventional oil and gas are found, was under way in France by the 1830s, and quickly spread across much of Europe, and America and Canada as well by the mid-nineteenth century. But over time cheaper whale oil, and then conventional crude oil, shut down most of the more costly shale oil production around the world.

From 2009 onward, though, with the oil price relatively stable around the $100 mark, this once uneconomic source of energy became appealing. And oil producers large and small – particularly in the United States – piled in. The consequences would soon be felt by the world.

We were aware of the rise of shale and the development of other sources of 'tight' oil and were not worried. New sources of oil and gas will be required in the coming decades to meet the world's growing energy needs. The natural decline of existing fields, and increasing energy use by the expanding middle classes across much of the developing world in Asia, Africa and Latin America, mean that more oil and gas will be needed in the decades ahead. Renewable energy sources, including those provided by Saudi companies, will be able to meet some of this demand, but by no means all.

It became clear by mid-2014 that the addition of this high-priced crude oil supply was outpacing demand. Sure enough, market forces kicked in and started pulling prices lower.

There was widespread expectation in oil and financial capitals around the world that Saudi Arabia would once again cut production, and revenues, to support oil prices and long-term demand for our exports. Isn't that what we had done in the 1980s and 1990s? Well, yes we did, but we suffered for it. By 2014, we'd learned our lesson. This time, things would be different.

Like many observers, OPEC was slow to appreciate the speed with which the shale oil industry in the US would develop. The initial shale boom was limited mainly to gas production, after all. Oil came a few years later, spurred by the expansion of shale oil drilling in Texas in addition to North Dakota's Bakken basin. In Midland, Texas, it looked like a rerun of the late 1970s oil boom as workers by the thousand flocked to find their fortunes, and the cost of everything from housing to drilling rigs was rocketing out of sight.

OPEC's 2011 *World Oil Outlook* said that 'shale oil should not be viewed as anything other than a source of marginal additions to crude oil supply'. By 2012, the story was different and OPEC acknowledged that 'shale oil represents a large change to the supply picture'. Indeed, thanks mainly to shale oil, US oil production increased by 850,000 barrels per day in 2012, 950,000 barrels in 2013, and a stunning 1.2 million barrels in 2014, according to the US Energy Information Administration. PricewaterhouseCoopers estimated that global shale oil production could reach 14 million barrels a day by 2035.

The additional shale oil drove US oil production to nearly 9 million barrels a day by year end 2014, 80 per cent more than it was producing on the eve of the 2008 financial crisis. That was roughly in line with Saudi Arabia's production level. When was the last time US production hit 9 million barrels a day? In 1986, the year crude oil prices crashed.

Initially, this new shale oil didn't have much impact on stubbornly high global oil prices. That's in part a result of the chaos and civil war that followed the brief Arab Spring among certain key oil-producing nations, particularly Libya and Iraq. Libya's oil production, for instance, went from a pre-civil war level of about 1.8 million barrels per day, to as low as 250,000 barrels per day in late 2013 and early 2014. So, for a time, the increase in shale was making up for the lost production in Libya.

One of the reasons that we hadn't been too worried about shale oil production was projections of robust demand growth, especially from Asia. By early 2014, however, it became clear that demand for crude oil was not picking up as expected. Global consumption of crude oil had fluctuated modestly, but wasn't making any sustained moves above the 90–92 million barrels per day level. To the surprise of many economists and investors, China's economic growth was proving much more modest than had been predicted. And America's anaemic 1–2 per cent growth looked strong only in comparison to the even slower rates of growth, if not actually economic contraction, experienced across Europe.

Things were coming to a head.

As 2013 came to an end, my advisers at the Ministry of Petroleum were offering a gloomy prognosis of the year ahead. We kept a close watch on supply and demand trends going forward.

Our concerns about rising supply outweighing global demand weren't immediately shared by the rest of the market. In fact, as we neared the 11 June 2014 OPEC meeting, market sources were predicting that we would now need to increase our output to meet what they saw as stronger than expected demand from the US and China, and the failure of Iraq and Libya to increase production. Prices peaked barely a week after the OPEC meeting at just shy of $116 a barrel for Brent crude.

It proved to be a high-water mark.

As the weeks passed, prices slumped lower. The question was, what would the future bring? I was acutely aware that in such situations all eyes turned toward me, the Saudi oil minister. Two decades in the job and two more as an officer of Saudi Aramco had taught me the value of taking bold, decisive action. But this time, not on our own.

We were open to working with other oil producers to coordinate a cut in production, as we had in years past. But any group action had to include major non-OPEC producers. And given our experience in the late 1990s and again in 2009, with Russia in particular, I wasn't optimistic that was going to happen.

And I wasn't going to be the one to make the first move. I also realized that it would take some time for our position to sink in with OPEC and other producers, and for them to take us seriously.

Meantime, I watched crude oil prices work their way lower, putting pressure on higher-priced, inefficient production. By the second week of September, Brent crude was trading below $98, and West Texas Intermediate was hovering just above $90. We attended a Gulf Cooperation Council meeting in Kuwait on 10 September. The question on everyone's mind was, how low can it go? I told reporters that it was normal for prices to fluctuate, and that I 'wasn't worried' about prices. I was criticized for saying that by some Saudi media outlets. They wanted to know, if it wasn't the oil minister's job to worry about the price of oil, whose job was it?

By mid-October Brent crude had dropped another $10 a barrel and showed no signs of stopping. Venezuela, among other producers, was facing mounting fiscal woes as the price of oil continued to slide. Rafael Ramírez, Venezuela's foreign minister and former oil minister, called for an emergency meeting of OPEC prior to our next scheduled meeting on 27 November to try and set a floor under prices. There wasn't much support for the idea within OPEC.

I was much more interested in a private call I received, asking me to meet with Ramírez discreetly on the sidelines of an international climate change policy forum in the first week in November. That meeting was to be held at the previously expropriated Hilton Hotel on Venezuela's Caribbean resort of Margarita Island. The meeting was a gathering of government ministers and leaders of civil groups in advance of the United Nations Conference of Parties meeting (COP20), scheduled for the following month in Lima.

Saudi Arabia and Venezuela had butted heads during the late 1990s over what we saw as their unwillingness to stick to quotas or disclose accurate production figures, but on a personal level I had a great deal of respect for Minister Ramírez and his understanding of the markets, especially compared to some of his predecessors.

I met Minister Ramírez in the lobby of the hotel and we went to the bank of elevators that would take us up to his suite for the meeting. The farcical nature of our efforts to reach his suite on the top floor was perhaps an omen of what was ahead of us. The lift stopped at the first four floors then promptly returned us to the lobby. The minister was embarrassed but we all started laughing and we finally made it to his room.

Having survived the elevator ride we were rewarded with a picture-postcard view of a moon-drenched Caribbean harbour as we sat down in our shirtsleeves on a warm autumn night and got to work. After introductions by Minister Ramírez I spoke first. Throughout my career I have been complimented for being a good listener. Indeed, I have found that there is a lot you can learn by listening carefully to what people are saying, and what they aren't, that will strengthen your own arguments or decision making rather than jumping in and trying to direct the conversation from the start.

This time, however, I needed to make myself as clear as possible. The stakes were too high. Maybe it is the patience, and perhaps even wisdom, conferred by age, but I have come to realize that when you are speaking for a nation and its policy, you can never say something just once. Or twice. Messages have to be repeated constantly to change the status quo.

I summarized the situation we were in with mounting supplies coming from high-cost sources and the weaker than expected demand. He nodded; that was their reading of the market as well. 'Now, we the OPEC members are called on to cut production,' I said. 'I don't think it's fair for us to defend prices just for the sake of defending prices. It will come at the expense of our market share.' I added, 'If we want to cut back then it has to be in collaboration with other non-OPEC producers who need to come to the table.' The next move was up to Venezuela.

Ramírez saw his opening. 'Prices are really important to us in Venezuela,' he said. 'I think we can do something about talking to other countries.' I had the feeling his president had wanted him to take this approach, and he was relieved that I was in agreement. We discussed the leading non-OPEC oil producers: Russia, Mexico, Kazakhstan and Norway. Since US crude oil is produced by independent companies, and the US has strict anti-trust laws, there was zero chance of a conversation, let alone agreement, with the Americans.

One of my team members later asked me how I rated the chance of Ramírez succeeding in his mission to bring non-OPEC members to the bargaining table and get them to cut production. I held up my right hand and made the sign for zero.

After the climate policy meeting concluded I flew to Mexico for an International Energy Forum conference on natural gas in Acapulco. There I met the Mexican energy minister, Pedro Joaquín Coldwell. As it turned out, I was following in Ramírez's footsteps. Minister Coldwell told me what he told the Venezuelan: Mexico was sympathetic to the need for a coordinated price cut. He also reminded me of how closely our countries had worked together in the late 1990s and again in 2009 to take production off the market. The problem now was that Mexico was in the process of taking steps to attract much-needed foreign investment to modernize its oil production in key fields. It couldn't very well do that and at the same time say it was cutting back production in the fields whose output was projected to increase to justify the added investment. I understood.

I took the opportunity to restate our position during a speech I delivered on 12 November. I said we wanted to work with 'other producers to ensure price stability for the interest of producers, consumers and the industry at large. Talk of a price war is a sign of misunderstanding, deliberate or otherwise, and has no basis in reality.' Some commentators focused on slight changes we were making in our oil pricing formula as evidence that we had launched a price war. Nonsense, I told them. 'Saudi Aramco prices oil according to sound marketing procedures, no more and no less. These take into account a host of scientific and practical factors, including the state of the market,' I said.

I thought I was being pretty straightforward. Many observers understood that I was reiterating our position.

Others were frustrated that I wasn't being more proactive in the face of oil prices that were down roughly 30 per cent from their mid-year highs. One commentator said I was being 'very Greenspan-like' in my 'intentional lack of clarity'. You can't win, sometimes.

The next major event on my calendar was the November OPEC meeting in Vienna. And there was another elevator absurdity. A couple of days ahead of the official OPEC meeting, we agreed to meet with representatives from Venezuela and with two non-OPEC members, Russia and Mexico. If there was going to be a coordinated global response, it was going to happen here.

The meeting was held at the Park Hyatt Hotel, where the Russian energy minister and his associates were staying. Prior to meeting with us in Vienna, Ramírez had flown to Moscow to meet the Russians separately to promote the idea of coordinated price cuts. His reception from the Russians was about as chilly as the late November Moscow weather.

To avoid attracting attention from the media, our Saudi team travelled in two cars to the Park Hyatt and entered through a rear door. It turned out to be the loading bay for the hotel kitchen, which we walked through on our way to the elevator that would take us to the upper floors. The lift was tiny, with just enough room for two people, so we went in two shifts.

Inside the suite, seated on one of two large sofas arranged in a semi-circle, were Igor Sechin, the Russian deputy prime minister and head of the giant, state-owned oil company Rosneft, and Alexander Novak, the Russian energy minister. On the other sofa was Minister Ramírez. We exchanged small talk as we waited for the Mexican delegation to arrive.

When Minister Coldwell joined us we moved into another room, where we sat around a table with our staffs behind us. As the meeting's organizer, Ramírez welcomed us all. He then looked to me across the table and said, 'Your Excellency, Minister Al-Naimi, would you like to start the discussion?' Unlike during my meeting on Margarita Island, I did not. I had made my position quite clear in recent weeks. I wanted to let the others show their hands. 'Let's hear from our non-OPEC colleagues,' I said, gesturing to Minister Coldwell.

The Mexican repeated what he had told me in Acapulco. He added some technical details about problems with the condition of some of their fields, but he emphasized that the need to attract foreign investment left them with little choice but to maintain their production levels. I nodded that I understood.

We all turned to the Russians. Igor Sechin spoke first, followed by Minister Novak. They talked about how their production had levelled off in recent years. They also weighed in with a list of technical problems they had been having. Their staff handed out a presentation that the rest of us flipped through. The bottom line was that they were not in a position to make any cut in production.

All eyes turned to me. Maybe they were hoping that their positions would put added pressure on me to conclude that Saudi Arabia would once again have to swoop in and make a dramatic reduction in output. A move from which they would benefit without having to share the pain of lost revenue. Not this time.

I gathered my papers. 'It looks like nobody can cut, so I think the meeting is over,' I said, standing up to shake hands and leave. My own team was clearly as unprepared for my response as the other ministers. I could hear them hurriedly collecting their things behind me. Coldwell, Novak and Sechin were doing their best to conceal their sense of shock that I wasn't interested in negotiating. Ramírez didn't look happy. We all shook hands and our team left the suite by the back elevator.

Ramírez spoke to the press later that day. He said that we had held a meeting, but no agreement was reached. He remained optimistic that some action would be taken at the official OPEC session. The market wasn't so sure. Oil prices fell several dollars a barrel after his press conference.

Sechin also addressed the press. In his written release he said, 'One should clearly differentiate the specific nature of the oil industry in the majority of OPEC states and Russia. Given the climatic, logistical and technological factors, Russia cannot immediately cut production, but is capable of taking structured measures with mid-term and long-term implications.' In his question-and-answer session, he said that the recent price slump was 'not critical' for the Russian economy, despite comments to the contrary from ministers in Moscow, and that Russia was not prepared to cut 'one barrel of oil'.

Separately, I met with the Iranian oil minister Bijan Zanganeh the day before the full OPEC meeting. This was much more of a meeting to update him on our position. Broadly, he agreed with me. I met with the other Gulf state members of OPEC that day as well. I told reporters that I expected the oil market to 'stabilize itself eventually'.

As late as the morning of the OPEC session some were still predicting that we would announce a major cut in production without waiting for non-OPEC coordination. Ramírez of Venezuela told reporters before the meeting that production cuts of as much as 2 million barrels a day were necessary to restore higher prices. He was not willing to let go of the memory of $100 oil. Algeria was also hoping for cuts.

Once we were inside the OPEC meeting hall events unfolded much as I had expected. Ministers aired their positions, and many expressed a need for OPEC to cut production. I asked each in turn if his country was willing to cut production. None was.

After lunch I restated our position that if we, Saudi Arabia or OPEC as a whole, cut production without the participation of major non-OPEC members, we would be sacrificing revenues as well as market share. For the long-term interests of us all it was vital that we let the market find its equilibrium between supply and demand. Too many new producers had entered the oil market for Saudi Arabia to play the role of swing producer to the world. We voted and agreed to maintain our production target.

Even though I had made our position clear several times, and the fact that we had been unable to reach agreement in our meeting two days earlier with Mexico and Russia, the oil and currency markets reacted as if this outcome could not have been predicted. Brent crude oil futures plunged 6.7 per cent to $72.58 a barrel. The Russian rouble hit a record low against the euro and a near record low versus the US dollar.

Despite the failure of OPEC and non-OPEC producers to reach an accord in late 2014, and the sharp drop in oil prices that followed, I remain an optimist. We are in a temporary state during which the world's most important commodity is being repriced for the future. New supplies will find new demand at the right price.

The bottom line is this: through periods of high prices or low, Saudi Arabia will remain the most trusted and reliable supplier of energy to the world.

Epilogue

I chose to end the account of my career in November 2014 for various reasons, not least because we had to end it somewhere and because the historic decision reached at OPEC in Vienna that month seemed as good a place as any. That said, just ahead of this memoir being finalized and printed in 2016, my circumstances changed. King Salman succeeded his brother King Abdullah in 2015 and, as is customary, after a certain period he also reorganized his government. As part of the sweeping reorganization, and after twenty-one years as minister, I was replaced by the former CEO of Saudi Aramco, Khalid Al-Falih. I wish Khalid all the best. He is an exceptionally talented individual. King Salman bestowed upon me the honour of adviser to the Royal Court.

Now seems an opportune time to offer a final reflection on my career and the changes in the oil industry during my lifetime. If you have finished reading this book, you will know by now that I joined Aramco as an office boy in 1947. It was a very different world and the company, and the Saudi nation, have come a long way since then. From the grinding poverty of the past, the Kingdom of Saudi Arabia is now a member of the G20. Life expectancy, educational standards, healthcare and infrastructure are unrecognizable compared to the situation I knew as a boy. It's been an amazing time – and the journey continues.

During my seven decades working in the oil and gas

industry, I've seen oil at under $2 a barrel and at $147 a barrel, and much volatility in between. I've witnessed gluts and scarcity, seen multiple booms and busts, and I've even survived the peak oil doom mongerers! These experiences taught me that this business and this commodity, like all commodities, is inevitably cyclical. While I always strived to keep focused on the long term, the fact remains that the short term is here to stay. Demand rises and falls. Supply rises and falls. Prices rise and fall.

When I became oil minister in 1995, the average oil price for the year was around $16 to $17 a barrel, which was considered reasonable by producers and consumers alike. As a result of various factors, including the Asian financial crash, the price subsequently collapsed, but through dogged determination and collaborative diplomacy, OPEC and non-OPEC producers worked together and it recovered. In fact, in the following years, we witnessed an incredible rise in the oil price, a result of strong economic growth across much of the developed and developing worlds.

When oil was up to around $100 a barrel, the price also seemed reasonable, for suppliers and consumers. But it was very high. That price unleashed a wave of investment around the world into what had previously been uneconomic oilfields. This went from the Arctic, to Canadian oil sands, to Venezuela's Orinoco tar sands, to deep-water frontiers. It also led to the development of shale-oil resources in some parts of the US. This resulted in robust global growth of conventional and unconventional oil supplies. And the price, inevitably, started to fall.

As I noted back in November 2014 at the OPEC meeting, there was a clamour by many for the group to cut its production to arrest the fall. But the oil market is much bigger than just OPEC. We tried hard to bring everyone together, OPEC and non-OPEC, to seek consensus. But there was no appetite for sharing the burden. So we left it to the market as the most efficient way to rebalance supply and demand. It was – it is – a simple case of letting the market work. To the casual observer this sounds reasonable, but it was a remarkable change of approach from OPEC. I will let history be the judge as to the success of our market-based policy.

The fact is that demand for oil was, and remains, strong. You can argue over small percentage falls or rises, but the bottom line is that the world demands, and gets, more than 90 million barrels a day of oil. Long term this will increase, so I have no concerns about demand.

While the parallels with experiences in past cycles can be instructive, every era is different, and 2014 onwards is not the 1980s. Oil markets are more sophisticated and complex. There are a lot of new players and financial instruments that simply didn't exist thirty-five years ago. Each oil market cycle comes with some uncharted territory. Even as the global oil market has become more efficient and dynamic over the past several decades, it continues to offer up surprises. Some are welcome, some are not. Volatility and overshooting of prices – both at the top and at the bottom of the market – remain key challenges for the future.

If and when the market goes awry, governments and industry need to find ways to work together to help it rebalance. We should allow markets to work, but we must also remain vigilant. We must seek to understand changing market dynamics better, and be ready to act when market failures and extreme volatility occur.

More broadly, on the subject of the oil industry going forward, I firmly believe that oil is here to stay for the foreseeable future. It may not surprise you to read that I believe fossil fuels are a good thing. They will continue to play a vital part in the overall energy mix, whether we like it or not, but don't misunderstand me. I am a big supporter of renewable energy, particularly wind and solar. For Saudi Arabia, solar will be a great source of energy for future generations. But I believe a mix of sources is the best and most secure way forward.

In my opinion, the problem is not fossil fuels themselves, but the harmful emissions we get from burning coal, oil and gas. The answer is not to leave the world's greatest, most plentiful and economic energy resources in the ground. I believe the solution is to work on technology that minimizes and ultimately eradicates harmful emissions. Some don't accept this view, but I have faith in technology. Advances in carbon-capture technology, for instance, are already happening on a small scale. The world has made progress, but much more work and collaboration is required. It is inconceivable that renewables alone can supply the growing global population with the critical energy it needs in the decades ahead. And it is simply not fair for advanced nations to dictate what developing nations can or cannot do to meet their energy needs.

Saudi Arabia, the United States, Europe, Asia and virtually every nation and region of the world have been developed using fossil fuels. The products derived from oil are essential parts of our daily lives. Our industry should be celebrating that fact, and should get better at explaining the vital importance of these precious natural resources.

As for me, I am proud of the role I played working for and heading Saudi Aramco, and of the twenty-one years I spent as oil minister. But all good things come to an end. I have no regrets – and I'd do it all again. By any measure I've had a remarkable life and career. Despite entering my eighties, and with seven decades of working in the oil business behind me, I remain a citizen of the future and an optimist.

But as for what tomorrow will bring? As I've often told journalists over the years, if I knew what the future held I'd be in Las Vegas or Macau – whichever is closer.

Acknowledgements

There are far too many people to thank by name when it comes to my life and career, ranging from family and friends to educators, colleagues and business partners. Nothing is possible without teamwork, and I am fortunate to have been advised, assisted and supported by excellent teams throughout my career in Saudi Aramco and at the Ministry of Petroleum and Mineral Resources, and beyond. My achievement is, in great part, down to our achievements together.

I would like to pay special tribute to the Saudi royal family for placing their trust and support in me. My career has been dedicated to my country and helping to improve the lives of its citizens.

With regards to this book, I would like to thank the following individuals and organizations for making it happen, most notably Saudi Aramco.

Firstly, I would like to offer my great appreciation to all the interviewees and contributors, in alphabetical order: Fahad Abdulkareem, Khalid Abubshait, Khalid Abuleif, Mahdi Al-Adel, Nassir Ajmi, Harry Alter, Mike Ameen, Nabeel Amudi, John Duke Anthony, Andres Antonious, Marit Arnstad, Saud Ashgar, Abdullah Al-Attiya, Abdalla el-Badri, Ali Baluchi, Faysal Bassam, Vic Beghini, Fatih Birol, Sam and Diane Bodman, David Bosch, John Browne, Doug van Buskirk, Carl Calabro, Guy Caruso, Dick Cheney, Sherard Cowper-Coles, Abdullah Dabbagh, Jon Deakin, Nasser Dossary, Douhan Douhan, Kate Dourian, Khalid Al-Falih,

Abdulaziz Falih, Bassam Fattouh, Wyche Fowler Jr, Charles Freeman, Frank Fugate, Steve Gallogly, Alice Gast, Luis Giusti, Alan Greenspan, Bruce Guile, John Hamre, Charles Hendry, Suleiman Al-Herbish, Maria van der Hoeven, Samer and Abdelaziz Hokail, Noé Van Hulst, Joe Ingrassia, Arthur Irving, Saud Jaloud, Robert Jordan, Abdallah Jum'ah, Frank Jungers, Peter van de Kamp, Samira Kawar, Nat Kern, Chakib Khelil, Othman Khowaiter, Walid Khadduri, Shafiq Kombargi, Adrian Lajous, S. W. Lee, Tom Lippman, Laney Littlejohn, Rilwanu Lukman, Bob Luttrell, Robert Mabro, Nasser Mahasher, Kuroda Makoto, Claude Mandil, Christophe de Margerie, Ernesto Martens, Toyoda Masakazu, Stan McGinley, Lourdes Melgar, John Mitchell, Abdulla Mohanna, Majid Al-Moneef, Mark and Judy Moody-Stuart, Jack Moore, Yasser Mufti, Alan Munro, Rami Al-Naimi, Reem Al-Naimi, Mohammad K. Al-Naimi, Nadhmi Al-Nasr, Bob Norberg, Lou Noto, James Oberwetter, David O'Reilly, David Ottaway, William Patey, Garland Paulk, Tom Philips, Robert Priddle, Jim Ragland, Bill Ramsay, Richard Redd, Bill Richardson, Abdalla Ruwaii, Muhammad Saggaf, Jawad Sakka, Ahmed Saleh, Hamad Sayari, James R. Schlesinger, Sa'ad Shaifan, Adam Sieminski, James B. Smith, Paul Stevens, Ahmed Subaey, Randa Takieddine, Larry Tanner, Ian Taylor, Luis Téllez, Rex Tillerson, Esam Trabulsi, Dhaifallah Utaibi, Frank Verrastro, Dan Walters, Arne Walther, John Watson, Flo and Tom White, Molly Williamson, Dan Yergin, Hiromasa Yonekura.

I would like to thank Ali Al-Twairqi, for spearheading the project, and Jamie Oliver for the interviews, editorial input, and for coordinating and delivering the project. My thanks also to Siobhan Blood for her tireless transcribing. My sincere appreciation to Scott McMurray from The

History Factory for helping to capture my story. And special thanks also to Abdallah Jum'ah for perusing and improving the manuscript.

Thanks also, in Saudi Aramco, Dhahran: David Cherrington, Kyle Pakka, Karl Kleemeier, and Scott Baldalf for the interviews he conducted. Also Osama Kadi for help with photography. In Saudi Aramco US: Alan Dodd, Arthur Clark, Sarah Miller, Robert List and Jack Moore. Also Steve Sawyer and Evan Harrje for interviews. And Abdullah Tawlah for his efforts. In Riyadh: Dr Ibrahim Muhanna, Abdullah Furaih, Fahad Yousif, Nayif Asiri and Abdullah Dhwayan. Thanks also to Yousef Mohimeed. Saudi Aramco worldwide: Nabeel Amudi, Fahad Abdulkareem, Adeeb Aama, Nasser Mahasher. Also Hideki Koike in Japan and Narges Meraj in The Hague.

In the US, thanks to Dan Yergin, Molly Williamson, Frank Verrastro and Bhushan Bharee. Also in the US, Bruce Weindruch, Michael Leland, and Alden Hathaway (The History Factory). In Mexico, kind appreciation to Lourdes Melgar. In France, Dunia Chalabi. In Austria, James Griffin. Thanks to Abdulhadi Mansouri. In London, thanks to Paddy Haverson and Charlie Brotherstone.

Thanks also to the British Library Middle East Department, the Middle East Centre Archive, St Antony's College, Oxford, Georgetown University and Lehigh University (especially Dr Alice Gast).

Special thanks for their support, Garland Paulk, Steve Paulk, Curtis Swaringam.

Last, but not least, thanks to Penguin Random House, particularly Joel Rickett and Celia Long, for seeing the potential in this book and making it happen.

References

Note: The Al- prefix has been ignored when ordering Arabic names in both References and Index sections.

Books

Barger, Thomas C. *Out in the Blue: Letters from Arabia, 1937–1940*, Selwa Press, 2000

Bower, Tom. *The Squeeze: Oil, Money and Greed in the Twenty-first Century*, HarperPress, 2010

Bush, George W. *Decision Points*, Virgin Books, 2010

Carter, Jimmy. *Keeping Faith: Memoirs of a President*, Bantam Books, 1995

Cave Brown, Anthony. *Oil, God, and Gold: The Story of Aramco and the Saudi Kings*, Houghton Mifflin, 1999

Cheney, Michael Sheldon. *Big Oil Man from Arabia*, Literary Licensing, LLC, 1958

Cheney, Dick. *In My Time: A Personal and Political Memoir*, Threshold Editions, 2012

Davidson, Christopher. *After the Sheikhs: The Coming Collapse of the Gulf Monarchies*, Hurst, 2013

Downey, Morgan. *Oil 101*, Wooden Table Press, 2009

Gerolymatos, André. *Castles Made of Sand: A Century of Anglo-American Espionage and Intervention in the Middle East*, Thomas Dunne, 2010

Hartshorn, J. E. *Oil Trade: Politics and Prospects*, Cambridge University Press, 1993

Hertog, Steffen. *Princes, Brokers, and Bureaucrats: Oil and the State in Saudi Arabia*, Cornell University Press, 2011

House, Karen Elliott. *On Saudi Arabia: Its People, Past, Religion, Fault Lines – and Future*, Random House, 2012

Lacey, Robert. *Inside the Kingdom: Kings, Clerics, Modernists, Terrorists, and the Struggle for Saudi Arabia*, Hutchinson, 2009

————. *The Kingdom: Arabia and the House of Saud*, Harcourt, 1982

Mabro, Robert. *Oil in the Twenty-First Century: Issues, Challenges, and Opportunities*, Oxford University Press, 2006

Marcel, Valerie. *Oil Titans: National Oil Companies in the Middle East*, Royal Institute of International Affairs, 2006

Maugeri, Leonardo. *Beyond the Age of Oil: The Myths, Realities and Future of Fossil Fuels and the Alternatives*, Praeger, 2008

McConnell, Philip C. *The Hundred Men*, Currier Press, 1985

McMurray, Scott. *Energy to the World*, 2 vols, Aramco Services Company, 2011

Munro, Alan. *Arab Storm: Politics and Diplomacy Behind the Gulf War*, I. B. Tauris, 2005

Pakka, Kyle L. *The Energy Within: A Photo History of the People of Saudi Aramco*, Saudi Arabian Oil Company, 2007

Peterson, J. E. *Historical Dictionary of Saudi Arabia*, 2nd edn, Scarecrow Press, 2003

Rice, Condoleezza. *No Higher Honour: A Memoir of My Years in Washington*, Simon & Schuster, 2011

Rumsfeld, Donald. *Known and Unknown: A Memoir*, Sentinel, 2011

Sampson, Anthony. *Seven Sisters: Great Oil Companies and the World They Made*, Coronet Books, 1983

Scott, R. *IEA: The First Twenty Years*, vol. I: *Origins and Structures*; vol. II: *Major Policies and Actions*, IEA, 1994

Seymour, Ian. *OPEC: Instrument of Change*, Macmillan, 1980

Stegner, Wallace. *Discovery! The Search for Arabian Oil*, Selwa Press, 2007

Taher, Abdulhadi H. *Petroleum, Gas and Development Strategies of Saudi Arabia*, Saqi, 2011

——. *Saudi Arabian Hydro-Carbons and World Affairs*, Saqi, 2013

Twitchell, Karl. *Saudi Arabia: With an Account of the Development of Its Natural Resources*, Princeton University Press, 1958

Vassiliev, Alexei. *The History of Saudi Arabia*, New York University Press, 2000

Victor, David G., Hults, David R., and Thurber, Mark C. *Oil and Governance: State-Owned Enterprises and the World Energy Supply*, Cambridge University Press, 2011

Vitalis, Robert. *America's Kingdom: Mythmaking on the Saudi Oil Frontier* (Stanford Studies in Middle Eastern and Islamic Studies and Cultures), Verso, 2009

Yergin, Daniel. *The Prize: The Epic Quest for Oil, Money and Power*, Free Press, 1991

——. *The Quest: Energy, Security and the Remaking of the Modern World*, Penguin, 2011

Other Sources/Papers/Articles

Ageili, M. Al-. The settlement of the nomadic tribes in the northern province: Saudi Arabia. Manchester University PhD thesis, 1986

Ahmady, T. Al-. The image of Saudi Arabia in the British press. University of Leeds PhD thesis, 1995

American Association for the Advancement of Science. Technology and consumption trends. http://atlas.aaas.org/index.php?part=1&sec=trends

American University, Beirut, www.aub.edu.lb

Arab-British Centre, www.arabbritishcentre.org.uk

Arab-British Chamber of Commerce, www.abcc.org.uk

Arab News

Argus Global Markets, various

Associated Press, www.ap.org

Attas, A. Al-. The role of the non-oil minerals sector in the economic growth of Saudi Arabia. University of Leeds PhD thesis, 2002

Bazoobandi, Sara. Political economy of the Gulf sovereign wealth funds: a case study of Iran, Kuwait, Saudi Arabia and United Arab Emirates. University of Exeter PhD thesis, 2011

BBC news, various

Bergendahl, Goran. Petroleum investment in the Arabian Gulf. Oxford Institute for Energy Studies, 1985

Bloom, D., and Finlay, J. Demographic change and economic growth in Asia. Harvard working paper, September 2008

BP *Statistical Review of World Energy*, various

British Library, Middle East division, www.bl.uk

Center for Strategic and International Studies (CSIS), csis.org

Centre for Global Energy Studies, www.cges.co.uk

Chatham House reports, various, www.chathamhouse.org

Chevron, various, www.chevron.com

China Sinopec, english.sinopec.com

Cordesman, Anthony. Economics, energy and the future stability of Saudi Arabia. CSIS, 1999

————. Islamic extremism in Saudi Arabia and the attack on Al-Khobar. CSIS, 2001

————. Saudi Arabia and Iran. CSIS, 2001

————. Saudi Arabia enters the 21st century: shaping the future of the Saudi petroleum sector. CSIS, 2002

Council on Foreign Relations, various, www.cfr.org

Economic Times, economictimes.indiatimes.com

Economist magazine, www.economist.com

Elawy, Ibrahim. Al-. The influence of oil upon settlement in Al-Hasa oasis, Saudi Arabia. Durham University PhD thesis, 1976

Energy Charter Secretariat. Putting a price on energy, www.encharter.org

Energy Information Administration, US. Various reports, country profiles, statistics, eia.gov

Energy Intelligence, various, www.energyintel.com

ExxonMobil, various

Fattouh, Bassam. Energy and Arab economic development (UN Development Programme, 2012)

———. OPEC policy and oil prices: long-term issues versus short-term management of the market. Oxford Institute for Energy Studies, 2009

———. OPEC pricing power: the need for a new perspective. Oxford Institute for Energy Studies, 2007

———. OPEC: what difference has it made? Oxford Institute for Energy Studies, 2013

———. Summer again: the swing in oil demand in Saudi Arabia. Oxford Institute for Energy Studies, 2013

Federal Research Division of the Library of Congress. Country Reports, Saudi Arabia. http://countrystudies.us/saudi-arabia/

Financial Times, ft.com

Foreign Reports, Inc., various, www.foreignreports.com

GCC, http://www.gcc-sg.org/eng

George Bush library, www.bush41library.tamu.edu

George W. Bush library, www.georgewbushlibrary.smu.edu

Gordon, D. Opportunities and challenges confronting Russian oil. Carnegie Endowment For International Peace, http://carnegieendowment.org. 2013

Grand Teton National Park, www.nps.gov/grte

Harit, I. The emergence of private authority in the oil industry: the case of oil concession agreements. Durham University PhD thesis, 2010

Henderson, S. After King Fahd. Washington Institute for Near East Policy, Washington DC, 1994

———. Inside Saudi succession. Washington Institute for Near East Policy, Washington DC, 2009

Hertog, Steffen. Petromin: the slow death of statist oil development in Saudi Arabia. School of Government and International Affairs, University of Durham, 2008

———. Shaping the Saudi state: human agency's shifting role in rentier state formation. *International Journal of Middle East Studies*, 2007

IEA, Paris, various, www.iea.org

IEF, JODI data. www.jodidata.org

IEF, Joint Statement, Jeddah Energy Meeting, 2008

IEF, various, www.ief.org

IMF, various, www.imf.org

Institute of Energy Economics, Japan, various, eneken.ieej.or.jp/en

Irving Oil, www.irvingoil.com

Ismail, N. The political and economic relations of the People's Republic of China and the Kingdom of Saudi Arabia, 1949–2010. University of Exeter PhD thesis, 2011

Jadwa Investment, reports. www.jadwa.com

James Carter library, www.jimmycarterlibrary.gov

Jarallah, A. Al-. Analysing the impact of the World Trade Organisation (WTO) on the sustainability of competitiveness of the petrochemical industry in Saudi Arabia. Durham University PhD thesis, 2010

KAPSARC, www.kapsarc.org

Kaufman, R. Will oil prices decline over the long run? European Central Bank, 2008

KAUST, www.kaust.edu.sa

Khelaiwi, K. Al-. The impact of oil revenue fluctuations on the Saudi Arabian economy. Durham University PhD thesis, 2001

King Abdullah City for Atomic and Renewable Energy, www. kacare.gov.sa/en

Kohl, Wilfrid. OPEC behaviour 1998–2001. *Quarterly Review of Economics and Finance,* 2002

Lahn, G. Targets to promote energy savings in the GCC states. Chatham House, 2012

Lehigh University. www.lehigh.edu

Ma'aden, various. www.maaden.com.sa/en

Mabro, Robert. The oil price crisis of 1998. Oxford Institute for Energy Studies, 1998

———. The oil weapon. Oxford Institute for Energy Studies, 2002

———. US national energy policy or wishful thinking? Oxford Institute for Energy Studies, 2001

Mahdi, A. S. S. US foreign policy and energy resources during the George W. Bush administration. University of Birmingham PhD thesis, 2010

Middle East Association, the-mea.co.uk

Middle East Centre, St Antony's, Oxford, www.sant.ox.ac.uk/mec

Middle East Economic Survey, various, http://archives.mees.com/volumes

Middle East Institute, www.mei.edu

Miller Center of Public Affairs. Interview with James Schlesinger, 1984

Ministry of Economy, Trade and Industry, Japan, www.meti.go.jp

Ministry of Energy, Canada, www.energy.gov.on.ca

Ministry of Petroleum and Energy, Norway, http://www.regjeringen.no/en

Mitchell, J., and Stevens, P. Ending dependence: hard choices for oil exporting states. Chatham House, 2008

Mommer, B. Venezuelan oil politics at the crossroads. Oxford Energy, 2001

Muhanna, Ibrahim Al-. From Paris to Riyadh. The evolution of oil producers and consumers relationship: from mistrust to building a common future. IEF, 2011

Mulligan Papers, various. Georgetown University, Washington DC

Museum of Pearl Diving, Bahrain

Nahedh, M. The sedentarization of a Bedouin community in Saudi Arabia. University of Leeds PhD thesis, 1989

Naimi, His Excellency Ali Al-, speeches, 1995–present

National Council on US–Arab Relations, ncusar.org

National Energy Policy Development Group, USA. National Energy Policy, 2001

New York Times, www.nytimes.com

Nihon Keizai Shimbun, www.nikkei.co.jp

OAPEC, www.oapecorg.org

Odah, O. Saudi-American relations 1968–1978: a study in ambiguity. University of Salford PhD thesis, 1988

OECD, www.oecd.org

Oil & Gas Journal, various

OPEC: Statute, production data, meeting minutes, various publications

OPEC Fund for International Development, various

Oxford Institute for Energy Studies, www.oxfordenergy.org

People's Daily, english.peopledaily.com.cn

Peterson Institute for International Economics, various

Petróleos de Venezuela, S.A., www.pdvsa.com

Petroleum Argus

Petroleum Intelligence Weekly

Platts Oligram News

Priddle, Robert. The wolf and the watchdog. International Energy Agency

Reuters

Richard Nixon library, www.nixonlibrary.gov

Roberts, Steve. Who makes the oil price? An analysis of oil price movements, 1978–1982. Oxford Institute for Energy Studies, 1984

Royal Dutch Shell

SABIC, various

Saudi Arabian Monetary Agency, KSA, www.sama.gov.sa/sites/SAMAEN

Saudi Aramco annual reviews, various

Saudi Aramco special collection

Saudi Aramco world magazine, various, www.saudiaramcoworld.com

Saudi Embassy, www.saudiembassy.net

Saudi Geological Society, www.sgs.org.sa

Saudi–US Relations Information Service, various, http://susris.com/

School of Oriental and African Studies, www.soas.ac.uk

Schott, J. Peterson. The Iran and Libya Sanctions Act of 1996: Results to Date, 22 April 2010, Institute for International Economics

Secretaría de Energía, Mexico, www.sener.gob.mx

Stanford University, www.stanford.edu

Statoil, www.statoil.com

Subcommittee on Monopoly of Select Committee on Small Business, US Senate, 83d Cong., 2nd session (Washington DC, 1952). The International Petroleum Cartel

Sumitomo Corporation, www.sumitomocorp.co.jp/en/

Thatcher archive, http://www.margaretthatcher.org

Thatcher, Margaret. Letter to King Fahd, 1983

Total S.A., Total in Saudi Arabia: facts and figures, http://www.totalsaudi.com/

UN Conference on Trade and Development, World economic situation and prospects, 2009

UN Food and Agriculture Organisation, report, 1956, http://www.fao.org/index_en.htm

UN Framework Convention on Climate Change, unfccc.int

UN Oil for Food Programme, http://www.un.org/News/dh/iraq/oip/facts-oilforfood.htm

UN Report on resources, 1952

University of California, Berkeley's Regional Oral History Office at The Bancroft Library. American perspectives of Aramco, the Saudi-Arabian oil-producing company, 1930s–1980s

US Department for Energy

US Energy Association, National energy security post 9/11, 2002

US Energy Association, Toward a national energy strategy, 2001

US Export Administration Regulations

US Federal Reserve, www.federalreserve.gov

US Senate, www.senate.gov

US State Department, www.state.gov

Van Hulst, Noé. Global efforts to stabilize the international oil market. International Energy Forum, 2008

Vela Marine International, http://www.vela.ae/

Wall St Journal, online.wsj.com

Washington Post, www.washingtonpost.com

Wikileaks, various

Wilson Center, Washington DC

World Bank, National oil companies and value creation. Working paper, 2011

World Bank reports, statistics, various

World Energy Council, www.worldenergy.org

World Gas Intelligence, various

Yousef, N. Al-. The role of Saudi Arabia in the World Oil Market 1974–1997. University of Surrey PhD thesis, 1998

Zayer, Fuad Al-. The future of oil and gas and the resultant challenges and opportunities for NOCs. Keynote address to the World National Oil Companies Congress, London, 25–26 April 2007

Index